ADVANCE PRAISE FOR JESUS CHRIST, PEACEMAKER

"Hands down the best book available on the nonviolence of Jesus and its implications for theology, spirituality, the church and the world today."

—Rev. John Dear, author, *Jesus the Rebel,*
Lazarus Come Forth! and *The Nonviolent Life*

"Terrence Rynne has the uncanny and enviable gift of seeing things with fresh eyes and in the process helps us understand anew timeworn topics such as the just war theory. Digging deep into the Gospels he retrieves the image of Jesus as Peacemaker and with the example and teaching of Gandhi he lays a new foundation for non-violence, not as a weak-spined evasion of social responsibilities but as a strategy, and above all, as a fundamental attitude of Christian faith and more-necessary-than-ever practice of peace-making. A more apposite tract for the time can hardly be written. I most strongly recommend it to those engaged in national defense as well as those working for reconciliation and justice."

—Peter Phan, Georgetown University

"Moving beyond a theoretical debate about the morality of war, Terrence Rynne insists that our vocation as Christians is to active, nonviolent, persistent, risky, creative peacemaking and shows clearly how an evolving Catholic theology of peace increasingly reflects that emphasis. *Jesus Christ, Peacemaker: A New Theology of Peace* is both interesting and convincing."

—Marie Dennis, International President, Pax Christi

"Terrence Rynne has written a book with a truly challenging message about what true discipleship asks of Christians in the realm of neighbor love, forgiveness, and the work of peacemaking. The book is rich in biblical and historical scholarship and Rynne presents a coherent and creative strategy for the church to follow in the way of Jesus, the Prince of Peace."

—Kenneth R. Himes, O.F.M., Boston College

"Since 1965 Catholic teaching has proclaimed, 'No to war, war never again.' Here is a book that truly recovers the original Gospel ethic: Jesus rejected violence for any reason whatsoever. Readers of this book will be guided into the way of peace taught and modeled by Jesus. Perhaps our Church will begin again to be a 'peace church' and deserve to hear Jesus announce to us "Blessed are the peacemakers."
—Bishop Thomas Gumbleton

"This powerful new book definitively illuminates the active nonviolence of Jesus—and how peacemaking is central to the way of faithful discipleship for every Christian. Terrence Rynne has performed an inestimable service for all of us by producing this clear and systematic theology of peace rooted in the nonviolent heart of the Gospel. If we take this book seriously—in our lives, our churches, and our society—we will finally be on our way to transforming the pervasive violence we face, and will do so as an act of faith in the God who calls all of us to nonviolence, peace and reconciliation."
—Ken Butigan, Executive Director, Pace e Bene Nonviolence Service

Jesus Christ, Peacemaker

Jesus Christ, Peacemaker

A New Theology of Peace

Terrence J. Rynne

ORBIS BOOKS
Maryknoll, New York 10545

ORBIS BOOKS
Maryknoll, New York 10545

Founded in 1970, Orbis Books endeavors to publish works that enlighten the mind, nourish the spirit, and challenge the conscience. The publishing arm of the Maryknoll Fathers and Brothers, Orbis seeks to explore the global dimensions of the Christian faith and mission, to invite dialogue with diverse cultures and religious traditions, and to serve the cause of reconciliation and peace. The books published reflect the views of their authors and do not represent the official position of the Maryknoll Society. To learn more about Maryknoll and Orbis Books, please visit our website at www.maryknollsociety.org.

Library of Congress Cataloging-in-Publication Data

Rynne, Terrence J., 1942-
    Jesus Christ, peacemaker : a new theology of peace / by Terrence Rynne.
        pages cm
    Includes bibliographical references and index.
    ISBN 978-1-62698-097-6 (pbk.)
    1. Peace—Religious aspects—Catholic Church.   2. Church history—Primitive and early church, ca. 30-600.   3. Jesus Christ.   4. Peace—Biblical teaching.   I. Title.
BX1795.P43R96 2014
241'.6242—dc23   2014005448

Contents

A New Theology of Peace

The time is ripe for a new theology of peace.

It is time to base a theology of peace on the sacred scriptures, on the life and teachings of Jesus—not on natural law thinking.

For the first four centuries of Christianity, Jesus' example and teachings, as documented by the gospels, guided Christians through their major political challenges. The gospels served as the basis of the peace theology of the first four centuries of Christianity. Then for the next sixteen centuries, ever since Saint Augustine, Christian peace theology has not been developed on the basis of the gospels but on the basis of natural law thinking.

Jesus' life and teachings portrayed in the gospels had great meaning and relevance for the first and early Christians—not just for their personal spiritual lives but also for the way in which they came to grips with the problems and challenges of their political lives. In the years just after Jesus' death, the first Christians—who were mainly Jews themselves—had to deal with the steadily building resistance of their Jewish countrymen against the Roman occupation. Scholars today believe that Mark's Gospel was written just before the Jewish revolt in 66 CE to give these first Christians a clear view of Jesus' life and teaching and to help them stand strong against the pressures to join in the revolt. Jesus' clear rejection of violence—from the first time he was tempted in the desert to his refusal to allow the people to fashion him into a revolutionary messiah to the way he dealt with the corruption of his society's leadership to the way he responded to their violence toward him—helped inspire the first Christians to take their stand. They refused to participate in the violent revolt. Benedict

XVI reminded us that Eusebius, writing in 339 CE, told us that "even before the beginning of the siege of Jerusalem the Christians had fled to the city of Pella beyond the Jordan," and "We also know that they did not take part in the revolt at the time of Hadrian."[1] Jesus' nonviolent way of dealing with hate and violence was normative for them and helped them through their political travail.

In the next era, from the end of the first century to the end of the third century, Jesus' example and teaching helped guide Christians as they dealt with the next most difficult political challenge facing them—violent Roman persecution. Their heroic way of life, a life of love for their enemies and a willingness to suffer for their faith, deeply impressed the peoples of the ancient world. Their example gradually inspired mass conversions to the Christian faith.

By the end of the fourth century, peace theology changed. For the next sixteen centuries, ever since the time of Saint Augustine, Christian peace theology has relied on natural law thinking. Augustine thought, unlike the earlier Fathers of the Church, that Jesus' teachings in the Sermon on the Mount did not give guidance on the questions of war and peace. He perceived them to counsel purity of interior intentions and not as guides for how to act. He therefore turned to the classical authors and in particular, Cicero, for guidance on issues of war and peace. Using natural law thinking—the belief that human reason can determine what is right and wrong by tracing the law written into the human heart in creation, Cicero and then Augustine came up with some guidelines, the criteria of the just war theory that allows humans to determine whether or not an individual war is just or not. As a result, the gospels, Jesus' life and teaching, were relegated to the private, spiritual domain and considered irrelevant for the complicated issues of statecraft faced by political leaders, irrelevant when it comes to issues of war and peace. The call to a Christian response to violence was silenced. The dynamism and inspiration of Jesus' life and teachings as they relate to issues of violence and political life were choked off.

Ever since the Second Vatican Council, however, the church has been calling for a new theology of peace, one with an "entirely new attitude," one based on the Sacred Scriptures. Until the council, natural law thinking as expressed in the just war theory provided the substance of authoritative teaching. Scripture was cited mainly as proof texts to

---

[1] Benedict XVI, *Jesus of Nazareth* (San Francisco: Ignatius Press, 2011), 24, 47.

buttress natural law reasoning. Just after the first session of the council, for example, Pope John XXIII issued his marvelous encyclical, *Pacem in Terris, Peace on Earth,* using natural law thinking. It was the first time the church fully embraced the concept of human rights. In fact, Pope John offered a new and helpful definition of positive peace in that encyclical: Peace is had when humans enjoy the full development of all the natural human rights for which they are designed. Peace is more than the absence of war. It is more like a cathedral; it has to be built.

The Catholic Church through the centuries has had great respect for the human intellect and the natural human desire for meaning and truth. The church maintained a natural law approach in order to be in dialogue with and show respect for those who did not share the faith. The conviction was that humans of good will, reasoning together, could come to a full understanding of what it takes to construct a world of peace. The scriptures are barely mentioned in *Pacem in Terris.* In fact, John cites scripture at the end only to confirm the natural law approach, citing Romans 2:15, the classic text for proving that there is a natural law. Charles Curran writes about this: "Grace is help from on high—In keeping with the theological thesis that fallen human beings without grace cannot observe the natural law for long. This reduces grace, Gospel and Christ to means for observing the natural law."[2] The American Catholic bishops in their important letter on peace, *The Challenge of Peace,* in 1983, attempted to base their teaching on a firm scriptural base but in the end returned to a natural law approach to formulate their recommendations.

The centerpiece of peace theology as a result of this approach has been the just war theory. The just war theory offers a way for rational people to think rationally about war, using rational principles from the natural law, the law written on the hearts of all humans. Most of the principles of the just war theory, such as just cause and proportionality, were first articulated by the Roman writer and philosopher Cicero in his work *De Officis* and then reworked by Saint Ambrose and Saint Augustine. As we will see, the just war theory has a place in a theology of peace—given its ability to found a dialogue with people of good will. It has to have, however, a subordinate place to a theology of peace that taps the power of the gospel call to peacemaking.

---

[2]Charles Curran, *Catholic Social Teaching* (Washington, DC: Georgetown University Press, 2002), 30.

What the world urgently needs is more than a theory for debating whether or not a particular war is justified or not. What the world needs is for Christians to follow the way of Jesus' suffering love for enemies, the way of the cross. A theology of peace based on the gospels emphasizes action, proactive action—peacemaking practices. Peacemaking practices will move in many directions utilizing the power of nonviolence—peacemaking practices that confront injustices and forge justice, peacemaking practices that remove the causes of war before war is ready to break out, peacemaking practices that reconcile peoples affected by long-term violence so that the cycle of violence is ended, peacemaking practices that sail into situations of domination and overcome them, peacemaking practices that confront conflict situations and resolve them. A theology of peace based on the gospels will produce not armchair theorists but active peacemakers

It is time to again base our theology of peace on the life and teaching of Jesus, not on the principles of Cicero. Doing so will put the just war theory into its appropriate subordinate place, something to use when thinking about war with others who do not base their lives on the way of Jesus. Basing our theology of peace on the life and teaching of Jesus will unleash the creativity and staying power of Christian discipleship—to go beyond what is "natural" and to explore the full, creative power of nonviolence in the ways that Jesus did. Doing so will allow the call to Christian discipleship to be heard again—loving one's enemies, creatively responding to those who do us harm, being willing to go the extra mile to resolve conflicts before they fester. The just war theory will no longer be equated with the church's stance on war and peace. Basing our theology of peace on the life and teachings of Jesus will bring forward, into primacy of place, the challenge of active peacemaking and the Christian's vocation to nonviolent action.

As Marilyn McMorrow writes, "The community of faith needs but has not yet developed a comprehensive theology of peace. Such a theology would be a central resource in illuminating peacemaking as an essential dimension of Christian faith. While important, the long-standing emphasis in traditional Catholic theology on the obligation to limit resort to force is not in itself sufficient."[3] She goes on to quote

---

[3]Marilyn McMorrow, "Creating Conditions of Peace: A Theological Framework," in *Peacemaking: Moral and Policy Challenges for a New World*, ed. Gerard F. Powers, Drew Christiansen, and Robert T. Hennemeyer (Washington, DC: United States Catholic Conference, 1994), 43.

the United States Catholic Bishops when they wrote that we have to "ground the task in the biblical vision of the kingdom of God and then place it centrally in the ministry of the Church."[4]

In recent decades there has been a convergence of testimony from scripture scholars concerning the nonviolence of Jesus. John Howard Yoder published two editions of his path-finding book, *The Politics of Jesus*, hailed by Stanley Hauerwas as the most important work of theology of the twentieth century. In each edition, published eight years apart, Yoder listed the scripture scholars who recognized the nonviolence of Jesus at the time each edition was issued—two long lists of distinguished scholars. To those lists in this decade one can add some of the current leading scholars: Marcus Borg, John Dominic Crossan, James D. G. Dunn, Richard Horsley, Gerhard Lohfink, John Meier, Donald Senior, Walter Wink, N. T. Wright, and Sandra Schneiders. A new theology of peace will be based on the scriptures and draw on the scholarship of these thinkers.

The official church teaching on war and peace has evolved rapidly over the last century. It is time for a theology of peace to catch up with those developments.

The old debate between pacifism and just war has been superseded by the concepts of peacemaking and peacebuilding. Recent popes are no longer taking a theoretical approach to problems of peace and war; they are taking an action-oriented approach, an active approach emphasizing, as did John XXIII, that peace needs to be built. It is not enough that people refrain from war, although the assumption against any justifiable war in the modern era grows stronger and stronger in successive papal teaching. It is only when people are in right relationships with one another that they can enjoy *shalom*, a full positive peace. As Maryann Cusimano Love writes: "Robust peace is the aim of all action. . . . Just war theorists too often only engage when war is looming, . . . blissfully unaware of the larger and broader task to cultivate a peaceful world."[5]

---

[4] National Conference of the Catholic Bishops, *The Challenge of Peace: God's Promise and Our Response* (Washington, DC: USCC, 1983), no. 25.

[5] Maryann Cusimano Love, "What Kind of Peace Do We Seek?" in *Peacebuilding: Catholic Theology, Ethics, and Praxis*, ed. Robert J. Schreiter, R. Scott Appleby, and Gerard F. Powers (Maryknoll, NY: Orbis Books, 2010), 75.

Just peacemaking is the new paradigm. Recent teaching draws on the teachings of the Jewish scriptures that the language of justice is action language, power language—a just person "justices," makes justice. The biblical symbol for justice is not a set of scales but "a mighty, surging river—bringing life to a parched land," as Christopher Marshall writes.[6] John Paul II, for example, said that when he went to India, he first studied the life and writings of Mahatma Gandhi. He found there the principles of active nonviolence that had freed India and that were helping remake the world through nonviolence. Pope John Paul proudly proclaimed upon his return that he had evangelized India through the works of Gandhi.[7]

Pope Benedict XVI was a very clear voice articulating this new paradigm. For example, he described nonviolence for Christians as "not mere tactical behavior but a person's way of being, the attitude of one who is convinced of God's love and power, who is not afraid to confront evil with the weapons of love and truth alone. Loving the enemy is the nucleus of the 'Christian revolution.' "[8] At his Good Friday sermon of 2011, he said:

> Above all we want to make the voice of Jesus heard. He was always a man of peace. It could be expected that, when God came to earth, he would be a man of great power, destroying the opposing forces. That he would be a man of powerful violence as an instrument of peace. Not at all. He came in weakness. He came with only the strength of love, totally without violence, even to point of going to the cross. This is what shows the true face of God, that violence never comes from God, never helps bring anything good, but is a destructive means and not the path to escape difficulties. . . . This is Jesus' true message: seek peace with the means of peace and leave violence aside.[9]

---

[6]Christopher Marshall, *Beyond Retribution* (Grand Rapids, MI: William B. Eerdmans, 2001), 53.

[7]*New York Times*, February 2, 1986, and February 12, 1986, as quoted by Lloyd I. Rudolph in "Gandhi in the Mind of America," in *Gandhi's Experiments with Truth,* ed. Richard Johnson (Lanham, MD: Lexington Books, 2006), 281.

[8]Pope Benedict XVI, *Midday Angelus,* 2007.

[9]Pope Benedict XVI, *Good Friday Sermon,* 2011.

The world has given us a sign of the times that cannot be ignored any longer: the power of nonviolent action. It is time for a theology of peace to recognize the power and effectiveness of nonviolent action—time after time and all over the globe, in the more than sixty years since Mahatma Gandhi.

It is time for a theology of peace that learns from one of the most striking signs of our time—the history of successful campaigns of nonviolence around the world. It is time for a theology of peace that lays out the principles of effective nonviolent strategy, teaches the skills of creative nonviolent conflict resolution, and mobilizes people for action—churchwide and parish deep.

Imagine if every Christian around the globe were well versed in the great stories of nonviolence, not only what happened through nonviolence in India, but also in South Africa, the Philippines, East Germany, Czechoslovakia, Northern Ireland, Poland, Chile, and in our own nonviolent civil rights revolution in the United States. What if all Christians were able to see through and resist the myths about violence: the myth that violence is effective; the myth that it is really, when it comes down to it, the only way to protect oneself and be powerful; the myths that power grows out of the barrel of the gun and that violence is the way the West is won. Imagine if the church felt the call to peacemaking in every fiber of its being. Imagine the tsunami of peacemaking practices and witness that would flood the world.

The Catholic Church has the numbers and the worldwide organizational reach and structure to make an immense contribution to building a world of peace. It is time for a theology of peace that draws on the real-life experience of local churches' peacemaking around the globe.

The Catholic Church numbers 1.2 billion people. Imagine the impact the Catholic Church could have if it articulated a theology of peace that reached and mobilized its members throughout the world, if every student graduating from a Catholic school and every Christian in the pews saw himself or herself, first and foremost, as a peacemaker and felt equipped to act as a peacemaker and a peace builder. The Catholic Church has a local structure and a central authority at one and the same time. As Scott Appleby writes, "The Catholic Church is in fact diffuse, decentralized and surpassingly local when left in its natural state, so to speak. . . . [It has] enormous potential as a fully vibrant, operationally unified and responsive transnational actor."[10] In some cases, such as in Southern Sudan, the Catholic Church is almost alone as an organized structure for mobilizing and protecting the ongoing civil life of the society. In other countries, such as the Philippines and Malaysia, the Catholic Church is actively collaborating with Muslims and people of other faiths to hold and build the peace. In other countries, such as the United States, the Catholic Church has the opportunity in a multicultural melting pot to offer an alternate community witness to the mainline conventions about the effectiveness and necessity of violence.

What if the Catholic Church embraced the call to peacemaking and spoke and witnessed to gospel nonviolence in the same way that it currently speaks to and witnesses to the issue of abortion? The Catholic Church would be proclaiming a message that the world urgently needs and is ready to hear—if it is borne out in consistent practices of peacemaking by Christians around the world.

---

[10]R. Scott Appleby, "Peacebuilding and Catholicism," in *Peacebuilding: Catholic Theology, Ethics, and Praxis*, ed. Robert J. Schreiter, R. Scott Appleby, and Gerard F. Powers (Maryknoll, NY: Orbis Books), 7.

1

The Nonviolent, Political Jesus

Many people are currently lamenting that so many have walked away from their Christian heritage and that the message of Christianity seems irrelevant to so many young people. Catholic writers in particular are lamenting these developments and bemoaning the fact that former Catholics now constitute the second largest religious (or formerly religious) group in the United States. To partially counter these trends, the Archdiocese of Chicago offered a free book, *Rediscovering Catholicism*,[1] to every adult who attended Mass at Christmas 2013 at any and all of the archdiocese's parishes and offered the services of all its clergy to dialogue with people about the content of the book—to spark a broad discussion of the underlying problems that have led to such a mass exodus from the church. The hope was that the book and the discussions would revivify a positive sense of Catholic identity. The strategy recognized the fact that many more people attend Christmas services than come to Mass on a typical Sunday and that those once- or twice-a-year people are likely candidates to be the next out the door.

Such efforts are not fundamental enough. If the nonviolent Jesus and the way of the nonviolent cross are made front and center, in season and out of season, churchwide and parish deep, Christianity and the church will immediately become relevant, enticing, and exciting. Why? First, the world's real problems are political. The issues people care about, get organized around, and give themselves to, are political. The nonviolent Jesus is political. The nonviolent Jesus addresses the political challenges of our time. He does not take us to a world of religion apart from the challenges of history, to a private world of

---

[1]Matthew Kelly, *Rediscovering Catholicism: A Spiritual Guide to Living with Passion and Purpose* (Cincinnati, OH: Beacon, 2010).

"lofty interior feelings" or a religion of personal salvation; he calls us to the heart of the world and its problems.

"A God who is not present in political life is dead to man's conscience because the decisions, or lack of them, which bring life and death to the majority of humankind now take place in the realm of politics," as James Douglass writes.[2] Second, the view that violence and only violence can keep us safe is the real belief and cultural value that keeps us deaf to the message of Jesus. Walter Wink writes, "Violence is the ethos of our time. It is the spirituality of the modern world. It has been accorded the status of religion, demanding from its devotees an absolute obedience unto death."[3] The nonviolent Jesus confronts that belief and cultural value head-on and demonstrates that there is another, much more effective way: the way of nonviolent, courageous, creative, suffering love. Third, people, young people in particular, want to be called to greatness, to deeds that are soul-sized. The nonviolent Jesus calls us to discipleship well beyond timid morality to actions that expand our souls and horizons to what we discover is, after all, the really real and authentically human.

Other recent prophets have pointed out this same truth and opportunity for the church and Christianity. Bernard Häring, the finest Catholic moral theologian of the twentieth century, writes:

> Those for whom . . . peace and peace mission remain only a marginal question in this historical moment condemn themselves to become altogether marginal. . . . At this juncture in history to neglect the message and practice of nonviolence could easily make the Church and her teaching irrelevant. . . . By giving a central role to the gospel and mission of peacemaking and nonviolence, they rid themselves of any possible insinuation of irrelevance in today's peaceless world.[4]

In the past century, the message of Christianity has been translated into successive idioms, corresponding to particular facets of the human condition that were felt to be important for particular times.

After the Second World War, existentialist thinkers, such as Camus,

---

[2] James Douglass, *The Nonviolent Cross* (London: Macmillan, 1968), 32.

[3] Walter Wink, *Engaging the Powers* (Minneapolis: Fortress Press, 1992), 13.

[4] Bernard Häring, *The Healing Power of Peace and Nonviolence* (New York: Paulist Press, 1986), 7, 11.

Sartre, and Beckett caught the mood of the times. After the evil and the horrors of the war and the Holocaust how could humanity go on as before? The human condition was felt to be, if not hopeless, then at best, absurd. Without any meaning or transcendence how could a person live an authentic human life? Albert Camus, in his book *The Plague* recognized that even in the void it was still important to fight evil but wondered how it was possible to fight violence and domination without becoming infected by the very evils that one was fighting. Rudolf Bultmann and others began to translate the Christian message into existentialist categories. Even if the world and its problems seemed overwhelming, at least individuals could live their lives authentically. To be authentic was the main thing. The recommended path: read the texts of the scriptures; let the presence behind the words approach you; and in that existential moment make a leap of faith into the void and gain your authenticity.

Later the human potential movement took hold. Given the anxieties, fragility, and alienation of the external, modern world, people began to turn within to look for a sure place of succor. If the problems of the world were too great to confront and solve, maybe at least one could work on oneself—to make one's own psyche whole and healthy. Christianity began to be rekeyed in terms of personal health and psychological wholeness. If people did not hear in their churches the call to psychological fulfillment that resonated with them, they began to look outside the churches to secular gurus to fill the void.

An approach that focuses only on one's own psychological health but does not lead to a deeper engagement with the world and attention to human suffering impoverishes, disempowers, and deadens the central Christian message. The central teaching and consuming passion of Jesus is the kingdom of God, a profoundly political term that calls people to face the problems of the world, not despair of the world or flee from it.

Before I reflect on the meaning of Jesus' teaching on the kingdom of God and the political power embodied in that term, I first look at the political, economic, social, and religious environment into which Jesus came and which he confronted with his life and teachings: "The more we want to know about Jesus, the more we should know about his world," Donald Senior writes.[5]

---

[5]Donald Senior, *Jesus: A Gospel Portrait* (New York: Paulist Press, 1992), 26.

The Political Situation at the Time of Jesus

The Memory of the Maccabean Revolt

An important fact influencing the political situation of Jesus' day was the memory of what had happened a hundred years prior to the conquering and occupying of Israel by Rome in 63 BCE. The Seleucid ruler, Antiochus IV, frustrated by a rebellion of the Jews, sacked Jerusalem and desecrated the Jerusalem temple by enshrining a statue of Zeus in the holy of holies. As a result, Judea erupted in revolt, led by the Hasmonean family of Mattathias and his sons. Judas, one of his sons, was nicknamed the "hammer," Maccabeus, because of his explosive resistance to the enemy. At the time their resistance seemed suicidal, but instead they were victorious. By 164 BCE the statue of Zeus had been cleared away, the temple rededicated, and a commemoration of the event, the feast of Hannukah, celebrated, and kept ever since. A century of Jewish independence was begun—a situation never to be repeated until the modern state of Israel in the twentieth century.

The memory of that victory over a foreign power lingered in the consciousness of Israel and colored its expectations of the character of the hoped-for Messiah. James Dunn writes:

> To be noted here is the common assumption that the royal Messiah would be a powerful ruler executing justice for all. A frequent motif is his warlike character in rooting out evil and destroying Israel's enemies . . . a lively hope for the restoration of the Davidic line and that the Davidic Messiah was widely thought of as a warrior king who would destroy the enemies of Israel.[6]

And Senior states:

> Although freedom would once again slip away with the coming of the Romans, the incredible victory of the Hasmoneans was never forgotten in Israel. Nationalists at the time of Jesus were convinced that just as Yahweh had granted success to the Has-

---

[6]James D. G. Dunn, *Jesus Remembered*, vol. 1 (Grand Rapids, MI: William B. Eerdmans, 2003), 620–21.

moneans against the Greeks, the same victory could be achieved against the Romans. The prescription would be a tragic mistake.[7]

As we will see, when the people following Jesus and then his disciples began to see Jesus as the promised Messiah, it became very difficult for him to break the idea that messiah equals warrior, that liberation means the use of violence, that successful change requires violence.

Roman Rule through Client Kings

Rome, the greatest military power the world had seen to that time, occupied Israel, from the time of Pompey's victory in 63 BCE through the lifetime of Jesus and for centuries thereafter. Occupation by a foreign power is the first and perhaps the most important political fact affecting the day-to-day life of Jesus and his people. Occupation, whether it be Britain in India during Gandhi's time or the United States in Iraq in our time, means domination, economic exploitation, the constant threat of retribution and violence, and the resulting feelings of impotence, anger, and resentment in the people. When Jesus was born, Octavian, Caesar Augustus, was the emperor. Because he, Octavian, had brought peace to the empire after twenty-five bloody years of internecine killing—first Octavian and Marc Antony against Brutus and Cassius to avenge Julius Caesar's assassination and then Octavian against Marc Antony and Cleopatra, the fated lovers whom he finally defeated at the Battle of Actium in 31 BCE—the Roman senate declared their gratitude to Octavian by naming him their first emperor and declaring him a god. The worship of the emperor became the fastest-growing religion in the world during Jesus' time and early Christianity. There was to be no other "Lord" but Caesar.

What Rome wanted from its conquered territories was, first, a steady stream of tribute and, second, peace and quiet. Local satraps were expected to send riches to Rome and quickly squelch any and all outbreaks of local resistance or violence. E. P. Sanders is quoted as saying, "Rome generally governed remotely, being content with the collection of tribute and maintenance of stable borders; for the most

---

[7]Senior, *Jesus: A Gospel Portrait.*

part it left even these matters in the hand of local leaders."[8] The famous Pax Romana was a peace of devastation. As Tacitus, a defeated noble in Britain, said: "and where they make a desert, call it peace."[9]

Rome ruled its far-flung empire through local leaders who were given some free sway but who were in actuality totally dependent on Rome for their power. Staying in the good graces of the emperor was their first duty. In 43 BCE Rome appointed Herod, later to be called the Great, the king of Judea, displacing the Hasmonean Jerusalem high priests who had ruled over the country since the fall of the Hasmonean kings. Subsequently, Herod took to himself through conquest a land comparable to what David had ruled—from modern Lebanon in the north to the Negev in the south. Herod carefully balanced Rome's demands with those of his Jewish subjects. It was made all the more difficult because of his background. Tom Mueller writes, "His mother was an ethnic Arab and his father was an Edomite, and though Herod was raised a Jew, he lacked the social status of the powerful old families in Jerusalem who were eligible to serve as high priest as the Hasmonean kings had traditionally done."[10]

Herod ruled ruthlessly. He used a system of spies and an army of foreign mercenaries to repress dissent. Josephus, the historian who had been born and raised a Palestinian Jew but who deserted his countrymen during the Jewish revolt of 67–73 CE and joined the invading Roman forces, writes:

> . . . while he was always inventing somewhat further for his own security, and encompassing the whole nation with guards, that they might by no means get from under his power . . . while some of his spies might be upon them from the neighborhood, and might both be able to know what they were attempting and to prevent it.[11]

Herod built monuments of colossal size and ambition. He built a city and a deep-water harbor from scratch in honor of Caesar on the coast

---

[8]E. P. Sanders, as quoted in Ben Witherington III, *The Jesus Quest: The Third Search for the Jew of Nazareth* (Downers Grove, IL: Intervarsity Press, 1997), 17.

[9]Tacitus, *Agricola* (Oxford translation, revised by Edward Brooks), 30.

[10]Tom Mueller, "King Herod Revealed," National Geographic, December 2008, 40.

[11]Josephus, *Antiquities of the Jews* (sacred-texts.com, translated by Williams Whiston, 1737), Chapter 15, 5.

of the Mediterranean, Caesarea. Even today the remains of the city are a wonder. A huge amphitheater and aqueduct survive, and the remains of an enormous breakwater built from massive concrete blocks are visible in the sea. The harbor attracted trade from all over the Mediterranean. Herod rebuilt the Second Temple, as Mueller explains, "using gargantuan foundation stones, some over 40 feet long and weighing up to 600 tons. What remains of this stonework, the Western Wall, is Judaism's most sacred place."[12] The Temple was a wonder of the world, and people from all over the world traveled to Jerusalem to see it. Herod built the Northern Palace at Masada, which cascades down a cliff face high above the sere Judean desert and the Dead Sea, a seemingly impregnable fortress.

How was Herod able to finance not only his ongoing tribute obligations to Rome but also these massive building projects? Through taxation of the peasants. Land was the main, almost the sole, source of wealth. The tax burden on the simple people of the land was backbreaking in Jesus' time—estimated at half of every harvest. Many went into debt as a result. As a result of debt, many were thrown off their parcels of land. Anger and bitter resentment toward the leaders boiled over into violent uprisings—especially in Galilee. When Herod died in 4 BCE (just after Jesus' birth), Judas the Galilean led an armed uprising that attacked the capital of Galilee, Sepphoris, the home of wealthy landowners allied with the Temple priesthood, and raided the armory there. Varus, the Roman general in the region, sent in a detachment of the army. They captured and burned the city of Sepphoris and took the inhabitants into slavery. Josephus described what happened next:

> Varus sent a part of his army into the country, against those that had been the authors of this commotion, and as they caught great numbers of them, those that appeared to have been the least concerned in these tumults he put into custody, but such as were the most guilty he crucified; these were in number about two thousand.[13]

Sepphoris was four miles, an easy walk over the hills, from Jesus' hometown of Nazareth. Jesus no doubt grew up hearing the story of

---

[12]Mueller, "King Herod Revealed," 42.

[13]Josephus, *War of the Jews* (sacred-texts.com, translated by Williams Whiston, 1737), Book 2, Chapter 5.

the "Day the Romans came," when Rome used its favorite tool to strike terror into the hearts of a seething people, crucifixion. Two thousand rebels nailed or tied, naked, to crosses for all to see, slumping, pulling themselves up again and again, slowly, painfully asphyxiating, gasping for breath, and at last giving up their spirits. The constant threat of blood and violence was in the air that Jesus breathed. The city of Sepphoris was rebuilt by Herod the Great's successor, Herod Antipas, during the years of Jesus' youth.

In the years before Jesus' lifetime, during his life, and for decades after, uprisings and rebellions continued, escalating each time in violence. In his writings Josephus traced the history leading up to the fateful, final destruction of Jerusalem in 70 CE.

During the 40s of the common era, the countryside saw the growth of banditry, apparently supported by the local populations. Judean common people evidently turned to the brigands for help in restoring justice, which they had despaired of securing from the Roman or high-priestly government. Though not a major threat to the ruling establishment, they caused enough havoc to induce the governor at the time to send troops and arrest and crucify not only them but also, as Josephus writes, "common people who were convicted of complicity with them and punished by him, an incalculable number."[14]

In the 50s of the common era, a terrorist movement arose called *sicarii,* or "dagger men"—after the curved knives or scimitars that they used in terrorist attacks against the ruling classes, especially the Jewish high-priestly aristocracy. Josephus describes the situation:

> But while the countryside was thus cleared, a different type of bandit sprang up in Jerusalem, the so-called *sicarii,* who murdered men in broad daylight in the heart of the city. Especially during the festivals they would mingle with the crowd, carrying short daggers concealed in their clothing, with which they stabbed their enemies. Then when they fell, the murderers would join in the cries of indignation and, through this plausible behavior, avoided discovery. The first to be assassinated by them was Jonathan, the High Priest. After his death, there were numerous daily murders.[15]

---

[14]Ibid., Book 2, Chapter 14.
[15]Ibid., Book 20, Chapter 8.

The issue of violence—what would happen to his people, if they continued down the path of escalating violence, knowing the viciousness of Roman reprisals—must have concerned Jesus deeply. Toward the end of his life the gospels indicate that Jesus wept over the city of Jerusalem and its likely fate given the escalating spiral of violence. "Oh, Jerusalem I wanted to take you under my wings as does a hen her chicks" (Luke 13:34) for Jerusalem's protection and safety. And "Oh, Jerusalem, if only today you had known the ways of peace" (Luke 19:42).

We know through Josephus that the people of Israel had, in addition to violent resistance, tried nonviolent resistance as well. The nonviolent tradition was not unknown to Jesus. In *Jesus and the Spiral of Violence*, Richard Horsley traces such nonviolent resistance movements back to two groups of intellectuals who, in the name of the Torah, resisted the Hellenizing reform and the Antiochian persecution of the 160s BCE under the Seleucids as expressed in the last vision of the book of Daniel.

A well-known example of nonviolent resistance against Herodian-Roman rule was prompted by two famous teachers, Judas and Matthias, and their students. Herod had erected a large golden eagle over the great gate of the Temple, consistent with the ways he violated Jewish laws that forbade setting up images and with his ongoing obsequiousness to and collaboration with Rome—the golden eagle was the key symbol of the Roman army. Forty young students went up and chopped down the golden eagle. Horsley writes:

> As a protest, the chopping down of the golden eagle from atop the main Temple gate is impressive, given Herod's tight security measures. It is evident that the whole event was deliberately conceived and carefully planned as a nonviolent protest. The very number of those arrested, forty young men, indicates how extensive the group was that planned the action. Those who carried out the action could not have been any more aggressive and bold in their defiance of Herod and his practices. Yet they did not offer any armed resistance to the military force sent to apprehend them, but courageously awaited the attack.[16]

---

[16]Richard Horsley, *Jesus and the Spiral of Violence* (Minneapolis: Fortress Press, 1993), 76.

Herod responded to their protest with the utmost brutality, burning the scholars and their students alive.

After Herod died, Rome divided his kingdom between three of his sons: Herod Archelaus received half of the kingdom, Idumea, Judea, and Samaria, and the other half was divided in two between Herod Antipas, Galilee and Perea, and Herod Philip, the far northern reaches of the country. When Herod Archelaus fell out of favor, Rome put in a procurator, Pontius Pilate, in his place.

Herod Antipas, the "tetrarch" (one-fourth) of Jesus' home territory, Galilee, is the Herod who executed John the Baptist and interacted with Pilate during the trial of Jesus; this is the Herod whom Jesus famously described as "that fox." He continued the tradition of his father, actively currying favor with Rome. He built a new capital of Galilee on the western coast of the Sea of Galilee and named it Tiberias, after the emperor who succeeded Octavian. He built it on top of a Jewish graveyard, making the town perpetually unclean for Jews. Ben Witherington writes, "And many of the devout refused to enter it, for in the Jewish law a corpse and thus a graveyard was the most unclean thing of all."[17] John Dominic Crossan surmises that the building of Tiberias was not only homage to Caesar but also an attempt to commercialize the fishing industry of the Sea of Galilee, develop another dependable source of revenue to flow into the stream of tribute to Rome, and offer Rome a reason to name him not tetrarch but monarch over the whole of Israel.

> If you were Antipas and wanted to become King of the Jews, you would have to increase your tax base in Galilee so that Rome might grant you that royal promotion. If Antipas did this as tetrarch of Galilee and Perea, Rome might think, what would he not accomplish as monarch of the entire Jewish homeland? Antipas could not squeeze more taxation from his peasant-farmers without risking resistance or even revolt. But having learned, as it were, how to multiply loaves in the valleys around Sepphoris, he would now learn how to multiply fishes in the waters around Tiberias.[18]

---

[17]Witherington, *Jesus Quest*, 18.
[18]John Dominic Crossan, *God and Empire* (San Francisco: Harper, 2007), 103.

It was against Pilate, the first direct Roman ruler, that another celebrated act of nonviolent resistance was carried out in Jesus' time. Pilate had introduced into Jerusalem at night images of Caesar attached to the army's military standards. That immediately stirred up great consternation among the people of Jerusalem, which spread to people in the surrounding countryside. A multitude of people went to Caesarea to implore him to remove the standards and uphold their ancestors' practices. Josephus writes:

> When Pilate refused them, they fell down prostrate on the ground, and continued immovable in that posture for five days and as many nights. On the next day Pilate sat on his tribunal, in the open market place, and called to him the multitude, as desirous to give them an answer and then gave a signal to the soldiers, that they should all by agreement at once encompass the Jews with their weapons, so the band of soldiers stood round about the Jews in three ranks. The Jews were under the utmost consternation at that unexpected sight. Pilate also said to them that they should be cut in pieces, unless they would admit of Caesar's images, and gave intimation to the soldiers to draw their naked swords. Hereupon the Jews, as it were at one signal, fell down in vast numbers together, and exposed their necks bare, and cried out that they were sooner ready to be slain, than that their law should be transgressed. Hereupon Pilate was greatly surprised at their prodigious superstition, and gave order that the ensigns should be presently carried out of Jerusalem.[19]

This case, in which the common people exhibited such disciplined and constant courage, even to the point of risking death, is an example of a successful nonviolent protest—unlike the case of the students tearing down the golden eagle. Nonviolent resistance to evil and domination did not, obviously, begin with Gandhi. It was alive and well in Jesus' own time and culture, one of the traditions for him to draw on when he formulated his own response to the oppression of his people.

Another remarkable example of nonviolent resistance by the Jewish people to the powers that be occurred in response to an initiative of the Emperor Caligula—who resented the fact that the Jews did not

---

[19]Josephus, *War of the Jews*, Book 2, Chapter 9.

give him honor as befits a god. He ordered his legate, Petronius, to lead a large force into Judea to build a statue of him in the Jerusalem temple. If the people resisted, Petronius was to subdue them by force. Petronius led two legions of the army to Ptolemais, intending to winter there and in the spring continue on his mission. The Jews heard about the plan, and "many tens of thousands of Jews came to Petronius at Ptolemais with petitions not to use force to make them transgress and violate their ancestral code."[20] Petronius sensed how determined the many Jewish people were about the plan and recognized that it could lead to a great slaughter, so he traveled to Tiberias with some friends and attendants to sense what citizens in the capital of Galilee were thinking. Josephus writes:

> As before, many tens of thousands faced Petronius on his arrival at Tiberias. . . . "Will you then go to war with Caesar?" said Petronius. "On no account would we fight," they said, "but we will die sooner than violate our laws." And falling on their faces and baring their throats, declared that they were ready to be slain. They continued to make these supplications for forty days. Furthermore they neglected their fields, and that, though it was time to sow the seed.[21]

Some of the leaders among the Jews then pleaded with Petronius to let Caligula know just how determined was the resistance against his plan, pointing out the fact that not only would there be great bloodshed but because the people had, in effect, gone on a rent strike, there would be no tribute forthcoming. In fact, the country could anticipate further violence from the growth of banditry when there was a great lack of food. Petronius agreed to write to Caligula and ask him to not go ahead with the plan to set up a statue of himself in the holy of holies in exchange for a promise to tend to agricultural matters.

The conflict was resolved when, in January of 41, Caligula was assassinated before Petronius could intervene personally with him.

The length of the demonstrations, some forty days, the size of the resistance, the withholding of not only consent but also cooperative labor, began to weigh on Petronius. The anticipated economic impact

---

[20]Ibid., Book 18, Chapter 8.
[21]Ibid.

of what was in effect a massive peasant strike made Petronius anxious to get the agricultural cycle under way. Once again, a nonviolent resistance campaign was effective and short-circuited what would have been an escalating cycle of violence.

Jewish Rule: Political and Religious Leadership

The Priests

In Jesus' time and world, the Temple was understood to be the center of the world. Holiness exuded outward, from the holy of holies in the Temple, to the rest of the Temple, to the city of Jerusalem, and then out across the rest of the country. The Temple was a combination, in contemporary terms, of Pennsylvania Avenue, Wall Street, and Rodeo Drive—the center of political, economic, and cultural power: political, because day-to-day rule emanated from Jerusalem; economic, because of the tremendous wealth of the Temple treasury, leveraged often by the priests to enhance their own wealth; cultural, because religion made the Temple the central reference point in people's lives, the place to which they made pilgrimage to offer sacrifice, to gain ritual purity, and to be united with the God of their fathers. The high priest was the only man who entered the holy of holies, once a year at Passover, to pour blood on the *hilasterion,* the mercy seat. The high priest had a double role: he had the cultic role of leader of the Jewish religion and the political role of convener and leader of the Sanhedrin, the council of elders and priests that had responsibility for the day-to-day rule of the country. Under Pilate that traditional role had been restored to the Sanhedrin, and the high priest was selected and named by Pilate. The appointment by Pilate undermined the high priesthood by changing it from a lifetime office to an appointed one, which could be changed at any time by the occupying power.

The family that was in power during most of Jesus' lifetime was that of Ananus b. Sethi.[22] His family would be in that position for some sixty years. He was high priest for nine years, and all five of his sons, including Caiaphas, the one who presided at the Jewish "trial" of Jesus, held the position. The family from the beginning of its appointment was not held in high regard by the people—partly because of their dependency on Roman power but also because they were not

---

[22]Ibid., Book 20, Chapter 9.

in the line of the Zadok priestly heritage and were not even from a respected, aristocratic family.

There is some evidence that priestly leaders in Jesus' time used their positions for their own enrichment, exploiting the riches of the Temple treasury to expand their land holdings. The religious leaders, according to Josephus, developed their own private forces, which they used in repressive and even predatory ways.

> Ananias had servants who were very wicked, who joined themselves to the boldest sort of the people, and went to the thrashing-floors, and took away the tithes that belonged to the priests by violence, and did not refrain from beating such as would not give these tithes to them. So the other high priests acted in like manner, as did those of his servants, without any one being able to prohibit them; so that some of the priests, that of old were wont to be supported with those tithes, died for want of food.[23]

The Pharisees

The Pharisees, in contrast, were respected by the common people. A lay renewal group that had been scandalized by the behavior of the priestly class, the group sought to bring the nation back to authentic piety and holiness by rigorous obedience to the prescriptions of the Torah. The Pharisees sought to make the practices of ritual purity and dietary laws prescribed for the priestly class apply to the people as a whole. Committed to renewal, they differed from the Essenes, who, although similarly scandalized by the priestly class, felt it necessary to withdraw altogether from society and move as a community into the desert. The Pharisees believed in renewing society from within.

The Pharisees, in their zeal for purity, accepted not just the written Torah but also all the inherited verbal and written interpretations and embellishments that had come down to them—which served as a "fence" to protect the written Torah. Keeping all the prescriptions of the inherited tradition made sure that one would never come close to violating the written Torah. (The Sadducees, another party within first-century Judaism, differed from the Pharisees on this count. They did not accept the inherited embellishments to the law but only the written Torah.) Because of their diligence and integrity, the Pharisees

---

[23]Ibid.

had considerable authority to interpret and even dictate the behavior of others. Under the later Hasmoneans they had enjoyed considerable power and influence. They even had the power of the sword behind them in those years. As John Meier writes, "They were willing to use the power of the state to impose their legal practices on the people—even bloody vengeance on their foes."[24] Under Herod, because they so vigorously resisted his moves to introduce Hellenism into the country, they found themselves out of power. After Herod the Great's death, under Pilate and the Sanhedrin, they enjoyed renewed power and influence.

The Pharisees believed that to be faithful to Yahweh and to renew Israel, it was important that the people remain pure and undefiled. Many things could make people impure—certain occupations, contact with dead bodies, contact with Gentiles, contact with bodily fluids, lack of physical wholeness from illness as in eunuchs or lepers, and perhaps what was most important for the Pharisees, not keeping the rituals surrounding food and not tithing according to the law.

The importance and power of a shared meal are known to all people. To share a meal is an expression of intimacy and fellowship. To invite someone to a meal, particularly in one's home, honors that person and expresses trust and acceptance. Sharing a meal was particularly important for people of the ancient Near East. Refusing to share a meal communicates disapproval and rejection. As Marcus Borg writes: "Such rejection was a form of social control whereby unseemly behavior was discouraged. Thus sharing or refusing to share a table in antiquity had a social function, expressing approval or disapproval of different modes of behavior."[25]

The number of rules that grew up around table fellowship was astounding—it was difficult to know them all, first, and even more difficult to observe them in their entirety. Two hundred twenty-nine of the 341 rabbinic texts attributed to the Pharisaic schools of Shammai and Hillel of the first century pertained to table fellowship, including stipulations of how to make sure that food was not rendered impure during its preparation or serving and rules concerning proper hand washing before meals.[26] The quest for holiness meant that one ob-

---

[24]John P. Meier, *A Marginal Jew: Rethinking the Historical Jesus*, vol. 3 (New York: Doubleday, 2001), 331.

[25]Marcus Borg, *Conflict, Holiness, and Politics in the Teachings of Jesus* (Harrisburg, PA: Trinity Press International, 1998), 94.

[26]Ibid., 97.

served these rules strictly. A person who observed them was a faithful follower of Yahweh. If a person did not follow them, that person was not holy, not an observant member of the community, and was on the outside looking in—along with the gentiles and others who were impure in various ways.

The second area important to the Pharisees, as they tried to extend the priestly purity laws to the people as a whole, was proper tithing. A small fee was expected to be paid to the Temple at every stage of the food production process—at the time of planting, the time of reaping, the time of distribution, and on through consumption. Not to pay meant that an individual was not observant, had separated himself or herself from the community. Jesus' reaction to these practices is hinted at in the line from Luke and Matthew: "But woe to you Pharisees. For you tithe the mint and rue and every herb, and neglect justice and love of God" (Luke 11:42; Matt. 23:23).

This concept of holiness through observance of the laws concerning the preparation of food and tithing led to practical limitations on table fellowship. One could not be a guest of a person who was lax with regard to payment of tithes or food preparation, and one could not be at a meal if there were guests present who would defile the meal. This approach to table fellowship was a vivid symbol of Israel's emerging destiny and political philosophy—separation. Borg writes, "Holiness as separation served a survival function by separating Israel from elements subversive of its solidarity. Table fellowship as a public embodiment of holiness seemed to many a 'survival symbol,' which, if shattered or eroded, would threaten the cohesiveness of Israel."[27]

The Pharisees' insistence on purity was actually a much broader agenda than simple rule keeping. It was a way of maintaining Jewish identity, defending against the inroads of paganism in order to eventually realize once again the dream of national liberation. The focus on the purity code was not about personal cleanliness but symbolic of purity for the tribe. As N. T. Wright explains, "The Jewish laws were not designed as a legalist's ladder up which one might climb to heaven but were the boundary-markers for a beleaguered people."[28] The Pharisees, as a self-appointed pressure group, in effect kept the fires of resistance burning and eventually stoked the fires, collaborat-

---

[27]Borg, *Conflict, Holiness and Politics,* 96.
[28]N. T. Wright, *The Challenge of Jesus* (Downers Grove, IL: IVP Academic, 1999), 58.

ing with those who turned to violence to secure national liberation through the fight against Rome. According to Wright:

> The followers of Hillel and Shammai, the two great sages of the Herodian period, disagreed not merely on the finer points of Torah observance, but on what a loyal Jew should do in the present political circumstances: should one actively resist Rome, or be content to study and practice Torah? . . . Strong evidence exists that the former, the position associated with the house of Shammai, was held by the majority prior to 66. In other words (a significant conclusion for any discussion of Jesus and the Gospels, and indeed Paul), the Pharisees in the period we are concerned with, between the death of Herod the Great and the outbreak of war in 66, were concerned with politics, not merely with piety; with resistance and revolution, not merely with private holiness.[29]

From the standpoint of the common people, however, the holiness code of the Pharisees meant that many, many people in Israel at the time of Jesus found themselves in effect on the outside looking in, impure for one reason or another: those in certain occupations such as shepherds or those who had to deal with gentiles, tax collectors; the sick—because sickness was perceived as punishment for sin, either one's own or one's ancestors; those who married outsiders—down to the tenth generation; those who did not keep the dietary laws; those who did not or could not pay the requisite tithes; the uneducated who did not know what those laws and prescriptions were. How many could there be who were still left inside the circle of purity? This situation was coupled with the fact that so many in Israel had lost their small land holdings—driven into penury or sharecropper status—because of the practices of the powers that be, the actions of the power structure in place; the Roman occupiers made sure they took their share of each harvest; the Herodians, with their massive building projects designed to keep favor with Rome and give them glory, took their share of each harvest; the priests took their share of each harvest for the Temple tax and for the animals to be sacrificed, and the priests themselves used

---

[29]N. T. Wright, Foreword to Marcus Borg, *Conflict, Holiness, and Politics in the Teachings of Jesus* (Harrisburg, PA: Trinity Press International, 1998), xii.

the Temple treasury to purchase land and further impoverish the small landowners. The Pharisees, with all their good intentions, through their insistence on additional food tithes flowing into the Temple treasury, further strengthened a terribly unjust system and exacerbated the plight of the people. As Senior wrote:

> The burden of taxation was almost unbearable. . . . The land was in the hands of absentee landowners. . . . The pressure of injustice was matched for many by a burden of religious guilt. . . . Those whose occupations brought them into contact with Gentiles were proscribed as officially unclean, shopkeepers and traders. . . . A world of mounting political tension, moving toward an inevitable holocaust—this was the world that Jesus ministered to.[30]

The Jewish religious/political power structure harmed the people more than Rome did. Religion, in effect, was being used to reinforce an unjust, oppressive system.

We begin to understand why, from the beginning of his public life, Jesus, as a faithful Jew, found himself in conflict with the power structure of the time—the scribes, who were those well versed in the scriptures, the Pharisees, the priestly class, the Herodians, and eventually Rome.

Jesus' Counternarrative: The Kingdom of God

Jesus read the Jewish scriptures and experienced the God of the Jewish religion in a very different way than the Pharisees of his time. As a result, he laid out a different way of dealing with the occupying power, Rome, a different way of responding to the needs of the common people, and a different way forward for the Jewish people. Jesus' teaching on the kingdom of God confronts both the Pharisees' holiness code, which maintained that the people should stay undefiled to ensure that the day of national liberation will come, and the unjust situation of the common people, which left them impoverished and outcast, that stems from that separatist holiness code. Jesus has compassion for the people and an alternative vision of what to do about Israel's political plight.

---

[30]Senior, *Jesus: A Gospel Portrait*, 44.

No Violence in God or Jesus

The first difference between Jesus' understanding of the Jewish scriptures and that of the Pharisees that shapes a different politics, is this: *There is no violence in God. There is no vengeance.*

We know that Jesus was deeply versed in the Jewish scriptures. The evangelists portray Jesus as one who speaks in a way that continually calls to mind passages from the Jewish scriptures. Luke's account of Jesus' encounter with two disciples on the road to Emmaus after the events of Holy Week tells us the lens he used to interpret the scriptures. They were despondent and confused. As they walked along, Jesus came up and walked beside them, but they did not recognize him. He began to do Bible study with them to explain to them how to read the scriptures. He said, "How slow you are to understand all that the prophets have told you. Did not the Christ have to suffer and then enter his glory?" (Luke 24:25–26). Then starting with Moses and going through all of the prophets, he explained to them the passages that were about himself. They said after he had left them, "Were not our hearts burning within us as he explained the scriptures to us?" (Luke 24:32). Jesus focused on the key to understanding the Jewish scriptures as a whole—on the violence willingly suffered by him, the messiah. What may have been most surprising to them in Jesus' explanation was that there was no retribution from God against those who committed the violence to his highly favored one. Instead, the violence that was willingly suffered led to glory. As Michael Hardin describes it:

> What may have astonished them the most was that the emphasis placed by Jesus on the meaning of his suffering and death did not result in some kind of retribution from God. It was the forgiveness expressed by God in the resurrected Jesus that collapsed all their previous theological ideas and assumptions. Their theologies dictated a violent or retributive response on the part of God. That never happened; instead peace, reconciliation, forgiveness and love were announced.[31]

The idea of a violent God had already been a problem for Judaism. The scriptures evidence an evolving understanding of God. The god

---

[31]Michael Hardin, *The Jesus Driven Life* (Lancaster, PA: JDL Press, 2010), 28.

portrayed in Joshua is vicious and vengeful—reflecting the mores and assumptions of the time. That is the way gods were expected to act. Gradually those perceptions were perceived to actually be projections of vengeful and violent human beings onto the godhead.

The God of the later prophets is distinctly different from the God who sanctions and even inspires violence in the earlier books of the Jewish scriptures. In Ezekiel, chapter 33, and Wisdom, chapter 11, the indiscriminately compassionate God begins to emerge clearly, leaving behind the conception of a God of vengeance and violence. God is faithful, constant, always loving, despite the hardness of heart of human beings. God in Hosea is seen according to Hosea's own experience—Hosea was faithful to his wife, Gomer, even after she was unfaithful to him. By the end of the book of Isaiah, the idea begins to emerge that not only will God not use force against humans, God will send a savior, a suffering servant, who will show humanity a new way to deal with humanity's violence—by enduring it and still coming back with love. The songs of the Servant of Yahweh who "submitted to be struck down and did not open his mouth though he had done no violence and spoke no word of treachery" (Isa. 53:7–9) became a great breakthrough for the divine revelation that "God's plan of salvation intends nothing less than to rescue sinners from their violence and all ideologies that try to justify violence," as Bernard Häring writes.[32]

Jesus talked of his Abba/Imma precisely in these terms of absolutely indiscriminate love. "Love your enemies and pray for those who persecute you so that you may be children of your Father in heaven, for he causes his sun to rise on the bad as well as the good and sends down rain to fall on the upright and the wicked alike" (Matt. 5:45). More important than the way Jesus talks about God is the way he acts—with the same indiscriminate, nonthreatening, positive outreach to all. He does not ask for repentance before he forgives. He reverses the expected order: first comes forgiveness and then often, as a result, repentance. To Zaccheus, the tax collector and the most notorious sinner in Jericho, who climbs a tree to catch a glimpse of Jesus passing by, Jesus says, "Zaccheus come down. Today I am going to stay at your house." Zaccheus said, "Sir, I am going to give half of what I have to the poor, and if I have defrauded anyone I will give them four times as much in return." Jesus said, "Salvation has come to this

---

[32]Häring, *The Healing Power of Peace and Nonviolence*, 43.

house today" (Luke 19:5–9). First the power of love, and then comes repentance and change. As Walter Wink puts it, "He did not wait for them to repent, become respectable, and do works of restitution in hopes of gaining divine forgiveness and human restoration. Instead he says their sins are forgiven. You are forgiven, now you can repent. There is nothing you must do to earn this. You need only accept it."[33]

Character is known through actions. Jesus imparted forgiveness directly. This contrasted with the temple cult where people came to offer sacrifices to be cleansed of their sins, where forgiveness came only after people signaled and acted out their repentance. "In his message of the kingdom, salvation and penance seem to have exchanged places," Raymond Schwager writes.[34] If God had seemed Janus-faced, showing beneficence with one side of his face and ready to condemn and wreak revenge and punishment with the other, Jesus showed that God has only one face. "What really blew the early church's mind was not whether Jesus was like God, but whether God was like Jesus," writes Hardin.[35]

No Wrath in God

Another way of saying there is no violence in God is "there is *no wrath* of God." The threatening, great God, Jehovah, coming on a cloud in judgment of the wicked is not found in Jesus' reading of the scriptures. The lust for the punishment of the bad guys is not God's; it is a human reaction projected onto God. There is judgment, but the judgment of evil is in the evil itself playing itself out to its own demise. Humans who refuse the offer of goodness judge themselves by the measure with which they judge others. That leads to complete self-absorption and can descend into what can only be called hell. Jesus' pronouncements of woe are about the Pharisees' self-deception denying the problem of violence in their own actions.

"God is always in himself the kind father who meets sinners with anticipatory love; only if sinners, despite the experience of grace, cling to their own criteria of judgment do they imprison themselves," Schwager writes.[36] Even the murder of his own son did not provoke

---

[33]Wink, *Engaging the Powers*, 266.
[34]Raymond Schwager, *Jesus in the Drama of Salvation* (New York: Crossroad, 1999), 38.
[35]Hardin, *Jesus Driven Life*, 86.
[36]Schwager, *Jesus in the Drama of Salvation*, 81.

the reaction of vengeful retribution. The risen Jesus appeared with the message of peace and forgiveness—even to those who had rejected the offer the first time. Forgiveness doubled. In the events after the resurrection we clearly see the nonviolent face of God. We see clearly the nonviolent Jesus. As Richard Rohr writes:

> The Risen Jesus. He blames nobody; he punishes no one. He doesn't even bring it up: all the betrayals, the abandonment, the torture, the unfaithfulness of almost everybody. Instead, he identifies forgiveness and peace with his very breath—constant, quiet, unearned—but always given.[37]

God's response to human obduracy is to deliver humankind to ourselves. We do make our own beds and lie in them. We do indeed make our own hells. God does not break in to punish us; we do it to ourselves. God's so-called wrath consists in granting full respect for our freedom. The possibility exists that humans could resist even redemptive and unfathomably forgiving love. Edward Schillebeeckx writes:

> Jesus did not attack the Yahwistic belief in God but the way in which this belief functioned socially in his time, to the detriment of the *anawim* [the poor]. . . . The Jewish-Christian tradition defines God as pure positivity; it rejects all names and images of God which injure and enslave human beings instead of liberating them.[38]

Even the passages in the New Testament that many scholars, such as Albert Schweitzer, had understood as describing the great judgment scene, the end of the world, the end of space-time as we know it, are now understood by the great preponderance of scripture scholars as a description of the end of the political order that Israel had known until that time. If Israel, the Pharisees, and the violent political party that was gathering steam in Israel in Jesus' lifetime kept at it, Jesus could see what was coming. Mark 13, for example, describes not the end of space and time but the coming calamity, the destruction of

---

[37]Richard Rohr, Foreword to Alain Richard, *Roots of Violence in the U.S. Culture* (Nevada City, CA: Blue Dolphin, 1999), xiii.

[38]Edward Schillebeeckx, *The Church: The Human Story of God* (New York: Crossroad, 1994), 58.

the Jewish people and their institutions, including the Temple—if the Pharisees and their allies intent on violence continued on their way of separation and resistance. Rome will be the hammer of their destruction. That grieved Jesus deeply, and he did all he could to point to a more fruitful way. According to Meier, "The end time was not some phantasmagoric destruction of heaven and earth or the complete end of human history. . . . Rather, Jesus was announcing the end of sacred history as Israel had known it up until now, and the definitive beginning of a new and permanent state of affairs."[39]

Jesus' concern was focused on the here and now, the events of history and where those events lead. He used language that is "apocalyptic," that is, taking historical and political events metaphorically to demonstrate the built-in trajectory of those events into the future. As James D. G. Dunn describes it: "Apocalyptic language has to be understood metaphorically in reference to historical and political events rather than literally in reference to the end of the world. . . . Neither Jesus nor his contemporaries were expecting the end of the space-time universe."[40] No wrath in God. No violence. Only unfathomable love. With that understanding of the God of his forefathers, Jesus could not countenance a political order built on exclusion, separation, and hatred of the enemy—in the name of their religion, in the name of their God. If there is no violence in God, that undercuts the age-old tendency of humans to label those who are outside a privileged circle as threats, as enemies, as evil—to dehumanize them and then make them objects of righteous, sacralized violence.

Jesus found the exclusionary stance, the labeling of others as outsiders and the consequent blessing of sacralized violence, to be a misreading of the arc of revelation experienced by the Jewish people in their history with Yahweh. As he read their shared history, he understood that Israel was indeed God's chosen people—but chosen as the hope of humankind. Through Israel the world was offered a God bigger than tribal religion. Yahweh is God of all the earth. Jesus therefore resisted with all his might the temptation to sink into tribal religion and its violence. In fact, he not only resisted; he offered an alternative—the kingdom of God, which, in him, was breaking into their midst.

---

[39]Meier, *Marginal Jew*, 624.
[40]Dunn, *Jesus Remembered*, 1:61.

The Meaning of "The Kingdom of God"

The Picture of the World in Jesus' Time

Before exploring what Jesus meant by the kingdom of God, it is important to note the view of the world that was prevalent among his people at the time. The picture of the world that people had was a two-story world. Above this world, coextensive with this one, is where God dwells, in heaven. Heaven is not, in this understanding, the place where good people go after their death. It is instead the place, contemporaneous with time on earth, where God is. Where God is, all is as it should be. Oftentimes the phrase used in the gospels is the "kingdom of heaven"—a different way of saying the kingdom of God but expressing the same idea. For the kingdom of God to come to this world means that this world is now going to be the way it should be—as things are in heaven. As Jesus taught us to pray: "Thy kingdom come. Thy will be done, on earth as it is in heaven" (Matt. 6:10).

Jesus' Kingdom of God Is a Power and a Place

The kingdom of God for Jesus is both a power and a place—a power that can transform the way things are and a place on the earth, a community, into which one can enter.

So the kingdom of God is first a message of power. Although there is evil, pain, suffering, death, and violence in this world, as great and as prevalent as they are—when and as God comes, they will be met with an even greater power and will be overcome. The nonviolent power of God's love and presence will engage with the violence of this world and overcome it. The darkness will be overcome with light. The violence will be defeated through nonviolent love. This message is not about some other world; it is precisely about this world. It is not a message of deliverance after death; it is about the here and now.

The kingdom of God is also a place, a community that one can enter. The kingdom is not just a power. Jesus did not simply resist; his kingdom was not just over against the current regime. The kingdom he was announcing included a constructive, alternative program and a community or movement that people could join. "Remember me when you enter your kingdom," a place, a new situation, a dynamic new community. By calling disciples and building a community of followers, Jesus was making the kingdom of God visible in their midst. The power was now embodied in people. When Jesus said to Pilate, "My kingdom is not of this world" (John 18:36), he did not mean it was in some other world than this earth; he meant his kingdom was not like Pilate's world—a kingdom based on violence and patronage.

In our day there is a kind of neuralgia in response to the term "kingdom" as there is to a feast day called Christ the King Sunday. The connotations of the word "kingdom" are not very congenial to modern ears—we have, for the most part, done away with kings. Most people in the modern world believe that democracy is a better fit for people who have claimed their political freedom, are trying to build societies of equality, and are moving away from the time when there was one ruler, one privileged class, one will imposed on all—or at least that is where we hope we have come. Perhaps it's acceptable that ceremonial kings and queens serve as identity symbols for people. They add a certain glamor to people's day-to-day, humdrum lives. The few kings and queens who are left in power at least have the counterweight of assemblies and constitutions to hem in their power. As a result of this cultural preference, some scholars prefer to use the terms "reign" or "rule," as in "God's reign" or "God's rule" to convey the idea of power while avoiding the out-of-date idea of a kingdom. Martin Luther King Jr. changed the term "kingdom" to the more contemporary "kindom," taking the king out of it while emphasizing the community-fostering nature of the idea. Although such attempts make some sense, it is preferable to maintain the term "kingdom," precisely because it emphasizes the "place" meaning of the term. A kingdom is a place that you enter, a realm.

This double meaning of the term "kingdom of God" is one of the reasons that centuries later Mahatma Gandhi found the term used by Jesus so compelling and appropriate. In one phrase it expressed a message of hope—that deep change is possible, that domination can and will be overcome if one sides with the truth, the latent power of the universe—and a message of belonging—that participating in the fight against injustice and violence was not to be carried out by solitary individuals but by a people who supported one another, an alternative community, a powerhouse of experimentation and action. He thought Jesus' expression the "kingdom of God" elegantly expressed the proper relationship between religion and politics.

The Kingdom of God Is Primarily Already Here

The first thing to note about the kingdom of God as Jesus announced it is that it is primarily already here. "For, in fact, the kingdom of God is among you" (Luke 17:21). "If it is by the finger of God that I cast out demons, then the Kingdom of God has come to you" (Luke 11:20; Matt. 12:28). "Jesus came to Galilee, proclaiming the good news of God, and saying, 'The time is fulfilled, and the kingdom of God has come near'" (Mark 1.14b–15; Matt. 4:17). The perfect tense, *egiken*, in Greek, Dunn writes, "indicates an action already performed and resulting in a state or effect which continues into the present. It is not a timeless nearness which is in mind; something had happened to bring the kingdom near. . . . The event that brought the kingdom near is the mission of Jesus."[41] That the kingdom of God has come into their midst in the person of Jesus is a fundamentally joyful message. The tradition suggested that the coming of the kingdom would be a great feast. With Jesus apparently there is plenty of feasting. At the same time, of course, the kingdom is not yet fully here. As Wright states, "Evil still stalks the earth."[42] There is still much to be done by those who have embraced the kingdom of nonviolence and loving action. But clearly the main emphasis in the gospels is on the fact that it is *here*.

For much of the history of Christianity, however, the emphasis has been the other way around. The emphasis was on the fact that Jesus was coming back, and then the kingdom would be really established at the end of space and time—in another world, not this one. The emphasis on an eschatological end—no need to work to change the way things are on earth because God will come in judgment at the end and make things right—tends to cause people to accept the status quo; it can become an apologia for mute acceptance of the way things are. Karl Marx's saying that religion is an opium of the people has some truth when religion makes the "sweet by and by" the really important thing. That is what Schweitzer's teaching on the eschatological judgment had the effect of doing. That is why it is so important that scripture scholarship has returned to the balance in the gospels themselves to understand Jesus' predictions of the end not as the end of the world but as the end of the political world as it was then known, the predict-

---

[41]Dunn, *Jesus Remembered*, 406.
[42]N. T. Wright, *Jesus and the Victory of God* (Minneapolis: Fortress Press, 1996), 659.

able fate of the destruction of Israel by Rome if the violent resistance continued to escalate. As Wright notes, "Jesus' warnings about imminent judgment were intended to be taken as denoting socio-political events, seen as the climactic moment in Israel's history. . . . In such a world to be nonpolitical is to be irrelevant."[43]

That the kingdom has come and is among us challenges us to act in the way Jesus acted. De-emphasizing that the kingdom is already here has very real consequences for Christianity. For example, the 1983 document of the American Catholic Bishops, *The Challenge of Peace*, which is a very important statement on peace, war, nuclear weapons, and deterrence, suffers from its overemphasis on the kingdom as "not yet." Because the kingdom is "not yet," not fully established, there is a place for war and the just war theory. Because God has not yet come fully in the Second Coming, one has to deal with the world as it is and not as we wish it would be. Although nonviolence may be laudably adopted by individuals, the real world contains enemies, and "realistically," violence has to be confronted with violence. When the kingdom is fully established, we can then follow Jesus' way of nonviolence. Until then it is just not practical.

The Kingdom of God Is Political

The second thing to note about the kingdom of God is that it is political. In Jesus' time the idea that religion and politics are separate was unthinkable.

The word "political" can be a slippery one and can be easily misunderstood when applied to Jesus. We in the United States, with our history of separation of church and state, are leery when the word "political" is applied to Jesus. We know that often in history when politics was fused with religion, "God's will" became the excuse for untold horrors and violence—from the Christian crusades to the terrorism of Al Qaeda. Many US Americans also shrink back from the way religion is used as a cudgel in the political debates over personal moral issues. Many conclude that "religion and politics don't mix." That conclusion, however, can have the effect of pushing religion out of the public square and relegating it to the personal, private sphere. Peace for the soul then becomes the sole purpose of religion. When

---

[43]Ibid., 97, 98.

religion is privatized in this way, it can have little influence on humanity's struggles for freedom and justice.

In what sense then is the kingdom of God political? The kingdom that Jesus preached had everything to do with the conflicts between Israel and Rome, everything to do with the conflicts between the common people and the ruling classes, everything to do with redressing the injustices inflicted on the peasant farmers, everything to do with the future shape and destiny of the people of Israel—political issues all. Whenever one is debating the issues of a community's well-being and future direction, one is involved in the world of politics. Politics here is being used in a broad, not a narrow, sense. As Borg writes, "Jesus did not seek a seat on the Sanhedrin or serve in the civil service or become involved in palace intrigues or guerilla warfare."[44] Those can be considered politics in the narrow sense. Jesus did, however, have grave concerns about, and involved himself in, the issues of the structure, the direction, and the purpose of his historical community—politics in the broad sense. Perhaps it would be less misleading to say that the kingdom of God operates not just in the private sphere but affects the public sphere as well.

The substance of Jesus' vision, the way he asked his followers to live, can also be called political. "Jesus calls his followers to share their bread, be reconciled with one another, love their enemies, and to honor the underdog and outsiders," John Howard Yoder writes.[45] The marks of a Christian were not in rituals or ahistorical gnosis or speculative religiosity. The marks constituted a distinct way of living day to day in community with others, ways of living in the polis—they were political.

The Three Political Impacts of the Kingdom of God

Jesus' announcement that the kingdom of God is in their midst has three distinct political impacts. The first impact relates to the way Israel is relating to the outside world in general and Rome in particular. The second impact relates to the people within Israel, especially the impoverished and the outcast. The third impact relates to the power structure of Israel—the "system" and its supporting institutions.

---

[44]Borg, *Conflict, Holiness, and Politics in the Teachings of Jesus*, 23.

[45]John Howard Yoder, *The War of the Lamb*, ed. Glen Stassen, Mark Thiessen Nation, and Matt Hamsher (Grand Rapids, MI: Brazos Press, 2009), 168.

The first political impact—Jesus is recommending an alternative way of dealing with enemies, in this case, the occupying power, Rome.

"Love your enemies and pray for those who persecute you" (Matt. 5:44) is a much more positive and aggressive stance than it appears to be at first hearing—we will explore that later. In this context, however, it is at least the beginning of an attempt to convince the Pharisees and others that there is another way to deal with the future of the Jewish people; it is a warning that the way they are choosing will be a dead end. Albert Nolan writes that Jesus' message was "to persuade the Jews that their present attitude of resentment and bitterness is suicidal. . . . The only way to be liberated from your enemies is to love your enemies."[46]

It was thought, at that time, that there were only three ways forward: fight, flight, or accommodate. The Essenes had chosen flight; they withdrew into the desert to build their own version of the Jewish religion. The priests and the Herodians had chosen accommodation; collaborating with the Romans meant they could continue to practice their religion, and as long as they did what the Romans wanted, they could wield a degree of power and even build some wealth for themselves. The Pharisees and, later, the party of violent resistance chose to resist, maintain their identity over against the pagans, keep it clear that they were enemies, and eventually to fight.

Jesus' kingdom of God pointed out a fourth way for Israel. Build an inclusive community, even including so-called enemies, by using the power of nonviolent, loving, willing-to-risk-suffering action. Later it will be called the Way of the Cross. If this could be done, Israel would fulfill its calling to be the light of the world. Instead of a way of narrow exclusion, Israel could practice the way of arms-wide-open inclusion and be the city on the hill that the rest of the world is looking for.

Looking back at this important juncture in history when Israel was confronted by Jesus with this alternative way—instead of the path of violence that it was beginning to take—it is legitimate to ask: Was Jesus' recommendation of an actively nonviolent path for a renewed Israel sound political advice?

Israel as a whole did not accept his advice. Instead, a remnant, one that evolved into early Christianity, took that path. It is astounding how quickly Christianity grew—precisely because it embodied a com-

---

[46]Albert Nolan, *Jesus before Christianity* (Maryknoll, NY: Orbis Books, 2008), 13.

munity that took care of its own, reached out in charity to so-called enemies, willingly accepted suffering and persecution even unto martyrdom, and experimented with ways to bring comfort and justice to the communities in which they were living. In a very insightful book, *The Rise of Christianity*,[47] Rodney Stark, a sociologist of religion, explored the archaeological evidence that confirmed the quick and widespread growth of Christianity throughout the Roman Empire. He concluded that Christianity grew so quickly because of the way Christians acted, a way markedly different from those around them. For example, Stark says that in the archaeological evidence, "We've unearthed sewers clogged with bones of newborn girls; the early Christians had to live with a trench running down the middle of the road in which you could find dead bodies decomposing. . . . Christians did speak against infanticide; they cared for each other and the weak in a society that otherwise blinded itself to human need."[48] The very poor, slaves, and outsiders were unimportant in Roman society. Assistance was confined to citizens. Into that world came Christianity. Christians loved one another and offered outreach to the less fortunate. That was what was magnetic about early Christianity. Stark goes on to compare the growth of early Christianity to the growth of the fastest-growing religions of our own time, such as Mormonism, and finds the same basic reason for their attractiveness and growth—their way of life. They care for one another and reach out to others with kindness and charity. Christianity grew because Christians in community followed the nonviolent Jesus in their daily actions.

In our day we are freshly reconsidering Jesus' alternative way of nonviolent, creative, loving, willing-to-suffer action and discovering the many ways it is sound political advice.

If the first political impact of Jesus's teaching about the kingdom of God concerned the way Israel was relating to the world outside Israel, especially Rome, the second political impact related to those inside Israel.

The second political impact of the kingdom of God lay in the way Jesus related to and treated those who were outcasts from society.

---

[47]Rodney Stark, *The Rise of Christianity: A Sociologist Reconsiders History* (Princeton, NJ: Princeton Univerity Press, 1996).

[48]Rodney Stark as quoted in Willard Swartley, *Covenant of Peace* (Grand Rapids, MI: William B. Eerdmans, 2006), 221.

Jesus gave the first speech of his public life in a synagogue in Nazareth where he grew up. He stood up to read and was given the scroll of the prophet Isaiah, and he found the place he wanted and began to read: "The spirit of the Lord is on me, for he has anointed me to bring good news to the afflicted. He has sent me to proclaim liberty to the captives, sight to the blind, to let the oppressed go free, to proclaim a year of jubilee from the Lord" (Luke 4:18–19). When he had finished, he rolled up the scroll, gave it back to the attendant, and said, "This text is being fulfilled today even while you are listening" (Luke 4:21). In other words, the kingdom of God has come into your midst, and it brings with it, through me, good news for the poor, the outcasts, and the oppressed. Jesus then set out to deliver on those promises through his healing, his exorcisms, his words of hope, and his practice of sharing meals with the very people who had been cast out of polite society. He chose a very different part of the Jewish tradition—the teaching of the prophets and the Deuteronomic jubilee tradition—to place in competition with the vision of the Pharisees.

The constant theme of the Deuteronomic vision and continued by all the prophets of Israel was to treat everyone justly and show compassion to the poor, the widows, the orphans, and the sojourners (the latter sometimes translated as "aliens" or "landless strangers"). In our day and age we might translate it as "immigrants."

From Deuteronomy: "You shall not withhold the wages of the poor and needy laborers, whether other Israelites or aliens who reside in your land in one of your towns. . . . You shall not deprive a resident alien or an orphan of justice; you shall not take a widow's garment in pledge" (Deut. 24:14, 17). These groups were consistently held up as needing special concern because these were the most vulnerable groups in the society. Widows have little power and are especially vulnerable because they have no male protection. Orphans are powerless and vulnerable because they have no parents to look after them. Sojourners or aliens (immigrants) are vulnerable because they have no tribal support to shield them.

On through the prophets, for example, Isaiah, justice for the oppressed and concern for the vulnerable is the ongoing mantra:

Ah, you who make iniquitous decrees, who write oppressive statutes, to turn aside the needy from justice and to rob the poor of my people of their right, that widows may be your spoil, and that you may make orphans your prey. (Isa. 10:1–2)

And Jeremiah:

For if you truly amend your ways and your doings, if you truly act justly with one another, if you do not oppress the alien, the orphan, and the widow, or shed innocent blood in this place, and if you do not go after other gods to your own hurt, then I will dwell with you in this place, in the land that I gave of old to your ancestors forever and ever. (Jer. 7:5–7)

The whole purpose of the jubilee tradition was to provide adequately for the poor and vulnerable and to keep the gap between the wealthy and the poor from growing greater. The Deuteronomy program for eliminating poverty is closely connected to the land. Landless strangers (aliens), widows, and orphans without land will live on the brink of survival. There was a constant provision for sharing in every field or harvest.

When you reap your harvest in your field and forget a sheaf in the field, you shall not go back to get it; it shall be left for the alien, the orphan, and the widow, so that the Lord your God may bless you in all your undertakings. When you beat your olive trees, do not strip what is left; it shall be for the alien, the orphan, and the widow. When you gather the grapes of your vineyard, do not glean what is left; it shall be for the alien, the orphan, and the widow. (Deut. 24:19–21)

And every third year a special tithe was to be stored so that the "Levites who have no allotment of land, as well as the resident aliens, orphans, and widows in your towns may come and eat their fill so that the Lord your God may bless you in all the work that you undertake" (Deut. 14:28).

The other important jubilee directives had to do with people who had lost their plots of land due to indebtedness. Every seven years title to the lost lands would be returned to the original owners. In addition, people who had to sell themselves into slavery or into tenant farming because of indebtedness, every seven years would be restored to their freedom and be given a stake so they could begin again—all to make sure that the gap between the wealthy and the not so wealthy would not continue to widen over time. These practices also underline the central truth that the earth, all the land, belongs to Yahweh alone. To whom he has granted land in Israel is divinely ordered and should be respected and maintained. The Deuteronomic tradition of justice is a distributive justice tradition—land and wealth should be distributed fairly to those in need. The Pharisaic holiness tradition with its tithing regulations is redistributive in the wrong direction—from those in need to those who already have the wealth. Sharon Ringe writes:

> [In] the Jubilee and Sabbath-year traditions of the Hebrew Scriptures . . . liberty is presented in economic, social and political terms: freedom for slaves, cancellation of debts and redistribution of land. . . . We are never given a blueprint of God's reign, but in the Jubilee images we get a glimpse of those points of intersection where daily life of human design encounters the truth of God's sovereignty.[49]

Jesus is embracing this central theme of the Jewish tradition as his own. "Be compassionate as your Father is compassionate" (Luke 6:36). Jesus presents a competing vision of the way that the poor and the outcasts in their midst should be treated. The Pharisees are quoting and commending Leviticus: "You shall be holy, because I, Yahweh your God, am holy" (Lev. 19:1–2). The Pharisees are contending that just as God's holiness is separation from all that defiles, so also for Israel holiness is separation from all that defiles. The future security of the nation depends on Israel's remaining pure and undefiled. With that vision they institute a series of laws around food and tithes that result in more and more people being put outside the circle of faithfulness, more and more outcasts separated from the fold. Jesus sets out to bring the outcasts back into the fold. Holiness for Jesus is not purity but compassion; not exclusion, but inclusion. That is the special meaning of his exorcisms and healings.

In Jesus' exorcisms the kingdom of God comes into the midst of the people through his contention with the powers of evil and violence.

---

[49]Sharon H. Ringe, *Jesus, Liberation, and the Biblical Jubilee* (Philadelphia: Fortress Press, 1985), xlv.

When he drives out the evil one, he says, "But if it is by the finger of God that I drive out evil spirits, then the kingdom of God has indeed come upon you" (Luke 11:20). Willard Swartley writes, "Jesus' deeds are acts of liberation: exorcisms and healings not only free people from the devil's grip, they also free people from social ostracism and challenge the religious laws that fetter freedom."[50]

Jesus' healings restore the person's health and place in the community. If leprosy makes a person unclean and as a result puts a person outside the circle of faithful Jews, Jesus heals lepers and tells them to report to the priests so they can be officially declared clean and restored to communion. If a woman with a discharge of blood is by that fact made unclean, he heals her and makes her "clean" and restores her to the community of faith. For those who are supposedly made impure because of what they eat or because they have not taken adequate care in the preparation of food, he declares that it is not what goes into people that makes them unclean but what comes out of their hearts—in effect denying and undercutting the entire edifice of branding people unclean through food laws. If particular jobs, such as shepherding or tax collecting, supposedly make people unclean and outcasts, Jesus associates with them. He even eats with them, shocking the Pharisees.

Jesus' way is not the way of exclusion; it is the way of inclusion. He is compassionate to the poor and the outcasts and claims that is the way to follow Yahweh, the God of their tradition. He says, "Be inclusive [*teleios* in Greek—unfortunately frequently translated "perfect"] as my heavenly Father is inclusive" (Matt. 5:48). Inclusive can also be translated "indiscriminate" or "unconditional." "Love your enemies and do good to them, and lend without any hope of return. You will have a great reward, and you will be children of the Most High, for *He himself is kind to the ungrateful and the wicked*" (Luke 6:35).

Would following this way of compassion and inclusiveness have meant the loss of identity that the Pharisees feared? Swartley writes that "religious orders throughout the world" have maintained distinctive identities while dedicated to compassion;[51] the two aren't mutually

---

[50]Willard Swartley, *Covenant of Peace* (Grand Rapids, MI: William B. Eerdmans, 2006), 94.

[51]Ibid., 150.

exclusive. The Pharisees desired a community with sharp and clearly defined boundaries. Early Christianity proceeded with a welcome-for-all style with indistinct boundaries and yet endured.

When Jesus announced to the people of Nazareth that the kingdom of God had come to them in his very reading of the passage from Isaiah that explained what the kingdom of God was all about, that it meant that the poor had the good news of liberation and justice brought to them, he omitted, or Luke omits, the last phrase of verse 2: "and a day of vengeance for our God." Yes to a year of jubilee; no to a day of vengeance. Jesus, in effect, may be saying that we have had enough vengeance. We need more jubilee.

The evangelists use one word consistently to describe Jesus' stance and emotion in the presence of those who are suffering. They say he felt *splachizomai*. His innards were moved with feelings of compassion for them.

Jesus set out to build the kingdom of God that had come into the world through him—from below, from the bottom up. He began with those who were at the bottom of the hierarchy of society and began to bind up their wounds, drive out their devils, give them back hope and confidence. He had a constructive program. He commissioned his disciples, first the twelve and then greater numbers, to go town by town doing the same actions—healing, relieving depression, bringing people together to share what they had with one another. "The itinerant Jesus actively addressed, engaged and wooed the whole of Israel," writes Meier.[52]

As he was building support for his vision of the nonviolent, compassionate kingdom of God from the grass roots, Jesus also had his eye on the leadership. He understood that more harm was being wrought on his people by their own religious leaders, at times unwittingly, than by the occupying power, Rome. Their own religious leaders were contributing to the suffering of the people—the poverty, the loss of lands, the feelings of alienation by those who could not live up to the Pharisees' interpretation of Torah—so Jesus gradually turned his attention to that leadership, the Pharisees, the priests, the scribes. He conducted what can only be called a nonviolent resistance campaign designed to reach them, convince them, and turn them around.

---

[52]Meier, *Marginal Jew,* 532.

The third political impact of the kingdom of God related to the re-ligious leadership of Israel and some of the ways the institutions of Israel were being run.

The two political impacts that we have already reviewed will need support from not just the common people but also the religious leadership of Israel. Adopting a different vision of how to deal with the occupying power, Rome, would require a change of heart for many of the Pharisees. Neither fight nor flight nor accommodate but only an alternative, inclusive community of nonviolent, loving service could break the cycle of violence. Many Pharisees were already leaning toward the way of violence against Rome. A nonviolent community would also require a significant change on the part of the priests. Many of them were wedded to the status quo of accommodation to Rome and securing what benefits they could for themselves. Second, Jesus showed, in competition with the vision of the Pharisees, an alternative way for Israel to deal with the poor and oppressed within Israel—follow the Deuteronomic way of jubilee, the way also of the prophets. Practice justice and show compassion to the most vulnerable within Israel. The Pharisees had much invested in their holiness code. Their ability to interpret the Torah in the way they saw fit and have it backed by what power for violence the Temple priesthood possessed made them a power within Israel. To change their approach required a significant change of heart and direction. The priestly establishment also had much at stake. The tithing system developed by the Pharisees benefited the Temple and the priests. The economic system as a whole that led so many into poverty through indebtedness also benefited them greatly. To change would take first embracing Jesus' vision and then changing the system.

Jesus was compelled to initiate a campaign to reach and convert the religious leadership of Israel. He set out to convince them to embrace his way of dealing with their external enemies and his preferred way of treating the vulnerable within Israel.

Jesus evidently had a fairly sure grasp on how power works. First, he seemed to understand that people in positions of power do not change their behavior unless they are forced to change when they see it as in their best interests to change. But at the same time he understood that force does not equal violence. Other powerful forces can be brought to bear besides violence. Second, he understood that exercising nonviolent power depends on a vanguard, a community of well-trained and disciplined advocates who care deeply about their cause and who will act for their cause. Third, Jesus understood the latent power in numbers. If a whole population can be rallied to a cause, those who are in leadership will at least take notice and at least pause. Fourth, he believed in the power of single-minded, charismatic leadership to make a difference in the power equation. Fifth, he recognized the power of being willing to suffer for one's cause. Sixth, he knew the importance of assertive dialogue with an opponent, the kind that can reveal the larger truth that can enlighten both sides of a conflict. Seventh, he seemed to understand the power of well-placed and well-timed symbolic action.

Step 1: Recruit a Vanguard

Jesus' full strategy for reaching the whole of Israel, common people and leadership, began to play out right from the beginning of the gospels. Jesus' first task was to recruit a vanguard, a group of followers who catch and believe in his vision of the kingdom of God come to Israel and who will dedicate themselves to action. He called the disciples. They are so captured by the man and the message that they leave their nets, their countinghouses, their parents, their former lives and join him. He demands full-throated, no-looking-back commitment from them. He devotes much patient time and energy educating them. He gives them their tasks of healing, casting out the devils of discord and confusion, preaching the gospel of God's love for the poor and vulnerable, and they return jubilant that people are not only listening but eager to embrace Jesus and his message. They are not an easy lot. It takes him until the end, for example, to disabuse them of the common belief about the Messiah, that he will lead a violent revolt. But they devote themselves to him, his message, and his way.

Step 2: Build Powerful Grassroots Support

Jesus' second task was to build strong grassroots support. Right at the beginning of Mark's Gospel we witness Jesus' strategy of building support from the people as a whole. It helps to trace the process. In chapter 1 of Mark we read that Jesus and four of his newly minted disciples headed straight for the largest, most important town on the Sea of Galilee, into the religious center and gathering place for the town at the time when most of the populace would be gathered for study and prayer. "They went into the town of Capernaum and Jesus began to teach in the synagogue during the Sabbath assemblies" (Mark 1:21). Straight away he sparked a wildfire of interest. "And Jesus' fame spread throughout all the country of Galilee" (Mark 1:28). Not content with reaching just one major town's population, Jesus then said: "Let's go to the nearby villages" (Mark 1:38).

He began to draw from a wider and wider area: "A great number of people also came from Judea, Jerusalem, Idumea, Transjordan and from the region of Tyre and Sidon, for they had heard of all that he was doing" (Mark 3:7–8). Jesus extended his personal outreach farther and farther, first across the Sea of Galilee to the east to the region of the Gerasenes (Mark 5:1) where many former Roman soldiers had settled. Then he ventured further into land occupied by gentiles, the border of the Tyrian country and into the towns of the Decapolis (Mark 7:32). Finally, he ventured to Caesarea Philippi, as far north as one could go and still be in Israel (Mark 8:27).

Everywhere he went he gathered crowds and made supporters. He had galvanized the power of numbers—to the extent that "the chief priests and teachers of the law . . . were afraid of him because all the people were captivated by his teaching" (Mark 11:18). As Wright notes:

> He was not so much a wandering preacher preaching sermons, or a wandering philosopher offering maxims, as like a politician gathering support for a new and highly risky movement. . . . Again we should not imagine that politics here could be split off from theology. Jesus was doing what he was doing in the belief that in this way Israel's God was becoming king. Throughout this work Jesus was seeking to gather support for his kingdom-movement.[53]

He was not only building support for his message of the kingdom of God as liberating the poor from domination—he is also building the messianic community.

The widespread support of the common people was his shield but also his opportunity. His success drew members of the power structure to investigate him for themselves. It was Jesus' opportunity to engage them.

Step 3: Engage Members of the Power Structure in Dialogue

The gospels were written after the fact, after Jesus had conducted

---

[53]Wright, *Challenge of Jesus*, 42–43.

intensive dialogue with the Pharisees and the scribes, after those attempts to reach these important members of the religious power structure, had, in the main, failed. The power structure, both religious and civil, had rejected Jesus and his message concerning the kingdom of God. Top religious leadership, the priests and the priestly party, had handed Jesus over to the Roman authority—who alone had the power to execute—to be killed. The Pharisees at this point were not featured in the gospels as directly involved in those proceedings. But nonetheless the memory is there that they did the initial investigations and instigated suspicion and fear among the upper reaches of the power structure. The gospel accounts do show some bitterness as a result. At the same time, however, they indicate just how intensely Jesus tried to reach them.

From the Pharisees' point of view there were some clear markers of faithfulness to their religion: faithfulness in keeping holy the Sabbath, reverence for the Temple, and keeping the commands of the Torah. Remember that the Pharisees accepted numerous oral traditions that served as a fence to protect the keeping of the written commands of the Torah—especially many that had to do with keeping Israel pure and undefiled, such as numerous laws concerning food and tithing. Those markers in turn symbolized "the political struggle to maintain Jewish identity and to realize the dream of national liberation," as Wright phrases it.[54] Representative scribes and Pharisees began to show up, though in the background, at places where Jesus was preaching. They are checking to see if he is a faithful Jew and if he keeps whole the special markers of their tradition.

A delegation of Pharisees kept watch to see if Jesus diligently fulfilled their expectations of orthopraxis. He took their presence as opportunities to invite them to understand his competing vision that was, in fact, faithful to their own deepest traditions—if only they could open themselves to it. One of the hallmarks of nonviolent action and power is its conviction that the opponent in a conflict situation is not an enemy. It always makes sense to find a way to build a bigger vision of truth so that the opponent can be invited into the circle of truth. At a deeper level human beings are in fact, one. A person of nonviolence never gives up hope that an opponent can change. Ched Myers writes, "The struggle for justice must always find a way

---

[54]Wright, *Challenge of Jesus*, 56.

to include its opponents in its vision of the future; just as no disciple is infallible, no adversary is disposable."[55] Centuries later that truth about nonviolent action played out graphically on many occasions. In India, because Gandhi refused to see the British as enemies, there is little ongoing bitterness to the British despite their centuries of cruel domination. So also in South Africa—because South Africa was in the end freed nonviolently, because of the painstaking process of truth and reconciliation after Mandela's election and because of the example of forgiveness practiced and demonstrated by Mandela and Tutu and others, there is a surprising lack of hatred by the population as a whole for the former practitioners of apartheid. So also in our own country. The leaders of the civil rights movement refused to demonize their opponents. Martin Luther King Jr. insisted that Bull Connor and Sheriff Jim Clark and George Wallace not be treated as enemies but as potential partners in a solution. Ralph Abernathy and Dr. King had been put in jail together seventeen times, and each time the two of them "spent the first day in prayer and fasting, so that they would bear no bitterness in their hearts toward their jailers."[56] As a result, Jim Clark later cultivated newly enfranchised Black voters in order to win reelection. George Wallace went from being an icon of segregation to an icon of reconciliation. In 1995 he came to a celebration of the Selma to Montgomery march and apologized. So also in Jesus' practice of nonviolent action: "He tried to win the scribes and Pharisees over to his view of God's action," Pheme Perkins writes.[57]

Reviewing the interactions between Jesus and the Pharisees described in chapters 2 and 3 of Mark's Gospel, for example, we see Jesus' use of the techniques of dialogue and disputation with which the Pharisees are accustomed. He does not treat them as enemies but as potential partners in the newly reconstituted Israel. In chapter 2, when the Pharisees see Jesus' disciples plucking ears of corn as they walked through a cornfield on the Sabbath, they said, "Look, why are they doing something forbidden?" (Mark 2:24). Jesus responded with "vigorous halakhic dispute," Dunn writes.[58] He quoted a legal prec-

---

[55]Ched Myers, *Binding the Strong Man* (Maryknoll, NY: Orbis Books, 2003), 184.

[56]Richard McSorley, *It's a Sin to Build a Nuclear Weapon* (Baltimore, MD: Fortkamp, 1991), 220.

[57]Pheme Perkins, *Love Commands in the New Testament* (New York: Paulist Press, 1982), 24.

[58]Dunn, *Jesus Remembered*, 283.

edent, citing the time when David and his followers, on the run from Saul, ate the loaves of offering that the priests alone were allowed to eat. On another level, however, Jesus referring to himself as the son of man who is lord of the Sabbath, invites them to consider a much larger truth in their midst and goes well beyond a simple legal tête-à-tête.

In the next chapter of Mark, the Pharisees were watching to see if Jesus would cure someone on the Sabbath—what they would have considered "work" and a violation of the Sabbath. Jesus called on a man with a withered hand to stand in the middle of the synagogue. He then tried to appeal to the better angels of the Pharisees' nature, asking them to look at the situation with eyes of compassion. Jesus said: "Is it permitted on the Sabbath day to do good, or to do evil; to save life or to kill?" (Mark 3:3). He is pointing out the deeper meaning of the Sabbath, making their narrow definitions of "work" beside the point. Wright explains that the Sabbath is "rest after trouble, redemption after slavery. . . . The claim was that the Sabbath day was the most appropriate day [for healing], because that day celebrated release from captivity, from bondage, as well as from work."[59] Healing of a man with a withered hand on the Sabbath was well within the central, deeper meaning of the Sabbath. The Pharisees were unmoved. Jesus looked round at them, and Mark wrote, "He was angry and grieved that they had closed their minds. He said to the man, 'stretch out your hand.' He stretched it out and his hand was restored" (Mark 3:5). The Pharisees closed their minds after Jesus was intent on helping them open their minds. He was angry and grieved at his and their failure. On their part, they went out right then and "began to plot with the Herodians against him, discussing how to destroy him" (Mark 3:6).

In his ongoing dialogue with the Pharisees over the meaning of the Sabbath and the legitimacy of healing on the Sabbath, John's Gospel shows Jesus bringing forth another legal precedent: "Moses ordered you to practice circumcision—not that it began with him, it goes back to the patriarchs—and you circumcise on the Sabbath. Now if someone can be circumcised on the Sabbath so that the law of Moses is not broken, why are you angry with me for making someone completely healthy on the Sabbath?" (John 7:22–24).

When some scribes of the Pharisee party saw him eating with tax collectors and, in their mind, sinners, they said to his disciples: "Why

---

[59]Wright, *Jesus and the Victory of God*, 394.

does he eat with tax collectors and sinners?" (Mark 2:16). Jesus overheard them, but he did not respond with anger or denunciation or with halakhic disputation. In this situation, he took another approach—he invited them to look at the situation more deeply, and he patiently clarified what he did and "why he did it in order to help his critics understand the meaning of his actions," as Thomas Schubeck writes.[60] Jesus responded to the Pharisees' question about why he ate with sinners by saying: "It is not the healthy who need the doctor, but the sick. I came to call not the upright, but sinners" (Mark 2:17).

At other times he used very strong language in response to the Pharisees, attempting to shake them up and have them look at their behavior and teachings from the standpoint of the central thrust of the Jewish tradition. "Fiery denunciation was a revered rhetorical tradition from the prophets Amos and Hosea onwards," Meier writes.[61] When the Pharisees and some of the scribes who had come from Jerusalem gathered around Jesus, they noticed that some of his disciples were eating with unclean hands, that is, without washing them, and they asked Jesus, "Why do your disciples not respect the tradition of the elders but eat their food with unclean hands?" (Mark 7:5). Jesus went right after their assumption that they had the right to make this kind of oral tradition the law of the land. He compared their strict standards of performance on what was considered a relatively trivial matter such as hand washing to their scandalously lax behavior on an extremely important matter in their tradition, namely respect for elders, care for their fathers and mothers. Specifically, he pointed to their endorsement of the practice of *korban*. In this practice, a person could declare that his wealth was dedicated to the Temple, that is, to God, and therefore be free from any obligation toward his parents. Convenient. As Myers explains, "Once this vow was made, assets belonged to the Temple treasury and, though still in the hands of the owner, could not be used. . . . The *korban* vow would preclude not only support but all the other things a son might do for a father. . . . Local Pharisees are merely an extension of the long arm of the Jewish establishment that oppresses the poor."[62] Jesus' response to their criticisms about hand washing is worth citing in its entirety:

---

[60]Thomas L. Schubeck, *Love That Does Justice* (Maryknoll, NY: Orbis Books, 2007), 57.
[61]Meier, *Marginal Jew*, 312.
[62]Myers, *Binding the Strong Man*, 221.

He answered: "How rightly Isaiah prophesied about you hypo-
crites in the passage of Scripture: 'This people honors me only
with lip-service, while their hearts are far from me. Their reverence for me is worthless; the lessons they teach are nothing but
human commandments.' You put aside the commandment of
God to observe human traditions." And he said to them, "How
ingeniously you get round the commandment of God in order
to preserve your own tradition! For Moses said, 'Honor your
father and your mother,' and 'Anyone who curses mother or
father must be put to death.' But you say: 'If a man says to his
father or mother: Anything I have that I might have used to help
you is Korban, that is, dedicated to God,' then he is forbidden
from that moment to do anything for his father or mother. In
this way you make God's word ineffective for the sake of your
own tradition which you have handed down. And you do many
other things like this." (Mark 7:7–13)

How devastating is his critique and how clearly he points out the
shallowness and the hypocrisy of insisting on such minor, man-made
rules as hand washing while supporting such a practice as *korban*
that violated a fundamental obligation of their holy tradition: care for
mothers and fathers. One would think that the Pharisees who heard
him would be not only stung but might reconsider their behavior and
the vision of the world that led them to that behavior. He speaks un-
varnished truth to power, with loving intent, and hopes it will be heard.

At times it appears from the gospel accounts that he did get through
to some of the scribes and Pharisees. In chapter 12 of Mark's Gospel,
Mark recounts that one of the scribes who had listened to his dialogue
with a group of Sadducees—who as a group denied that there was
any resurrection from the dead—and appreciated Jesus' answers, approached Jesus with a further question: "Which is the first of all the
commandments?" Jesus answered him with the words that were in
fact the *Shema*, the prayer that all Jews were to recite several times a
day concerning love of God, but also innovatively combined it with
love of neighbor:

This is the first: Listen, Israel, the Lord our God is the one, only
Lord, and you must love the Lord your God with all your heart,
with all your soul, with all your mind and with all your strength.

The second is this: You must love your neighbor as yourself. There is no commandment greater than these. (Mark 12:28–31)

The scribe repeated what Jesus said approvingly and added: "This is far more important than any burnt offering or sacrifice." Jesus, seeing how wisely he had spoken, said, "You are not far from the kingdom of God" (Mark 12:34). At least one of the scribes who sat listening to him approved of Jesus and Jesus of him.

There are other traces of support from the Jewish power structure: Nicodemus, a Pharisee and an elder, came under cover of night to confer with Jesus about how to enter the kingdom of God and later brought a hundred pounds of myrrh and aloes to aid in his burial (John 3:1–21, 19:39), and Joseph of Arimathaea, another leader among the people and a wealthy man, donated a tomb and personally took Jesus down from the cross, wrapped him in a shroud and, with Nicodemus, put him in the tomb (Luke 23:50–53). But for the most part, Jesus did not succeed in reaching the religious leaders through the power of his dialogue, disputations, or fiery condemnations. "He must have wished that his message would have thrilled the Pharisees and priests just as much, if not more, than it would the poor and oppressed and sinners," Senior writes.[63] Jesus decided to take another tack and ratchet up the intensity of his campaign to reach them.

Step 4: Intensify the Campaign Pressure Using Creative, Strategic Action

From Galilee he "resolutely set his face towards Jerusalem" (Luke 9:51). He decided to confront the power structure right in the seat of political, social, and religious power: Jerusalem. Jesus had told his followers what he was risking, but he felt compelled to make his case as clearly and forthrightly as possible to those in charge. Mark's Gospel in fact has Jesus predicting three time that he will be handed over to the chief priests and scribes and will be condemned to death, the last of which reads:

Now we are going up to Jerusalem, and the Son of Man is about to be handed over to the chief priests and the scribes. They will condemn him to death and will hand him over to the gentiles,

---

[63]Senior, *Jesus: A Gospel Portrait*, 127.

who will mock him and spit at him and scourge him and put him
to death; and after three days he will rise again. (Mark 10:33–34)

As they walked along on the road to Jerusalem, Jesus walked on ahead,
and "the Twelve were anxious and those who followed were afraid."
(Mark 10:32).

Jesus evidently had a gift for choosing actions that struck people
forcefully and memorably. He chose actions that spoke his message
even more clearly than did his words—symbolic, prophetic actions.
Much later in history others would come along who had similar gifts
as they led or participated in campaigns of nonviolence.

Mahatma Gandhi chose in 1930 to lead his people in a Salt March—
initially derided by the British as a meaningless exercise. It galvanized
the nation and caught the attention of the world because of the power
of its symbolism. The British held a monopoly on salt. Every person
in the hot land of India knew the importance of salt for their survival
and had to pay a tax to the British for each ounce of salt consumed.
Refusing to pay the salt tax, manufacturing their own salt—every
person in India could catch the meaning—Britain was exercising its
domination and bleeding the country dry. Every person in India—old,
young, women in their kitchens boiling salt—could participate in this
part of the resistance movement.

Our own civil rights movement featured many such moments of
powerful, symbolic action. Michael Nagler writes, "In Birmingham in
1964, marchers for voter rights came upon police and firefighters—they
knelt and prayed. Bull Connor gave the order to unleash the hoses
and the firefighters could not, they cried."[64] The surprising, symbolic
action that immediately conveyed meaning to the firefighters was the
marchers stopping their movement, kneeling down and praying. It
said to the firefighters—we are defenseless, but we have soul power
that cannot be stopped even by fire hoses, and we are one with you
under God. Do your worst to us, if you so choose—but you do have
a choice. We will not respond with violence. You have hearts not of
stone but of flesh and blood, just as we do. The action touched the
firefighters' hearts.

Jesus' table fellowship with outcasts, for example, was such a
symbolic, prophetic act. It conveyed the message of the kingdom of

---

[64]Michael Nagler, *Is There No Other Way?* (Maui, HI: Inner Ocean Publishing, 2001), 79.

God even more powerfully than his words—that in him the kingdom of God had come into their midst to bring justice and compassion to those in society who were most in need—those who had been cast out instead of included and embraced. On the road to Jerusalem he initiated another powerful action. When Jesus was drawing near to Jerusalem, near Bethphage and Bethany, he sent two of his disciples to the village opposite to untie a young donkey, which he then rode into the city. He then rode the donkey over the Mount of Olives, across the Kidron valley, and up to the Temple mount—the action spoke more loudly than words that his was a royal claim, a new kingdom, a new kind of king, who exerted power without violence, without a sword. The movement evoked the passage of Zechariah:

> Rejoice greatly, O daughter Zion! Shout aloud, O daughter Jerusalem! Lo, your king comes to you; triumphant and victorious is he, humble and riding a donkey, on a colt, the foal of a donkey. He will cut off the chariot from Ephraim and the war horse from Jerusalem; and the battle bow shall be cut off, and he shall command peace to the nations; his dominion shall be from sea to sea, and from the River to the ends of the earth. (Zech. 9.9–10)

As Borg observes, it is in fact a countersymbol and a counternarrative to the movement of Pilate who, right about this same time, is coming down from Caesarea and entering Jerusalem for the Passover on his war horse.[65] The picture depicted in Zechariah is of a king who destroys the weapons of war, a king of peace, a king of simplicity, a king of the poor. As Benedict XVI wrote: "But even in Zechariah's day, and still more by the time of Jesus, it was the horse that had come to signify the might of the mighty, while the donkey has become the animal of the poor."[66]

The crowd shouted "Hosanna! . . . Blessed is the coming kingdom of David our father. Hosanna in the highest heaven" (Mark 11:10). As Jesus caught sight of the city, he wept. He was still hoping against hope that the leaders would abandon their path of separatism that in effect fosters violence and embrace his message of the peaceable

---

[65]Borg, *Conflict, Holiness and Politics in the Teaching of Jesus,* 189.

[66]Benedict XVI, *Jesus of Nazareth* (San Francisco: Ignatius Press, 2011), 16.

kingdom, but he begins to see that the odds are not favorable. If they continue down their chosen path, he can see what will happen and that scenario brought him to tears. He said:

> If only you had recognized the ways of peace. But it is hidden from your eyes. . . . Your enemies will dash you and your children to the ground; they will leave not one stone standing . . . because you did not recognize the time of your visitation. (Luke 19:42–44)

Another action highly charged with meaning was his driving the money changers and others out of the Temple. Mark wrote:

> Jesus entered the Temple and began to drive out those who sold and those who bought in the Temple. He overturned the tables of the money changers and the seats of those who sold pigeons; and he would not allow anyone to carry anything through the Temple. And he taught and said to them: "Is it not written, 'My house shall be called a house of prayer for all the nations? But you have made it a den of thieves'." (Mark 11:15–17)

In Greek, *lestai* is probably better translated as brigands or violent ones, those who kill while plundering. It is the same word used to describe Barabbas in Mark's Gospel, where it is specified that Barabbas is in prison with rebels who committed murder during an uprising.

The money changers are there to protect the holiness of the Temple by exchanging profane coinage for "holy" coinage. Pilgrims are coming from all over the world bringing coinage from various lands. The money changers change it into acceptable coinage. "The Temple tax was paid in Tyrian half-shekels and shekels, not Greek or Roman coinage which carried pagan mottoes," Dunn explains.[67] Those who are selling birds for sacrifice made sure that the sacrificial doves are without blemish—further protecting the holiness of the Temple. Their efforts are part and parcel of a system that is "manifesting the clear distinction between the holy nation/profane nations[. Their] activity served and symbolized the quest for holiness understood as

---

[67]Dunn, *Jesus Remembered*, 637.

separation, a quest at the root of resistance to Rome," Borg writes.[68]

In Jesus' understanding of his tradition, Jerusalem with its Temple was meant to be the city on a hill whose light would reach all nations. Israel's mission was to bring the truth about Yahweh as God of the whole earth to all the nations. Instead, the Temple had become a bulwark of separatism, a center of resistance to Rome and a den breeding violence and violent agitators. "Jesus saw as a pagan corruption the very desire to fight paganism itself," Wright notes.[69] Jesus dramatically appealed to Jewish leaders to abandon their dangerous stance of separatism that issues in violent resistance and to embrace the way of the kingdom of God—love of enemies, nonviolent inclusion, and justice for the poor. Jesus could see the stiffening of the resistance to his message on the part of the priests and the scribes, but he pressed on. He continued to teach in the Temple every day. He knew he risked their retribution, but he stayed faithful to his vision of the kingdom.

Many have pointed to the passage in John's Gospel that describes this same prophetic action of Jesus as proof that Jesus was not against violence and in fact was violent himself. John's text:

> When the time of the Jewish Passover drew near, Jesus went up to Jerusalem, and in the Temple he found people selling cattle and sheep and doves, and the money changers sitting there. Making a whip out of cord, he drove them all out of the Temple, sheep and cattle as well, scattered the money changers' coins, knocked their tables over and said to the dove sellers, "Take all this out of here and stop using my Father's house as a market." (John 2:13–16)

John's extra detail, that Jesus fashioned and used a whip, is what puzzles some readers. This puzzlement stems from confusing force and coercion with violence—the fact that Jesus was determined, perhaps even angry, and that he expressed himself with an act of force, which is simply exerting one's power on a situation to change it, is confused with violence, which is intentionally hurting, either physically or psychically, another human being. In this case Jesus was in a conflict and acted assertively. He used the whip to drive out the animals. If there

---

[68]Borg, *Conflict, Holiness and Politics in the Teaching of Jesus*, 188.
[69]Wright, *Jesus and the Victory of God*, 596.

had been any hint of violence in his actions, the Roman soldiers who were in the fortress Antonia, which overlooked the Temple, would have intervened, especially at the time of Passover when they had explicitly come down with Pilate in force from Caesarea to make sure there were no outbreaks of resistance. They did not intervene. Jesus' action was a focused, prophetic, nonviolent act. The synoptic gospels have him coming back to the Temple the next day to teach.

We have stressed that there are two major political impacts on Israel in Jesus' teaching on the kingdom of God—the first has to do with the way Israel is relating to the outside world, especially Rome. Jesus is taking active steps to avoid anticipated, calamitous violence. The religious/political leaders of Israel are stressing a way of purity and separatism in the name of eventual national liberation and are, in Jesus' time, beginning to endorse the option of violent resistance. Jesus is calling them back to their central mission—to bring salvation to all the nations. He is preaching a way of inclusion, nonviolent action, and compassion—even for so-called enemies. That way will help Israel fulfill its calling.

The second impact of the kingdom of God teaching relates to the way that the religious leaders of Israel are treating people within Israel. They again are stressing a way of separatism, maintenance of purity, for the population as a whole. The Pharisees want ordinary people to practice a way of purity that was originally meant for the priestly class, to maintain a rigorous regimen of food preparation and hand-washing purity and a tithing system relating to food growing, preparation, and consumption. The purity system that they have implemented has the effect of driving many people out of the circle of the pure ones, creating a huge outcast population. The tithing system also exacerbates the debt and poverty problems of the people.

Jesus is preaching the message of the kingdom of God, a message about their God who treats all with outgoing love. No one has to win favor with God—God graces them first. There are no outcasts in the kingdom of God. The one and same purity system affects both the way nations outside of Israel and the way people within Israel are treated. Jesus is attempting to change the system that cuts two different ways. In the action in the Temple he is symbolically resisting both effects of the purity system.

The term *lestai* can be also translated as "thieves." That translation brings out the fact that Jesus' action is resisting the way people within

Israel are being treated. The whole Temple system is a machine for systematically taking money from the pockets of the poor and putting it into the pockets of the Temple leaders, the priests. If one translates *lestai* as practitioners of violence, the Temple is harboring the separatist aspirations that will issue eventually in violent resistance. The double meaning of the term means that Jesus' proclamation of the kingdom of God in their midst also cuts both ways. It is at one and the same time a critique of separatism in the name of national liberation and a critique of separatism through a purity system that breaks the backs of the poor and makes for a whole population of outcasts.

Jesus' message of the kingdom of God not only is attempting actively to avoid calamitous violence; it is also a way of changing the structures of violence built into the main Jewish institutions of his time that cause so much suffering to his people—Temple practices, taxation system, and Torah interpretations. The kingdom of God message is not a message for individuals only, it is also a message for societal and political institutions. As in our time, Hélder Câmara, the bishop of Recife, Brazil, known as a bishop for the poor, said: "I give bread to the poor, and they call me a saint. I ask why the poor do not have bread, and they call me a communist."[70]

Jesus does not give up. Immediately after depicting the expulsion of the dealers from the Temple, Luke writes: "He went in the Temple every day. The chief priests and the scribes, in company with the leading citizens, tried to do away with him, but they could not find a way to carry this out because the whole people hung on his words" (Luke 19:47–48).

Step 5: Continue to Act in Situations of Conflict; Continue to Treat Opponents with Love and Respect and Be Willing to Suffer

Over the long history of Judaism, in the centuries just before Jesus' time a theory began to be developed that suffering might be, in some mysterious way, redemptive. Suffering might be not only that *from which* people were to be delivered but also the way *by which* they might be delivered. The Servant Songs in Isaiah, chapters 40–55, bear particular witness to this. We have already reviewed striking and storied examples of nonviolent resistance that occurred in and around

---

[70]As quoted in John Heagle, *Justice Rising: The Emerging Biblical Vision* (Maryknoll, NY: Orbis Books, 2011), 72.

the time of Jesus—the students who tore down Herod's golden eagle from the top of the Temple; the large group of Pharisees who risked their necks in resistance to Pilate when he put Roman standards in the Temple; the massive peasant resistance to Caligula's plan to put a statue of himself in the Holy of Holies. People were willing to risk their lives to stay faithful to their beliefs. That willingness had such power that Pilate changed his mind. Petronius agreed to take their case back to Caligula when he saw that the peasants were willing to endure hunger and banditry and were even willing to be slaughtered, if need be, for their cause. That impressed and changed Petronius. The way of nonviolent resistance that courted and even endured suffering was not unknown to Jesus. These stories of nonviolent resistance depict very brave people, willing to stand against the might of Rome and take the consequences. They also depict a way forward that can be effective. Herod responded to the students who took down his golden eagle and then waited to be arrested with the utmost cruelty—burning them to death. But Pilate's response was different. He changed his mind and backed down—even though he had all the violent power at his command. He ceded to soul power. The peasants reached the conscience of Petronius, and he agreed to return to Rome to plead their case with the emperor Caligula. Jesus' commitment to nonviolent action was not a complete innovation. "It was an intensification of the nonviolence of Jeremiah, Ezekiel and the singer of the servant passages of the book of Isaiah," according to Yoder.[71] What comes next in Jesus' campaign to reach and change the religious leaders of Israel? He risked his life. He returned to teach daily in the Temple. Luke writes: "All day long he would be in the Temple teaching, but would spend the night in the open on the hill called the Mount of Olives. And from early morning the people thronged to him in the Temple to listen to him" (Luke 21:37–38). And "The chief priests and the scribes were still looking for a way of doing away with him because they were afraid of the people" (Luke 22:2). Even in the face of the threat of violence Jesus stayed faithful to his calling and his mission to turn around the nation and have them see the new way of the kingdom come into their midst. When Judas came to the chief priests and the officers of the guard to discuss a way of handing Jesus over to them without people knowing about it, they jumped at the chance.

---

[71]Yoder, *War of the Lamb,* 100.

The fact that the Jewish religious/political leaders kept a deaf ear to Jesus' message is, after all, not surprising. They had too much at stake and too much to lose. The Pharisees had the respect of the people. They had been accorded the power to interpret and enforce the laws of the Torah and the oral interpretations that earlier teachers of the law had developed. The priests depended on them not only to keep the faithful pacified but also to ensure a steady stream of revenue to the Temple and therefore to themselves. The chief priests and the elders in the Sanhedrin also had much to lose. Rome had allowed them day-to-day political rule over the country. They were able to generate substantial wealth for themselves as long as the country remained pacified and subservient. They even had some hope that, if they played their cards right, at the right moment there might be a chance to gain national liberation from Rome—and indeed in the year 66 CE a group of militant priests stopped the sacrifices to the emperor and sparked the revolt against both the Roman governor, Florus, and the rest of the priestly aristocracy. After all, the Maccabees had done it a century before. As Caiaphas the high priest articulated it so well, better to keep things as they were and not upset Rome. "It is better for one man to die for the people" (John 18:14). They could lose their power and privileges. It is not surprising that in the end, Jesus' campaign to reach them did not succeed and that they turned to violence. What is surprising is the way Jesus met their violence. He continued to reject the way of violence throughout his ordeal. He met violence with dignity, self-possession, and nonviolence.

Jesus had had a sense of the violence he was about to endure. His fear and prayer in the Garden of Gethsemane were intense. He "uses a word that emphasizes the dark depths of Jesus' fear: *tetaraktai*—it is the same verb, *tarassein*, that John uses to describe Jesus' deep emotion at the tomb of Lazarus as well as his inner turmoil at the prophecy of Judas' betrayal in the Upper Room."[72] Jesus shrank back from what he sensed was coming and asked that, if possible, the cup of suffering pass him by—before summoning up the courage to stay faithful to the message of the kingdom by meeting violence head on. When the chief priests and the captains of the guard came for him in the Garden of Gethsemane under cover of darkness, he responded to them with dignity: "Am I a bandit that you had to set out with swords and clubs.

---

[72]Benedict XVI, *Jesus of Nazareth*, 155.

When I was among you in the Temple day after day you never made a move to lay hands on me. But this is your hour; this is the hour of darkness" (Luke 22:52).

The gospels of Mark, Matthew, Luke, and John all describe one of his disciples meeting the violence with violence, taking out a sword and cutting off the ear of a servant of the high priest. Luke has Jesus say vehemently: "Enough of this!" (Luke 22:51) and then healing the servant's ear. Matthew has Jesus say: "Put your sword back, for all who draw the sword will die by the sword" (Matt. 26:52). Jesus certainly knew the siren song of violence. It was the first temptation the devil had put before him in the desert at the beginning of his public life. He rejected the violent option then, and he rejected it here. Matthew has Jesus go on to say: "Or do you think I cannot appeal to my Father, who would promptly send twelve legions of angels to my defense?" (Matt. 26:53). That would be thirty-six thousand angels. Can the sword not be used in self-defense? The guards have arrived in the garden with their swords. "if opponents use violence to attack Jesus, should his disciples use violence to defend him? The answer is quite clear. Even when opponents use the sword to attack Jesus, the disciples must not use it to defend him. But if not then, when? If not then, never!" writes Crossan.[73]

As the trial scenes unfold, Jesus continues to respond forthrightly and with dignity. When a soldier feels free to slap him for the way Jesus answered the high priest, Jesus responded calmly but assertively, "If there is some offense in what I said, point it out; but if not, why do you strike me?" (John 18:23).

In Jesus' dialogue with Pilate, he explicitly renounces the so-called natural right of self-defense—because he has brought into the world in his person and message a kingdom that is unlike Pilate's; it does not depend on violence or the threat of violence to exert power. His kingdom is not of this world, meaning Pilate's world. His kingdom relies on the power of truth and nonviolent resistance, or what many centuries later will be called "soul force." Jesus says to Pilate: "Mine is not a kingdom of this world; if my kingdom were of this world, my men would have fought to prevent my being surrendered to the Jews. As it is, my kingdom does not belong here" (John 18:36). He goes on to explicitly say what gives him his power: "I was born for this, I came

---

[73]Crossan, *God and Empire*, 178.

into the world for this, to bear witness to the truth and all who are on the side of truth listen to my voice." (John 18:37). Miroslav Volf writes:

> In the Johannine narrative a counter trial is taking place. In the exchange with Pilate, Jesus argues against the truth of power and for the power of truth . . . and alters the content of the term king. . . . His kingship does not rest on the violence of eliminating contenders for power, or holding them in check by treating them as things not part of his rule. Renouncing the power of violence, Jesus advocated for the power of truth.[74]

Jesus' kingdom of God stood over against the world that used violence and embedded violence into its political structures.

After he had been condemned to death and led to the place called The Skull, Golgotha, where they crucified him, Jesus—consistent with his entire message concerning the way one should respond to one's so-called enemies, and consistent with his message about the centrality of forgiveness in the kingdom of God—said: "Father, forgive them; they do not know what they are doing" (Luke 23:24). He died as he had lived. His last words expressed love and forgiveness for those who were killing him.

Scripture scholars differ on exactly when the Gospel of Mark, the first of the written gospels, was written, but they agree it was written around the time of the Jewish revolt, probably just beforehand, in the mid 60s CE, when there was intense pressure on the new Christians to join the violent revolt and participate in the violence. Scripture scholars agree that it was written to give the early Christians the courage to resist those overtures and pressures. Mark describes for them how Jesus, their Christ, endured and responded to threats and violence. He paints for them a portrait of how they should act in their difficult situation so that they can take heart and follow the way laid out by him—especially in the way he lived his whole life, but also how he met his final days, a way of brave, nonviolent love and forgiveness. There is every indication that the early Christians indeed did not participate in the revolt. According to Josephus, the Essenes did, and a great number of the Pharisees did, and they were all destroyed. Eusebius in 339 CE "tells us that even before the siege of Jerusalem the

---

[74]Miroslav Volf, *Exclusion and Embrace* (Nashville, TN: Abingdon Press, 1996), 264, 267.

Christians had fled to the city of Pella beyond the Jordan," according to Pope Benedict's account.[75]

Jesus lived and died modeling the power of truth and nonviolence. The term *nonviolence,* of course, can be misleading. It can mean passivity or resigned acceptance of the way things are. Jesus, as we have seen, was anything but passive. He was consistently the initiator of the action, the protagonist of his story. He was restless to change the way things were. To be resigned to the kind of structural violence that was built into the political/religious system of second Temple Israel was, in fact, to condone that violence. He not only rejected violence as a personal option; he also fought the structural violence that was embedded in the institutions of his nation. His nonviolence was the nonviolence of resistance and building up of the human community, the nonviolence of the *peacemaker.*

His nonviolent action also demonstrated the paradoxical power of suffering when it is at the service of resisting violence. The violent one says to his or her opponent: "Do what I want, or you will pay. I will make *you* suffer." The practitioner of nonviolence says: "Do what I want, or *I* will pay. *I* will suffer." This is not suffering for suffering's sake—that would be masochism. It is suffering that comes because one is fighting a fight but doing it in a way that breaks the cycle of violence. If the conflict turns ugly and the opponent turns to violence, the nonviolent resister refuses to do so and instead accepts the harm that comes down on himself or herself. This suffering is not passive. It is intense resistance but resistance with different weapons—the weapons of truth and self-suffering. The power of the suffering lies in its ability to reach the human heart—the hearts of bystanders and even the heart of the perpetrator of the violence. Centuries later, Gandhi, Martin Luther King Jr., and many others will demonstrate and use the power of self-suffering to reach the hearts of the violent. Gandhi consistently maintained that it was not enough to change peoples' minds. The witness of nonviolent, suffering love is designed to go further—to reach hearts. Unless hearts are reached, there is no basic change in behavior. Dr. Martin Luther King explained the power of suffering in a Christmas sermon on peace:

> We will match your capacity to inflict suffering by our capacity to endure suffering. We will meet your physical force with

---

[75]Benedict XVI, *Jesus of Nazareth,* 24.

soul force. Do to us what you will and we will still love you. . . . But be assured we will wear you down by our capacity to suffer, and one day we will win our freedom. We will not only win freedom for ourselves; we will so appeal to your heart and conscience that we will win you in the process, and our victory will be a double victory.[76]

Jesus continued to live his life in his final days in the way that he had lived it all through the years of his public life. He continued to model the kingdom—loving outreach for all, unearned love and forgiveness, and heroic meeting of violence with nonviolence. His teaching on the kingdom of God is a recipe for overcoming the power of violence. As Yoder writes, "We overcome violence partially by delegitimizing its moral pretensions, partly by refusing to meet it on its own terms, partly by replacing it with other more humane strategies and tactics of moral struggle, partly by innocent suffering, and partly by the special restorative resources of forgiveness and community."[77]

Yes, but did not Jesus' way of nonviolent building of the kingdom of God fail? His life and his message were apparently all for naught. They killed him. He did not change the minds and hearts of the leadership. The structural violence built into Israel's institutions that caused such suffering for the people—Temple practices, taxation system, Torah interpretations—did not change. It is true that a crucified messiah at first was an apparent contradiction in terms and a stumbling block for those who believed in him—until they began to remember and appreciate the way he lived and what he taught in the light of their own scriptures. What remained was precisely his practice, his way, and his message. What also remained was the community that he had formed to follow in his way. The apparent failure began to be, in fact, a triumph, as the early Christians remembered his call to discipleship and began to practice his way.

The gospels have Jesus say again and again that his followers will have to take up the way of the cross and follow him. Unfortunately the meaning of the phrase "take up your cross and follow me" has all too often been rinsed of its political, real-world power and the cross

---

[76]Martin Luther King Jr., "A Christmas Sermon on Peace," in *A Testament of Hope: The Essential Writings of Martin Luther King Jr.*, ed. James Melvin Washington, (San Francisco: Harper and Row, 1986), 256.

[77]Yoder, *War of the Lamb*, 41.

made into a means of individual soul saving. It has been all too often been made into a Jesus-and-me myth, an almost morbid concentration on his sufferings and death, apart from his life and the reason why he died—because of what he was trying to accomplish with his life and the fact that he incurred the wrath of the power structure of his time. Edward Schillebeeckx writes, "'Under Pontius Pilate' implies a political element. We may not isolate the death of Jesus from his life, his career, message; otherwise we turn its redemptive significance into a myth, sometimes even a bloody and sadistic myth."[78] To follow the way of the cross, means to follow his *way of life*—even at the risk of death. His way of life was to bring the kingdom of God to earth, to attempt, by might and main, to change the structures of violence built into society, to demonstrate an alternate way of inclusive justice and love, and thereby to actively avoid calamitous mass violence. Whenever people act in this way, they threaten the power structures and run the risk of retaliatory violence.

The disciples remembered him saying to them as he prayed to his Father: "Consecrate them in the truth; your word is truth. As you have sent me into the world, I have sent them into the world, and for their sake I consecrate myself so that they may be consecrated in the truth. I pray not only for these but also for those who through their teaching will come to believe in me" (John 17:17–20).

Pope Benedict XVI wrote: "Again and again, humankind will be faced with this same choice: to say yes to God who works only through the power of truth and love, or to build on something tangible and concrete—on violence. . . . Ecce homo . . . in him is displayed the suffering of all who are subjected to violence, all the downtrodden."[79]

Right from the beginning of the early church, Christians followed this way of bold witness, a posture of nonretaliation, and a willingness to endure violence. The early Christian communities celebrated Jesus' death as a victory over violence. Häring writes, "The way to overcome violence is indicated to them by discipleship."[80] In the Acts of the Apostles, for example, Stephen lives according to this pattern. Brought before the Sanhedrin, he proceeded to recount the history of their people from Abraham through Moses and David and the proph-

---

[78]Edward Schillebeeckx, *Christ: The Experience of Jesus as Lord* (New York: Crossroad, 1980), 120.
[79]Benedict XVI, *Jesus of Nazareth*, 197.
[80]Häring, *Healing Power of Peace and Nonviolence*, 46.

ets, all as pointing to the revelation that came with Jesus, whom they killed. Stephen then said: "You are always resisting the Holy Spirit just as your ancestors used to do" (Acts 7:51). The members of the council stopped up their ears in anger, took him out of the city and stoned him. As he died—in the hearing of Saul, soon to be Paul—he echoed the spirit of Jesus and said: "Lord, do not hold this sin against them" (Acts 7:60).

The apparent failure of Jesus' mission gives way to the promise of legions of his followers practicing his way of life and his way of the cross. Rudolph Pesch says, "Let us try to understand the death of Christ as the hour of birth of a new nonviolent society of the people of God in the New Covenant."[81]

Jesus consistently practiced what he proclaimed as his mission—to bring the kingdom of God into the world. He also taught the principles of nonviolent action in other ways—his Sermon on the Mount teachings on how to deal with violence, his teaching on love for the enemy, and his teaching on the role of forgiveness for his followers. It is to those teachings that we now turn.

---

[81]Rudolph Pesch, as quoted in Häring, *Healing Power of Peace and Nonviolence*, 54.

2

Jesus' Teachings on Nonviolent Action

The Sermon on the Mount: How to Overcome Violence

You have heard it said, an eye for an eye and a tooth for a tooth, but I say to you, "Do not [*antistenai*] violently resist one who does evil to you. If anyone strikes you on the right cheek, turn to him the left; if someone goes to court to take your cloak, give him your coat as well; and if anyone presses you into service for a mile, go a second mile with him." (Matt. 5:38–41)

The teaching on "an eye for an eye and a tooth for a tooth," *the lex talionis*, had been a great improvement for civilization over the approach of Lamech, which held that if someone took an eye, you could take their whole being. An eye for an eye suggested limiting retribution to equivalency—no more than equivalent harm done for harm endured. This had the effect of moderating the degree of retributive violence in the culture.

Jesus is leaping well beyond that approach with his teaching. The first key in interpreting this passage is to get the correct translation of the word *antistenai*. Most often it has been translated as "do not resist" or nonresistance. As a result, this precious advice on how one should resist violence has not been adequately appreciated. People take it to mean that Jesus is recommending being passive in the face of evil. Don't resist and allow yourself to be taken advantage of. Don't resist and let people walk all over you. Don't resist and thereby counsel women to stay in abusive relationships. Don't resist and encourage weakness and cowardice. Or in a political setting—not being strong just invites attack. "Si vis pacem, para bellum," that is, "If you want peace, prepare for war." And so on and so on. How can Jesus, who, fought evil with his whole self—even risking death and humiliation—be counseling nonresistance to evil? The answer—he is not. *Antistenai* should not be translated as nonresistance. Walter Wink cites the scripture passages that feature *antistenai*—which in the Greek, literally means to "stand against"—and finds that *antistenai* describes the way contending armies come at one another until they meet and then "take a stand" or fight. Jesus is saying in this passage that one should not *violently* resist one who does you harm.

Wink goes on to reflect on how *antistenai* came to be translated as nonresistance. It began with the translation of the Bible into English commissioned by King James, the King James Bible.

> The Bible translators in the hire of King James . . . knew that the king did not want people to conclude that they had any recourse against his or any other sovereign's tyranny. James had explicitly commissioned a new translation of the Bible because of what he regarded as "seditious . . . dangerous, and trayterous" tendencies in the marginal notes printed in the Geneva Bible, which included endorsement of the right to disobey a tyrant. Therefore, the public had to be made to believe that there are two alternatives, and only two: flight or fight. And Jesus is made to command us according to these king's men, to resist not. Jesus appears to authorize monarchical absolutism. Submission is the will of God.[1]

Ever since, English translations have simply been following suit. Ever since, the passage has remained a mystery and a stumbling block—as people go on assuming that Jesus is counseling nonresistance to evil.

The second key for understanding the passage is to understand the type of language that is being used in the passage. Many have assumed that the Sermon on the Mount as a whole and this passage in particular contain Jesus' new set of laws for the Christian community. As Moses stood on the mountain and proclaimed the law for the Jews, so Jesus

---

[1]Walter Wink, *The Powers That Be* (New York: Doubleday, 1998), 100.

is the new Moses, standing on a mount and laying down a new and even stricter set of rules. Robert Tannehill wrote a very important article in 1970. He asked a very simple question—"turn the other cheek; give your coat as well as your cloak when someone sues you; go the second mile when you have been impressed into service—what kind of language is this?" His answer: Jesus is offering three concrete examples of very difficult, oppressive, even violent situations. All three examples would have been quite recognizable to his audience of the time. Three narrowly drawn, recognizable examples of being up against it. The function of the language, three in a row, invites the hearer to add additional examples to the list—other examples that they may have experienced. Jesus is not laying down a law. Tannehill said these are "focal instances." The language is evocative, inviting thought and imagination. The language puts the hearers in a situation and then invites the hearers to imagine how they would deal with the situation. The extremeness of the sayings is also part of the way the language functions. Each instance stands in deliberate tension with the way people normally live and think. The extreme language shocks and provokes. The language "arouses the moral imagination, enabling hearers to see their situation in a new way and to contemplate new possibilities of action."[2] Jesus is giving some examples of being treated unfairly and then suggesting to his hearers that they—because they have known him and are his followers and have seen how he has handled such situations—might deal with them more creatively and differently than most.

The third key for understanding the passage is to understand the historical situations from which the examples come. Taking them one at a time: "if someone strikes you on the right cheek, turn to them your left." In this culture the left hand is used only for unclean tasks. So imagine how someone can strike another on the right cheek with his or her right hand. The only way to do it is with the back of your hand. Jesus is describing someone backhanding another across the face. John Stott writes, "The blow with the back of the hand is still today in the East an insulting blow."[3] A backhanded slap in the face is a gesture meant to humiliate, insult, and degrade another. It is an

---

[2]Robert Tannehill, "The 'Focal Instance' as a Form of New Testament Speech: A Study of Matthew 5:39b–42," *Journal of Religion* 50, no. 4 (1970): 382.

[3]John R. W. Stott, *The Message of the Sermon on the Mount* (Leicester, UK: Intervarsity Press, 1978), 107.

action, typically, of a superior to an inferior—a master to a slave, an elder to a child, a Roman to a Jew. Jesus is asking his hearers to imagine themselves on the receiving end of that blow—what would they do? He suggests a creative way to resist. Imagine the inferior in the situation looking the one who has committed the insult in the eye and then turning to that person the other cheek—saying, in effect, "I am not cowed. And you are acting in a way that is beneath yourself. So go ahead, if you really want to lower yourself, now punch me in the face. You still will not intimidate me. But I will not strike you back. I will maintain my dignity." Such a response is not a surefire way to avoid further trouble. But it is a response that just might work. The other person might be brought to his or her senses. The one insulted does not respond to the violence with violence but with a gesture that says, "I am willing to endure additional pain, a fist to my face, to reach you with a message about my and your common humanity." Jesus is certainly not counseling rolling over passively in a situation of violence. He is saying instead, "Stand up for yourself, but don't respond in kind." Jesus is suggesting that his followers act as he acted—with creative nonviolence.

The second example of duress—someone takes you to court. You are already so reduced in circumstances that all you have left to your name, of value, is your cloak. The cloak was the heavy outer garment in which a poor man in the cold would sleep. Deuteronomy 24:10–13 stipulates that a creditor could take the cloak as collateral but would have to return it every night. We have already reviewed the situation in which many poor peasants found themselves during Jesus' time. Debt and exorbitant interest on loans led to loss of ancestral lands. Staying out of, or getting out of, debt and securing one's daily ration of bread are the two central issues in the life of the peasants in Jesus' time—as reflected in the Lord's prayer. It is no surprise that the first act of the Jewish revolutionaries in 66 CE was to burn the Temple treasury where the debt records were stored.

What if, in response to being dragged into court and handing over your cloak, you handed over your coat as well? The term translated as "coat" is what is under the cloak, next to the skin—undergarments. What if you handed over not only your cloak but the rest of your meager clothing as well? Imagine how the tables would be turned on the creditor. He stands there holding your cloak in one hand and the rest of your clothing in the other. Perhaps he will recognize that his actions have led another human being to this state, defenseless as the day he was born. The legal system that countenances such a lawsuit that leaves a person in such dire straits is also called into question. As Wink comments: nakedness was taboo in Judaism, and shame fell less on the naked party than on the person viewing or causing the nakedness.[4] The action might give the creditor a chance to see, for the first time, what he is causing through his usurious moneylending practices. Such an action unmasks the cruelty embedded in the structures of the society and its pretensions of justice.

The background for the third example of the series is Rome's occupation of the country. The Roman soldier had the right, according to Rome's code, to press into service at any time a member of the occupied country to carry his pack of sixty to eighty-five pounds. To limit resentment from the local population, the code stipulated that impressment of an individual could be only for one mile. Forcing someone to carry the pack more than a mile was a violation of the military code and could warrant punishment from the centurion. Jesus is asking his hearers to imagine themselves being pressed into service—what would they do in that situation. In each of these examples Jesus is suggesting ways for them, in situations of oppression, to take back the initiative. Jesus says imagine when you come to the end of the first mile, you take the initiative and make the choice to carry the soldier's pack a second mile. In that action you would be saying to the soldier—you see me as a person without power, a veritable beast of burden for your army. I am letting you know I have not lost my dignity. I am a person who can make choices. I choose to go a second mile. By the way, we do not like the fact that Rome is dominating us and bleeding us dry, but I want you to know that I have nothing against you personally as a fellow human being. Jesus' audience can easily envision the soldier being confused, perhaps begging the Jew not to carry his pack—with the thought of his centurion hearing of the incident.

Jesus in this passage is putting forth an alternative way to the presumed limited choices of an oppressed people, a direction that is neither fight nor flight nor accommodation. It is instead a way to resist without being infected by the very violence that one is resisting. People have an unlimited array of possibilities once they are able to see their way past the violent response. Jesus calls his disciples to act

---

[4]Wink, *Powers That Be*, 104.

against domination using their creative imaginations, their courage, and their strength. They can break the cycle of violence and humiliation and at the same time leave open the opportunity for the oppressor to join them in a larger circle of love and truth. This has been called a spirituality for the oppressed. It is no doubt a spirituality for the spiritually strong.

Contemporary exegesis of the Sermon on the Mount, and in particular this passage, understands the text as Jesus' summons to his disciples to act like he acts, which in turn is to act as God acts. Jesus' teaching is not a new legalism. His disciples have observed him. They have heard his teaching on the kingdom of God coming into their midst. They have heard him speak of his Father as one who approaches humans with a free offer of love and grace—unearned. And they have seen him deal with people in the same way—none are outcast, none are beyond the pale. All are embraced—even when they choose to turn away from him, he does not give up on them. So living the Sermon on the Mount is to live in a different way—beyond the way that people "naturally" act. Act not because of laws but out of love that gives strength and knows no bounds. It is to live in the free air of those who know they are loved without limit and who as a result can pass that spirit on to others. It is no wonder that Mahatma Gandhi, after first reading the Sermon on the Mount, as a young adult in London, said that it went "straight to his heart." It confirmed for him the best of his own tradition, and it made him admire Jesus as the "Prince of the Satyagrahis," a man of action, a man of creative, loving nonviolence He continued to meditate on it for the rest of his life.

There have been many reasons given through the centuries for disregarding creative nonviolence as the way to respond to evil and violence. One of the most popular ways, developed in the early middle ages, was to make a distinction between a counsel and a precept or commandment. A precept applied to everyone, whereas a counsel, an ethical invitation that is not binding, applied to those who were special, those who had dedicated their lives to God.

Edward Schillebeeckx wrote:

> Catholic moral theologians often argue away the Sermon on the Mount in a hairsplitting fashion. . . . The whole utopian force of the Sermon on the Mount, through which even the most modern ethic can come under the criticism of the gospel,

is neutralized by this distinction. Furthermore it would lead to a double category of Christians: second-rate Christians . . . and the other Christians who follow the counsels as well . . . the nucleus of the New Testament ethic.[5]

Over time this distinction led to a great gulf between the roles of the clergy and the laity. Lay people, through custom and law, were consigned to second-rate status in the church. Their role was to keep the commandments. Clergy and religious were deemed first-rate, the truly dedicated and elite of the church. Their role was to pursue the life of perfection and take vows to follow the "counsels of perfection." Jesus' teaching on how to deal with violence in the Sermon on the Mount survived in the church as a mere residue. Staying free of violence was assigned to the clergy and the monks. They were expected to refrain from violence. Clergy who fell from grace and took up arms were accepted back into communion with the church only after years of penance. This division between classes of Christians, and the residue of the Sermon on the Mount teaching assigned to the clergy, survives even into our own times. In the United States clergy are exempt from the draft. The clergy, it is assumed, should have nothing to do with killing in war.

Through these distinctions between precept and counsel, and the clergy and the laity, the great, challenging call of the Sermon on the Mount was muffled and then stifled. Jesus' way of active nonviolent resistance to evil was deemed not for all. Even those who were deemed worthy to follow a higher way lose the active dynamism inherent in the teaching. It becomes merely not engaging in violence personally. The way of life that Jesus embodied—active resistance to the structures of violence in his society and active peacemaking in an attempt to avoid calamitous violence—that vocation is just about lost to the church altogether, except for the heroic few who through the ages continued to hear the call of the Sermon on the Mount. C. F. Andrews, the Anglican priest who was a great friend and follower of Gandhi in India, in his book *The Sermon on the Mount,* pointed out that in the early church there was no double standard or two-class approach.

---

[5]Edward Schillebeeckx, *Christ: The Experience of Jesus as Lord* (New York: Crossroad, 1980), 591.

One further historical fact is this, that none of the Apostles ever attempted to set up a double standard of this kind in the earliest days of the Church. . . . The first preachers of the good news of the Kingdom took men and women, of the lowliest type, freed men and slaves, just as they were, and by the power of the Holy Spirit transformed them in their own surroundings, making saints out of quite ordinary people.[6]

Warren Kissinger shows how all the ante-Nicene fathers of the church as well as Augustine understood the Sermon on the Mount to be the way of life applicable to all Christians, not just a select few.[7] Gandhi himself could not believe that Christians did not prize and embrace the teachings of the Sermon on the Mount as applicable to all. He said: "For many of them contend that the Sermon on the Mount does not apply to mundane things, that it was only meant for the twelve disciples. Well I do not believe this. I think the Sermon on the Mount has no meaning if it not of vital use in everyday life to everyone."[8]

Note that Gandhi says—in everyday life. Lay people, even with their day-to-day responsibilities for raising families and making a living, will find nonviolence of vital use in their daily interactions within their families, on the job, with their neighbors, with their children. It is a most practical method for facing and resolving conflicts. Moreover, in the bigger picture, it is lay Christians who are in position, in their corners of the world, to transform the world as it is—to one that more closely resembles the kingdom of God as Jesus proclaimed it.

The second most common way of dismissing the Sermon on the Mount has been to say that it is not "realistic." It underestimates the power of sin and evil in the world and does not understand how the world of power politics, "realpolitik," works. The Sermon on the Mount might be a legitimate approach to interpersonal conflict but not for the world of power blocs.

C. F. Andrews insisted that no one understood the power and stranglehold of evil in the world more clearly than did Jesus. He un-

---

[6]C. F. Andrews, *The Sermon on the Mount* (London: G. Allen and Unwin, 1942), 96–97.

[7]Warren Kissinger, *The Sermon on the Mount: A History of Interpretation and Bibliography*, ATLA Bibliography Series, no.. 3 (Metuchen, NJ: Scarecrow Press and the American Library Association, 1975), 5–15.

[8]Mahatma Gandhi, *Harijan*, March 23, 1940.

derstood also just how much of a counterweight was required to resist the powers of evil and violence. Andrews wrote:

> Our Lord Jesus Christ gave repeated warnings to his disciples concerning the immense strength of these forces of evil in the world which would have to be met and conquered. It was just because his pure eyes saw so clearly that he did not underestimate them for a moment. . . . Experience has shown us clearly, even in our own lifetime, what incredible sacrifices have to be made when evil is so strong in the world.[9]

As Jesus set his face to Jerusalem, he knew he was walking into the maw of state-sponsored violence. He had a vivid sense of the evil that would most likely come down on him. But he kept walking.

The critique of nonviolence as not "realistic" was enunciated especially by Reinhold Niebuhr, one of the United States's leading Christian theologians of the twentieth century. Niebuhr contributed greatly to theology in that he was one of the first theologians to put violence at the center of the theological enterprise and the problem, especially in an age of nuclear weapons, from which humankind needed to be delivered. Niebuhr had a deep sense of the world's evil. It confirmed in him a dark version of the teaching on original sin. His awareness of the depths of evil in the world moved him from a pacifist stance in the thirties to an ardent cold warrior stance in the 1950s and '60s. In those years he became a leading adviser to US presidents. In his book *Moral Man in an Immoral Society*, he contended that individuals may be able to partially live up to the ideals of the Sermon on the Mount but not groups, not nations, not power blocs—because as individuals merged into groups, their ability to act morally became compromised and their immorality more intense. He opined that it was simple "common sense" that groups of people, as well as nations, had to defend themselves from their enemies and, in that self-defense, often had to turn to violence.

In response, Thomas Merton wrote on the threefold conviction that underpinned Jesus' and Gandhi's view that nonviolence was not only possible but necessary. In so doing, he took on Niebuhr's concept of original sin. Merton wrote:

---

[9]Andrews, *Sermon on the Mount*, 94–95.

The threefold conviction: that in the hidden depths of our being we are more truly peaceful than destructively aggressive, that love is more natural to us than hatred, and that truth is the law of our being. This reflects the traditional Christian doctrine of original sin, which, properly understood, is optimistic. This doctrine does not teach that man is by nature evil, but rather that evil and hatred are an unnatural disorder.[10]

John Howard Yoder wrote an extensive critique of Niebuhr's central contentions. For example, in response to Niebuhr's contention that individuals became less moral when they merged into groups, Yoder wondered if Niebuhr ever had an experience of church—an experience of a community that worked to help individuals grow in their commitments to others, a community that helped people learn how to better love one another. As for Niebuhr's use of "common sense" as the arbiter of what is moral or immoral, Yoder wondered if, for Niebuhr, "common sense"—which could be equated with conventional wisdom—trumped the teachings of Jesus.[11]

Just how realistic nonviolent action is cannot be decided intellectually or established in debate. It can only be tested and verified in the crucible of historical events when it is tried. As we will see, one of the most important signs of our time that has led to a shift in the church's teaching on war and peace has been the remarkable success of organized nonviolent campaigns since Gandhi articulated and employed nonviolence in his fight to free India from British imperialism. Nonviolent action is more and more clearly seen not just as an ethic governing relationships between individuals but also an ethic for guiding the behavior of groups, including states. Martin Luther King Jr. wrote: "Gandhi was probably the first man to lift the love ethic of Jesus above mere interaction between individuals to a powerful and effective social force on a large scale."[12]

After experiences with the use of violence in places such as Vietnam, Serbia, and Iraq, many people are beginning to have profound doubts

---

[10]Thomas Merton, *Conjectures of a Guilty Bystander* (Garden City, NY: Doubleday Image Books, 1958), 85.

[11]John Howard Yoder, *Christian Attitudes to War, Peace and Revolution*, eds. Thomas J. Koontz and Andy Alexis-Baker (Grand Rapids, MI: Brazos, 2009), chs. 18-20.

[12]Martin Luther King Jr., *Stride toward Freedom: The Montgomery Story* (New York: Harper and Row, 1958), 85, 97.

concerning the so-called effectiveness of violence. At the same time, after seeing the impact of nonviolent movements in places as disparate as India, the Philippines, Serbia, South Africa, the Ukraine, Chile, and Poland, many others have awakened to the viability and effectiveness of nonviolence. The effectiveness of violence as the final arbiter for resolving conflicts between peoples is more and more suspect. As violence slides in value, nonviolence ascends. Raymond Schwager writes, "The time seems to be slowly becoming ripe for recognizing the hidden truth about violence."[13] In addition, more and more people sense the value of exploring the power of nonviolence and to researching and developing new applications of nonviolent strategy in a greater and greater array of conflict situations—from relations between individuals, between organizations, in businesses, in families, in schools. The nonviolence taught in the Sermon on the Mount might turn out to be the most realistic stance of all.

Love Your Enemies

The second special teaching in the gospels that founds a theology of peace is Jesus' teaching "Love your enemies."

> You have heard it said, "You will love your neighbor and hate your enemy." But I say to you, love your enemies and pray for those who persecute you; so that you may be children of your Father in heaven, for he causes the sun to rise on the bad as well as the good, and sends the rain on those who do good and those who do evil. Why should God reward you if you love only those who love you? Even the tax collectors do that. And if you speak only to your brothers, are you doing anything out of the ordinary? Even the gentiles do that. You must be all-embracing [frequently translated as "perfect"]—just as your Father is all-embracing [perfect].(Matt. 5:43–48)

This passage has been traditionally referred to by scripture scholars as one of the "hard sayings " of Jesus, as in—who can live up to this very challenging message? Or, isn't this beyond the capacity of ordi-

---

[13]Raymond Schwager, *Must There Be Scapegoats? Violence and Redemption in the Bible* (New York: Crossroad, 2000), 234.

nary mortals? It is also thought by most scholars to be the "*ipsissima verba*," the very words of Jesus, not the evangelist's words, not a creation of the early church but uttered by Jesus himself. Donald Senior writes, "Here the reader can hear the authentic voice of Jesus. If any saying in the gospel can claim to be an unaltered saying of Jesus it his statement on love of enemies. . . . Jesus' command to love your enemy directly affronts a sectarian attitude prevalent in his own time."[14] It is not necessary to overstate the contrast between Jesus' teaching and the teaching of the Jewish scriptures. To do so is to fall into the trap of saying "Jesus' teaching and therefore Christianity teaches a loftier ethic than Judaism." In fact, the phrase, "You shall love your neighbor and hate your enemy" is never used in the Jewish scriptures. Matthew is not quoting a Bible text. He is, however, referring to a sentiment common among those in the Jewish tradition who are trying overly hard to maintain clear boundaries of identity for their community. It is used, for example, by the Essenes. The sectarian literature discovered at Qumran, reads: "Members of the community are to love all the sons of light, each according to his lot among the council of God, but to hate all the sons of darkness, each according to his guilt in the vengeance of God."[15] Traces of the idea of loving your enemy are found in the Jewish tradition. For example, in the Joseph tradition, in the telling of the story of Joseph and his brothers, God is the one who rescues a person who does not retaliate but does good to his enemy. "If you therefore walk in the commandments of the Lord, my children, He will exalt you and bless you with good things forever. And if anyone seeks to do evil to you, do good to him and pray for him and the Lord will rescue from all evil."[16] Jesus came, as he said, to fulfill the law and the prophets. He is not demeaning the Jewish tradition; he is intensifying it.

In other places in the Jewish tradition, "love your enemy" is simply nonretaliation, not taking vengeance on those who have done harm. The reason in this tradition for not taking vengeance is because God will eventually take vengeance. People can be freed from the negative feelings of hate and vengeance if they simply leave the judgment to God.

---

[14] Donald Senior, *Jesus: A Gospel Portrait* (New York: Paulist Press, 1992), 90.

[15] Victor Paul Furnish, *The Love Commandment in the New Testament* (Nashville, TN: Abingdon Press, 1972), 46.

[16] T Jos xviii, 1–2, as quoted in Pheme Perkins, *Love Commands in the New Testament* (New York: Paulist Press, 1982), 33.

This is very different from the love your enemy passage of Matthew's Gospel which depicts God sending the sun and the rain on the good and bad alike. There is no mention of God's vengeance here. Instead, Jesus says that his Father has infinite patience. He will later expound on this same point in the parable concerning the wheat and the weeds growing up together in the field. Pheme Perkins writes:

> Rather than assure the audience that divine patience is about to end, the Synoptic saying presents the "patience of God" as a divine perfection. A perfection that humans might seek to imitate rather than to end. Thus this divine attitude need not raise questions about the fate of evil in the world. Instead it becomes in Jesus' teaching a sign of the presence of the rule of God.[17]

The first difference between Jesus' message of "love your enemies" and other traditions is the motive Jesus gives for loving enemies—"so that you may be children of your Father in heaven, for he causes the sun to rise on the bad and good, and sends down the rain on those who do good and those who do evil." Act this way because God acts this way. Instead of looking at the world as a place dominated by evil, Jesus sees the world as a place where good and evil are all mixed up. Jesus sensed God's nearness, his patience with humanity. He depicts God patiently waiting for the change in the enemy's heart to be brought about through the love shown to them by Christian disciples.

The teaching "love your enemy" is not exclusive to Jesus. Other traditions of Jesus' time, Hellenistic traditions, no doubt influenced the Jewish tradition of his day. For example, the Stoic tradition counseled love of enemy as a way to demonstrate superiority of virtue. Only the most virtuous maintain their equanimity and refrain from retaliation in the face of enmity from others. Seneca writes in his treatise *On Anger* that love of enemy can be the ethic that a wise man can assume as he takes public office. In this case his aim is the good of society, not exaggerated self-love. It is nobility of heart that keeps him from giving way to anger. "He is a great and noble man who acts as he does, the lordly wild beast that listens unconcernedly to the baying of tiny

---

[17]Perkins, *Love Commands in the New Testament*, 38.

dogs."[18] Clemency means refraining from vengeance and can be an effective strategy for knitting a frayed society back together. Unlike the gospel passage however, the strategy is usually utilized to strengthen and maintain domination over one's subjects.

Another tradition, the Socrates tradition, has a wise man refraining from retaliation while taking punishment, as a way of criticizing the unjust society of which he is a part. "He accepts these blows without resisting in order to proclaim the rottenness of society, not only in words but in his body."[19] Still another tradition counsels love of enemy in terms of nonretaliation as a way for a minority group or a person on a lower rung of society to survive—put your heads down, be nice to your superiors, and keep your head on your shoulders. Seneca tells the story of a Roman nobleman whose son had been condemned to death by the emperor for no valid reason and then asked the father to dinner. "The poor wretch went through with it, although he seemed to be drinking the blood of his son. . . . Do you ask why? He had a second son."

The love your enemy tradition was not exclusive to Jesus and Christians. It may have been influenced by some of these contemporaneous traditions. Jesus' teaching on love of enemy, nonetheless is quite distinctive. The first difference, as we have seen, is the motive Jesus gives for why his disciples should act in this way: because it is how they can be sons and daughters of his Father. The motive is a theological one, revealing the inner life of God. God acts in this way toward enemies.

Second, "love of enemies" in Jesus' understanding is not merely refraining from violent retribution, nonretaliation. It is very active outreach to, forbearance for, and inclusion of enemies. It is part of a missionary posture. Jesus says: pray for your persecutors, salute them, embrace them. This way of treating enemies is a logical extension of the central tenet of the kingdom of God teaching, namely, that salvation is for all. None are to be excluded from our common life, not even enemies. Christians are not only to be in solidarity with victims; they are also to include the perpetrators. Eventually the disciples will understand the meaning of the cross in precisely these terms. As Miroslav Volf writes, "At the heart of the cross is Christ's stance of not

[18]Seneca, as quoted in Luise Schottroff, Reginald Fuller, Christoph Burchard, and M. Jack Suggs, *Essays on the Love Commandment* (Philadelphia: Fortress Press, 1978), 29.
[19]Schottroff et al., *Essays on the Love Commandment*, 22.

letting the enemy remain an enemy and of creating space in himself for the offended to come in. . . . The victim who refuses to be defined by the perpetrator, forgives and makes space in himself for the enemy."[20]

Who falls into this category of enemy? To understand who the enemies are that Jesus is referring to, it helps to place this passage in its historical and political context. Matthew is writing his gospel after the destruction of the Temple and Jerusalem by the Romans in 70 CE Zealots, priests, and Sadducees had lost their political power as a result of the war. The Pharisees came out of the war with their power and authority strengthened. They moved on with their lives, without the Temple, by focusing on the Torah. Warren Carter writes: "Under the leadership of Rabbi Yohannan ben Zakkai (and later Gamaliel II) a group of Pharisaic leaders met at the coastal town of Yavneh (also called Jamnia). They asserted their authority to interpret the law, to regulate Jewish life and to order worship in the synagogue."[21] Through this movement the Jewish religion was kept alive in perpetuity—without a Temple and without a land. At the same time the Jewish Christian movement began to separate itself from the synagogues. Conflicts arose. Matthew, in the Sermon on the Mount, is giving Christian believers their guide for living—in the context of conflict and even persecution. At the same time the Jewish Christian community had embarked on its mission to the gentiles. "Love your enemies and pray for your persecutors." Who are the enemies? Clearly, "enemies" refers first to those who are doing the persecuting, the aggressive members of the Jewish community, and those in the gentile community who are opposing the evangelizing Christians.

The further meaning of "enemies" is conveyed by Jesus in the parable of the Good Samaritan. Samaritans were a hated enemy of the Jews. In the previous century the Maccabees went into Samaria and burned the Samaritans' breakaway Temple at Gerizim. Samaritans hated the Jews for this and for other cultural and religious reasons. The feelings went deep. In Jesus' lifetime, a lone pilgrim crossing from Galilee through Samaria to the Temple in Judea was killed by a band of Samaritans. A larger band of Judeans went into Samaria and executed those who had killed the pilgrim. Imagine the surprise

---

[20]Miroslav Volf, *Exclusion and Embrace* (Nashville, TN: Abingdon Press, 1996), 126.
[21]Warren Carter, *What Are They Saying about Matthew's Sermon on the Mount?* (New York: Paulist Press, 1994), 57.

of the Jews who heard the story of the Good Samaritan who stopped and cared for the injured man—enduring much aggravation, time, and expense. It was not the priest or the Levite, authorities in their religion, who stopped to help. It was the Samaritan. The one whom they considered their enemy proved to be their neighbor. The reversal is dramatic. Jesus is making it clear in this parable that it is not just individuals with whom we might have personal animosity that are enemies. It is also all those who have been demonized by society as enemies—for cultural, religious, or political reasons. They too are to be treated with outgoing love, care, and inclusion.

The third key for understanding the passage is to appreciate those to whom it is addressed. At the beginning of the Sermon on the Mount we read in chapter 5, verse 1 that Jesus "sees the crowds," goes up the mountain, and when the disciples come to him, teaches "them," that is, the disciples. The disciples have already heard Jesus' teaching on the nonviolent, political kingdom of God. They have witnessed how Jesus welcomes and embraces all—so-called sinners and the just alike. In the Sermon on the Mount Jesus means to give them further instruction on how they are to act and what their discipleship entails. To whom is Jesus addressing this very challenging teaching? His disciples—those who have heard him, followed him, been graced by him. This teaching is given to the disciples not as individuals for their individual spiritual practice; it is addressed to them in community. They are to help one another model this behavior through their common, supportive practice. They are not alone. In other words, the teaching in the Sermon on the Mount and, in particular, the passage about "loving your enemies," is for those who have decided to be disciples of Jesus. Disciples of Jesus act, and are expected to act, in ways that others will find difficult or strange or not "natural." Loving one's enemies is for those who have already heard and committed to Jesus' message of the kingdom of God.

Joachim Jeremias summarized the ways that the message of "love your enemies" had been discounted over the last century—as ethical perfectionism, as an impossible ideal, as an interim ethic. He then pointed out what others had not seen as clearly. Disciples can love their enemies because they have been emboldened by the prior message of the kingdom of God. Disciples are those who have responded to God's grace, inspired by the example of Jesus and supported by a community of disciples—all of whom are weak, but all of whom are capable of great things under the inspiration of the Spirit.[22] They are called to a higher way of life. The Sermon on the Mount is not a compendium of timeless truths designed to compete with other philosophers' systems of ethical truth. It is not, in this sense, an expectation for all. It is the guide for those who have heard and responded to the call to follow Jesus in discipleship and who have been filled with Jesus' spirit of love.

Finally, it helps to see the built-in relationship of love of enemies with evangelization and conversion. As Jesus says in John's Gospel: "By this all will know that you are my disciples, if you have love for one another" (John 13:34). Love for one another and love for enemies will be recognized by people outside the community. And as also in the Gospel of John: "I chose you and appointed you that you should bear fruit and that your fruit should abide" (John 15:16). Perkins says of this: "The passage encourages Christians not to give up under persecution. . . . They will have to witness to Jesus before a hostile world. Thus the community is being entrusted with continuing Jesus' own mission."[23] The enemy will become a friend. The unbeliever will become a believer—through the disciples' love of them and for one another.

It is not surprising that Pope Benedict XVI has said that: "Love of enemy is the nucleus of the Christian Revolution."[24]

The irony is that the message that is meant for those who are explicitly committed disciples, when tried by others outside the fold of faith, turns out to be a way that is surprisingly effective. Is this the wisdom Jesus was referring to when he said: "I bless you, Father, Lord of heaven and earth, for hiding these things from the learned and the wise and revealing them to little children"? (Matt. 11:25). Is this the wisdom the world needs and is seeking?

A man such as Gene Sharp, who, in our day has done so much to spread the message of nonviolent action, is an example of one who is not inside the fold of Christian faith but nonetheless has discovered the practical power of nonviolent action. Sharp has written many books on nonviolent action, such as *Gandhi as a Political Strategist; The Politics of Nonviolent Action; A Hundred Ways to Unseat a Dictator*. He is a man who has served as a guru for the revolution that unseated Milosevic in Serbia. His books have been translated into Serbian, Egyptian,

---

[22]Joachim Jeremias, *The Sermon on the Mount* (Philadelphia: Fortress Press, 1963), 34–35.
[23]Perkins, *Love Commands in the New Testament*, 109.
[24]Benedict XVI, *Good Friday Sermon*, 2011.

and many other languages. One of his key disciples, a retired colonel in the US Army, traveled to Serbia to instruct the young people who constituted the Otpor Revolution leadership in the principles and practice of nonviolence. Sharp also served the same role for the first leaders of the Egyptian Revolution—well before the first demonstrations in Tahrir Square in Cairo. Sharp is guided by what is practical and positive for humanity. He has found the message of nonviolent resistance to be eminently practical politics.

Describing how love for the enemy works in practical terms, Theodor Ebert in a book edited by Sharp, wrote, "No man can wield power for long without justification of his conscience. . . . The hardest iron will melt in the flame of love. . . . Three factors are at work: the length of time during which spiritual power is applied, the intensity of its application and the varying degree of susceptibility of the opponents."[25] Ebert recognizes the dynamism and the power of active, nonviolent regard for one's enemies. Even though he may not be an avowed disciple of Jesus, he makes the message of the Sermon on the Mount come alive.

> You must therefore be perfect [all embracing], just as your heavenly Father is perfect [all embracing]. (Matt. 5:48)

The last phrase of the "love your enemies" passage in the Sermon on the Mount rounds off the message and summarizes how Jesus wants his disciples to live. But it needs to be translated correctly. Otherwise, it can seem to negate the teaching concerning the kingdom of God. Often the Greek word *teleios* is translated as "perfect"—"Be perfect as your heavenly Father is perfect." This translation implies that disciples are called to punctilious observation of external rules. It has led many into onerous scrupulosity, an anxious pursuit of perfect observance. How can anyone be as perfect as God? a Sisyphean, impossible task. Translating *teleios* as "perfect" changes the whole tone and meaning of the passage. As we have seen, Jesus is not laying down laws in the Sermon on the Mount; he is issuing an invitation. He is giving a life guide for disciples who are living in the kingdom of God. He is not sentencing people to a life of compulsive observance of legal minutiae.

---

[25]Theodor Ebert, "The Crisis," in *Civilian Defense, An Introduction*, ed. T. K. Mahadevan, Adam Roberts, and Gene Sharp (New Delhi: Gandhi Peace Foundation, 1967), 196, 197.

ORBIS ✈ BOOKS

Maryknoll, New York 10545

COMPLIMENTARY REVIEW COPY

Send 2 hard copies or e-mail the link to an online review when published.

Marketing Department
ORBIS BOOKS
Price Bldg, Box 302
Maryknoll, NY 10545

To interview an author, please contact Bernadette Price at
(914) 941.7636 ext. 2435 or bprice@maryknoll.org

Visit our website at
www.orbisbooks.com

Thank you for your consideration.

CANADA

BND (Bayard Novalis Dist.)
10 Lower Spadina Ave., Ste 400
Toronto ON M5V 2Z2
Tel: 877.702.7773
Fax: 416.363.9409
books@novalis.ca

UK/EUROPE

Alban Books, Ltd.
14 Belford Rd., West End
Edinburgh EH4 3BL
Tel: 31.226.2217
Fax: 31.225.5999
sales@albanbooks.com

AUSTRALIA

Rainbow Book Agencies
303 Arthur Street
Fairfield, VIC 3078
Tel: (39) 481-6611
Fax: (39) 481-2371
custserve@rainbowbooks.com.au

In fact Jesus' message of the kingdom of God was meant to overturn the Pharisees' narrow way of purity and exclusion observance. Consequently, scripture scholars have weighed in on the appropriate translation. Walter Wink, for example, explains that the term *teleios* is used in Greek literature to signify the form in art that makes the whole attractive. He suggests that "all encompassing" is a better translation of the term *teleios*. "Be all encompassing as God is all encompassing in his compassion." Donald Senior suggests a similar translation: "*Teleios* in Matthew's context means whole, complete, loving with God's limitless compassion."[26] Stott in his book *The Message of the Sermon on the Mount* suggests "all embracing" as the appropriate translation.[27] All of these translations are in harmony with the rest of the passage. For a disciple of Jesus, no one is outside the pale; no one is unreachable; no one is an enemy.

Forgiveness

A third special teaching that founds a new theology of peace is Jesus' teaching on forgiveness. The teaching of Jesus on forgiveness echoes and extends the teaching on love of enemies.

> Then Peter went up to him and said, "Lord, how often must I forgive my brother if he wrongs me? As often as seven times?" Jesus answered, "Not seven, I tell you, but seventy times seven." (Matt. 18:22)

Matthew follows this declaration with the parable of the unforgiving debtor who owes his master ten thousand talents, an unimaginably large debt. The debt is forgiven by his master, but the one who is forgiven does not extend the same graciousness to one who owes him a hundred denarii, a minuscule amount in comparison. Christian forgiveness has a number of facets.

The first facet of Christian forgiveness is its two-sided nature—as exemplified in the parable of the unforgiving servant. It is both a gift and a mandate. Christopher Marshall writes, "In the New Testament forgiveness is a gift before it is a task and a gift and task and then a

---

[26]Senior, *Jesus: A Gospel Portrait*, 92.
[27]Stott, *Message of the Sermon on the Mount*, 107.

reverse loop from task to gift: failure to forgive nullifies the benefits of God's forgiveness."[28] As in the words of the Lord's Prayer: "Forgive us our debts, as we have forgiven our debtors"(Matt. 6:12). As James Dunn writes, "Characteristic of the discipleship to which Jesus called was the two-sided theme of forgiven as forgiving, forgiven therefore forgiving."[29] One cannot be forgiven if one does not forgive, and human forgiveness is the consequence of divine forgiveness. How people can find it in their hearts to forgive great evils—for example, a mother who forgives the murder of her son—is a great mystery. In Timothy Gorringe's words, "It is a creative act, *sui generis*, which heals by restoring people to community."[30] In the story of St. Nicholas Parish in Evanston, Illinois, recounted in the film *A Justice That Heals*,[31] a young parishioner was shot and killed by a gang member from a nearby community. The mother of the boy who was killed wrote a letter to the killer in prison and expressed to him her forgiveness. She did not know that he had sent a letter of profound apology to the family at the same time. The letters crossed in the mail. Eventually, the whole parish participated in the outreach to the young man. He repented, was deeply changed, and reformed his whole way of life. How could she find it in her heart to forgive when others in her family could not find the same spirit in their hearts? She attributed it to her own ineffable sense that God forgives her and us—so she had to find a way to forgive as well.

Second, forgiveness is not ignoring or overlooking evil. It begins with explicitly naming and confronting evil—and then meeting it with unconditional love. Daniel Philpott writes, "Forgiveness is an *imitatio dei*, an imitation of God . . . with eternal, unconditional love, the only sort that could be greater than the evil of the worst atrocities. . . . In full reconciliation, forgiveness is accompanied by apology and reparations."[32] In modern-day political peacemaking, acts of forgive-

---

[28]Christopher Marshall, *Beyond Retribution* (Grand Rapids, MI: William B. Eerdmans, 2001), 75.

[29]James D. G. Dunn, *Jesus Remembered*, vol. 1 (Grand Rapids, MI: William B. Eerdmans, 2003), 589.

[30]Timothy Gorringe, *God's Just Vengeance* (Cambridge: Cambridge University Press, 1996), 265.

[31]Jay Shefsky, dir., *A Justice That Heals*, 2000.

[32]Daniel Philpott, "Reconciliation: A Catholic Ethic for Peacebuilding in the Political Order," in *Peacebuilding: Catholic Theology, Ethics, and Praxis,* ed. Robert J. Schreiter, R. Scott Appleby, and Gerard F. Powers (Maryknoll, NY: Orbis Books, 2010), 117.

ness turn out to be critical for healing a society that has been wracked by violence and atrocities. Successful Truth and Reconciliation commissions begin with the recitation of the crimes done to real, individual persons, followed by admittance of the crimes by the perpetrators, bringing into the light of day not only the fact of the acts but also public recognition of the psychic wounds that continue to afflict those who suffered. Desmond Tutu's book *No Future without Forgiveness*,[33] makes it clear that the process of reconciliation begins with explicit recognition of the evil done so that the people harmed have the opportunity to emerge from their grief and have the opportunity to start again, and if they can find it in their hearts to forgive, start again with those who have perpetrated the violence.

The third facet of Christian forgiveness is related to the second—that it is a community practice. For a community to be healthy and outgoing it has to have the ability to recognize harm done between members, face those wrongs and find a way to go beyond them and find reconciliation between members. It needs lively conflict resolution skills. If a community continues on without acknowledging and confronting internal dissension and conflict, it begins to take on an air of false, forced unreality. N. T. Wright states:

> Centuries of Christian usage have accustomed readers of the New Testament to think of forgiveness as primarily a gift to the individual person . . . cart before the horse. . . . Israel saw exile precisely as the result of, or punishment for, her sins. Israel brought back from Exile would mean that her sins were being punished no more. . . . Forgiveness of sins is another way of saying return from exile. For a first-century Jew forgiveness of sins could never be a private blessing; it was the redemption for which Israel was hoping.[34]

In the early history of the church an important theme was how to correct someone who went astray in a way that would reintegrate that person into the community—first confront them and offer a hand of welcome and forgiveness, and if that did not work, then send a delegation to do the same and so on—early forms of restorative justice and

---

[33]Desmond Tutu, *No Future without Forgiveness* (New York: Doubleday, 1999).
[34]N. T. Wright, *Jesus and the Victory of God* (Minneapolis: Fortress Press, 1996), 268.

healing circles practice. A healthy community depends on forgiveness regularly both given and received.

When the man in the Mennonite community in Pennsylvania murdered three young girls at their school, the Mennonite community immediately reached out to the family of the man who committed the murder, striking people across the country as a surprising and noble practice. The community acted that way because they have continually nurtured the virtue of forgiveness in their midst. The act did not come out of nowhere; it was part and parcel of their ongoing community practice.

A new theology of peace needs a strong dose of effective conflict resolution. As Kenneth Himes writes:

> Missing in the tradition is a theory of conflict resolution. . . . A weakness of Catholic social teaching stemming from its communitarian vision is that conflict is viewed as more apparent than real. . . . Popes often appeal to parties in conflict to use reason. . . . The failure to acknowledge the deeply conflictual nature of human reality has permitted Catholic social teaching to remain underdeveloped in strategies of conflict resolution.[35]

Fourth, the act of forgiveness is not just a cancellation, it is also a constructive act. It frees the one forgiving from their ongoing, justified anger and resentment. Philpott writes, "Forgiveness is an act of love in which the victims of wrongdoing renounce their justified anger and resentment against the perpetrators along with all claims that the wrongdoers owe something to them for their deed."[36] As the one forgiving looks at the perpetrators in a new way, as a person in good standing, "They will too the restoration of the perpetrator's soul."[37]

Finally, the forgiveness that Jesus calls disciples to practice breaks the cycle of violence. Jesus taught that disciples should forgive seventy times seven times, echoing the passage in Genesis that quoted Lamech saying he would exercise revenge seventy times seven times, that is, infinitely. As such, forgiveness is a free creative act nonpareil. Volf writes:

---

[35]Kenneth Himes, "Peacebuilding and Catholic Social Teaching," in *Peacebuilding: Catholic Theology, Ethics, and Praxis,* ed. Robert J. Schreiter, R. Scott Appleby, and Gerard F. Powers (Maryknoll, NY: Orbis Books, 2010), 282.

[36]Philpott, "Reconciliation," 116.

[37]Ibid.

Forgiveness is a genuinely free act which does not merely react. Forgiveness breaks the power of the remembered past and transcends the claims of the affirmed justice and makes the spiral of vengeance grind to a halt. . . . The climate of oppression in which Jesus preached was suffused with the desire for revenge.[38]

If evil is contagious and if violence is contagious, so is love of enemy contagious and so is forgiveness contagious. A new theology of peace needs to incorporate, celebrate, and explore fully the healing power of forgiveness for today's violent world.

To conclude this section on the special teachings of Jesus that should be the foundation for a Christian aspiring to be a disciple of Jesus and for a gospel-based theology of peace, reflect on the words of Wright:

Jesus summoned his followers to a strange kind of revolution—a double revolution, in fact, through which Israel would become the light of the world . . . not through fighting a military battle like Judas Maccabeus, but through turning the other cheek, going the second mile, loving her enemies, and praying for her persecutors. This agenda was a revolutionary way of being revolutionary. . . . At the heart of that subversive wisdom was the call to his followers to take up the cross and follow him, to become his companions in the kingdom-story he was enacting.[39]

Perisson as the Key to a New Theology of Peace

In the Matthew's Sermon on the Mount, Jesus says, "For I tell you if your righteousness does not *surpass* that of the scribes and Pharisees, you will never get into the kingdom of Heaven" (Matt. 5:20), and "For if you love those who love you, what reward will you get? Do not even the tax collectors do as much? And if you save your greetings for your brothers are you doing anything *out of the ordinary*? Do not even the gentiles do as much?"(Matt. 5:46–47).

The key to a new theology of peace is embracing the concept and practice of *perisson*. The gospels were written in koine Greek, an everyday, straightforward style of the Greek language. *Perisson* in Greek

---

[38]Volf, *Exclusion and Embrace*, 120.
[39]Wright, *Jesus and the Victory of God*, 564.

means "more." The disciples are called to do more than the tax collectors, to do more than the Pharisees, to do more than the gentiles. Jesus is saying that even tax collectors love their brothers, those who are within their circle of friendship, tribe, or family. That is a good, but it really is no big deal. Even the gentiles greet and embrace their brothers. That is a good but it really is not very exceptional. But my disciples, now they are really something. They are called to a much higher calling. They are called to love, greet, and embrace their so-called enemies. They are called to put themselves on the line in situations of conflict and enmity, communicate their love and regard for the enemy, remove the enmity, and make the enemy a friend. My disciples are called to go well beyond the ordinary, the minimum, the usual. They practice *perisson*, a righteousness that goes well beyond that of the scribes and Pharisees. They are called to be active peacemakers. C. F. Andrews, the Anglican priest who was one of Mahatma Gandhi's closest friends, highlighted the idea of *perisson* as the key to understanding a new theology of peace in his book *The Sermon on the Mount*.[40]

The Sermon on the Mount is addressed to the disciples of Jesus. It is their charter for how to live in the kingdom of God that Jesus has inaugurated. Jesus' call to discipleship was quite different from the call of a leading rabbi to his followers. Discipleship as Jesus understood it was not a call to a theoretical discipline but a call to action. According to John Meier, the Greek "verb, 'to follow' (*akoloutheo*) describes their activity in the gospels more than the verb 'to learn' (*manthano*). They were called literally to leave home and family to follow Jesus on his journeys, to share and be formed by Jesus' own prophetic ministry of proclaiming the kingdom. . . . Jesus' absolute demand of discipleship is unique in ancient scholastic traditions."[41] Their work was not study but practice. Jesus was not for the disciples a teacher of correct doctrine but more a master-craftsman whom they were to learn from and imitate. Michael Hardin writes, "Discipleship was not matriculation into a Rabbinical college but apprenticeship to the work of the Kingdom."[42]

The gospels are similar to ancient biographies that portray the chosen subject's character by narrating his words and deeds. Jesus'

---

[40]Andrews, *Sermon on the Mount*.

[41]John P. Meier, *A Marginal Jew: Rethinking the Historical Jesus,* vol. 3 (New York: Doubleday, 2001), 71–72.

[42]Michael Hardin, *The Jesus Driven Life* (Lancaster, PA: JDL Press, 2010), 79.

deeds and words follow a pattern of fidelity to God and selfless love toward other people. To follow in discipleship is to follow that same pattern. The gospels "insist on living according to the same pattern of life and death shown by Jesus," Volf writes.[43] The disciples are those who followed Jesus' way, back then, and it also refers to those who are trying to follow his way today. To practice "turning the other cheek"—not understood as acting as a doormat, but in its original meaning of creative, brave standing up to oppression—to practice love of enemies; to practice forgiveness seventy times seven times—these are directives for discipleship. They are also directives that form and found a theology of peacemaking.

The ethic of Jesus in the Sermon on the Mount is strikingly different from natural law behavior because it is rooted in God's love even for rebellious sinners. This belief in the God of Jesus, the one who takes the initiative toward enemies, pursuing them until they either change or harden their hearts, is the dynamism that energizes disciples to do *more* than the expected, *more* than what natural law thinking demands. As Perkins writes:

> Ethical reflection in the New Testament has a style that is different from the "tell me the rules to get the reward model." Jesus kept talking about what God intended his creation to be. . . . Many of his words are like these. They almost look like laws, but they only work for people who live out of a different consciousness than that of the Pharisees.[44]

Many years ago Louis Monden, in his book *Sin, Liberty and Law*, reflected on what happens when all of ethical thinking concentrates on the line between what is right and what is wrong; what is moral and immoral; what is allowed and what is sin. Where do people live their lives? The answer—right at the line. This ethical thinking is concerned with keeping people safe. As long as people stay on the right side of the line they are safe. If they stay out of sin, if they don't cross the line, they are assured of heaven after this life. "Many even seem to hold implicitly, as a first principle, that God has no right to

---

[43] Volf, *Exclusion and Embrace*, 24.
[44] Perkins, *Love Commands in the New Testament*, 6.

expect anything out of the ordinary from the ordinary person."[45]

Monden was criticizing the moral theology of his time. After the Council of Trent, Catholic moral theology had as its purpose the training of priests to fulfill their roles in the confessional, emphasizing the lines between right and wrong in all kinds of settings, giving priests tools to be pastorally responsive and accurate judges of guilt—so they could assign penance according to the degree of severity of sin. The manuals of theology focused on the minimal requirements for salvation. The Tubingen school, on the other hand, which included such luminaries as Karl Adam and Romano Guardini, taught that moral theology should focus not just on sin, law, and penance but on the call of God in grace and the response to that call by Christians. It should focus on the fullness of the life to be lived by the Christian in the world and be based on a strong biblical foundation. Bernard Häring, recognized as the finest Catholic moral theologian of the twentieth century, took the teachings of the Tubingen school, synthesizing biblical and spiritual theology with moral theology, and produced his path-finding three-volume work on the *Law of Christ*. In that work he returned moral theology to being centered on Jesus' call to build the kingdom of God in the midst of a sinful, violent world.

In the Sermon on the Mount, Jesus invites disciples to help build the kingdom of God in a sinful world by going beyond what is typically expected. It is an ethic of creative, courageous, proactive peacemaking. As Glen Stassen states, "The Sermon on the Mount gives us norms that are not legalistic prohibitions but grace-based practices, kingdom breakthroughs, transforming initiatives."[46] A focus on the fullness of the life to be lived by a Christian in the world will be a life of *perisson, more*. A life of *perisson* does not hover at the line between right and wrong, doing the minimum required to survive this life and get to heaven. Lives of p*erisson* push into the upper limits of human potential. Wink writes, "When people participate in nonviolent resistance they experience something of their higher selves; for nonviolence is a characteristic of the coming reign of God, and a foretaste of its transcendent reality."[47] They will be, with the support of a community of practice, extraordinary lives. As Christopher Marshall states:

---

[45]Louis Monden, *Sin, Liberty and Law* (New York: Sheed and Ward, 1965), 117.

[46]Glen Stassen, *Just Peacemaking: Transforming Initiatives for Justice and Peace* (Louisville: Westminster/John Knox Press, 1992), 10.

[47]Wink, *The Powers That Be*, 162.

Best thought of as new moral challenges not new laws, in response to the coming of the kingdom . . . new heights . . . because something unprecedented is breaking into history that changes everything, not impossible ideals but realistic goals because they are empowered by the new reality of God's redeeming power that has broken into the world.[48]

A new theology of peace begins with the experience of a disciple who is called to embrace the way of Jesus, a way that confronts oppression using the tools of nonviolent resistance, a way that works to build a peaceful human condition well before calamitous violence has a chance to erupt. Such creative peacemaking is nourished through fellowship, prayer, and communal social action. Such a theology of peace will be quite different from one that is based on natural law thinking and its offshoot—the just war theory.

"The just war theory is the rule-based approach to the problem of violence," Lisa Sowle Cahill states.[49] Just war theory emerges from taking a natural law approach to the problem of war and violence. It reflects on humans as they are: their nature and what they need for flourishing. It then develops criteria that all people, using the light of their natural reason, can agree make sense when confronted with the decision about going to war. The criteria are developed with an eye to limiting war. It assumes that war is not a positive and to wage war is an exception to the rule of peaceful behavior that is humanity's natural condition. By stringently applying the criteria, such as just cause, proportionality, legitimate authority, and so on—responsible parties can make a judgment concerning the justifiability of a given war.

The just war theory has a place in a new theology of peace. It gives Christians a place to meet those who are not Christian disciples on a ground of common human reasoning. It is, however, a place that should be subordinate to the way of Christian discipleship. Jesus gives Christian disciples a way to act that goes way beyond what the dictates of human reason, unaided by the light of grace, will prescribe. It is a call to *perisson*, that is, a call to *more*. The New Testament teaching on love of enemy and creative nonviolence calls Christian disciples to not wait until a decision about waging war is

---

[48]Marshall, *Beyond Retribution*, 17.
[49]Lisa Sowle Cahill, *Love Your Enemies* (Minneapolis: Fortress Press, 1994), 13.

nigh. It calls disciples to be active peacemakers. Active peacemaking means working as Jesus did—he worked to build a society that would reject violence as a solution to oppression, and he hoped thereby to avoid calamitous violence. He worked to build an inclusive society that avoided labeling people as enemies. He modeled and taught a better way to resolve conflicts—a way of nonviolent, creative action, "turning the other cheek," and active love of enemy. He worked to build a jubilee society, where the poor and the powerless would benefit from equitable distribution of the earth's bounty. He brought the kingdom of God into our midst and called disciples to make the kingdom a full reality.

A new theology of peace will give pride of place to this New Testament teaching, to Christian discipleship and the call to be proactive peacemakers. The Catholic position on war and violence will no longer be equated with the just war theory. The Catholic position will embrace a much bigger call, a call to *perisson*, a call to *more*.

A Final Reflection on the Reaching of the New Testament on Peace and Nonviolence

The final reflection concerns Jesus' own way of handling violent situations. The gospel writers usually portray the violence against Jesus as clandestine, out of the public eye—secret meetings between those who became his mortal enemies. For example, by the beginning of the third chapter of Mark, Mark depicts the Pharisees and the Herodians, the party of those who inherited the power of Herod the Great, huddling together: "So the Pharisees left the synagogue and met at once with some members of Herod's party, and they made plans to kill Jesus." At least five other times in the gospels, his enemies are described as meeting and planning how they can catch Jesus in a way that shields them from the wrath of the people. Their violent intentions are secret and hidden—until Judas gives them their opportunity in the dead of night. On two occasions, however, the gospels portray Jesus directly confronted by angry, steamrolling violence. It is instructive to reflect on how he handled those situations.

The first situation takes place in his hometown of Nazareth. Jesus had just told them that prophets are never welcomed in their own hometowns and gave them the examples of Elijah and Elisha to demonstrate that fact. Luke wrote:

When the people in the synagogue heard this, they were filled with anger. They rose up, dragged Jesus out of town, and took him to the top of the hill on which their town was built. They meant to throw him over the cliff, but he walked through the middle of the crowd and went his way. (Luke 4:28–30)

How did he do that? They were murderously angry, but he walked right through the middle of them and went his way. Sharon Ringe comments on the passage:

> The graphic portrayal of the violence of their attack—attempting to run Jesus off a cliff—is without parallel in the New Testament. It might be understood as an escalation of the practice of casting a victim into a pit before stoning. If the people have concluded from Jesus' interpretation of his prophetic task that his appearance and proclamation are those of a false prophet, their response would be warranted by Torah.[50]

But still, how did he walk through their midst?

Perhaps we will gain further insight by reflecting on the second example.

> The teachers of the law and the Pharisees brought in a woman who had been caught committing adultery, and they made her stand before them all. "Teacher," they said to Jesus, "this woman was caught in the very act of committing adultery. In our law, Moses commanded that such a woman must be stoned to death. Now, what do you say?" (John 8:4–5)

Jesus is right there in the middle of a crowd of self-righteous religious leaders who are about to stone a woman to death under the sanction of their religion. What does he do? He bent over and silently wrote something in the dust—we don't know what he wrote, and it does not seem important. He let the situation cool, put them back on themselves. He then said, "Whichever one of you has committed no sin may throw the first stone at her" (John 8:7). Then he bent over again and resumed

---

[50]Sharon H. Ringe, *Jesus, Liberation, and Biblical Jubilee* (Philadelphia: Fortress Press, 1985), 41.

writing. He did not intensify the standoff by staring at them or challenging them. Instead, he let this words sink in. John wrote: "They all left one by one, the older ones first" (John 8:9). The younger ones' hyped-up energy evidently took a little longer to cool.

> Jesus was left alone with the woman still standing there. He straightened up and said to her, "Where are they? Is there no one left to condemn you?" "No one, sir," she answered. "Well then," Jesus said, "I do not condemn you either. Go, but do not sin again." (John 8:10–11)

In both of these situations of intense violence, Jesus was clearly not intimidated. He did not respond to the violence with threats or with counterviolence. He coolly faced the crowds. In the one situation he walked right through their midst. In the other case he countered their violence calmly and creatively, changing the dynamic of the situation and resolving it without bloodshed. The nonviolence, the calm, the courage, the creativity of Jesus—all were clearly displayed.

A typical challenge to nonviolence is capsulized in the standard question—"Yes, but what would you do if . . . someone threatened to kill another in your presence." Although it is usually stated with a closer to home proprietary overtone as in—"What would you do if your mother or your sister . . . ?" The assumption behind the question is that if you are not a coward, you would use violence preemptively to stop the threatened violence. John Howard Yoder wrote a whole book on the question, "What would you do if . . . ?" spelling out the assumptions behind such a question and offering a number of possible strategies other than violence.[51] The woman caught in adultery and threatened with stoning is such a situation—one that Jesus faced and resolved without violence.

Jesus' passing through the midst of the crowd in Nazareth is reminiscent of an incident described in a recent biography of Gandhi. Gandhi was doing all he could do to change the attitudes of his co-religionists toward the untouchables in their midst. That raised the ire of *sanatani* (strictly observant) Hindus, those who felt that Gandhi was straying from an important tenet of their tradition. A crowd of five thousand stopped him as he walked along and threatened him

---

[51]John Howard Yoder, *What Would You Do?* (Scottdale, PA: Herald Press, 1983).

with violence. Gandhi walked right through their midst. Later, another posse of *sanatani* Hindus sought to stop his car. Gandhi offered to give their leader a ride to the rally he was about to address. They went on together without violence.[52] How did Gandhi meet and walk right through violent situations? His centered, unruffled calm, his smile and clearly benevolent feelings toward his attackers were his protection.

In Christian history, Ambrose stated that, even though he did not believe he could use violence to protect himself—that would be against Jesus' teaching—a Christian had to protect the innocent from harm. Not to protect the innocent from harm made the one neglecting his duty even more guilty than the one perpetrating the harm. Augustine agreed with him on both counts—not using violence to protect oneself and the obligation to use violence to protect the innocent from harm. That teaching was the theory that opened the door to Christian participation in violence, even participation in war. Christian leaders have repeated that teaching of Ambrose and Augustine now for centuries. In fact, on this teaching hinges the entire "just war" theory. Note, however, that both Ambrose and Augustine assume that protection means violence. Protection of the innocent is equated with violence. They forgot the way Jesus defended the woman taken in adultery from violence through creative nonviolent action. They forgot how Jesus told Peter to put his sword away when Peter was only doing what Ambrose and Augustine would have commanded him to do. Peter was trying to protect the most innocent of innocents. They overlooked the fact that there is always an alternative to violence— one that typically works more successfully than violence in response to violence, one that breaks the cycle of violence—it is the power of creative nonviolent action.

The life of Jesus, the *way* he lived—that is what is normative for a Christian. Christianity was called "The Way" in its early years. It has been pointed out that the Creed unintentionally skips the life of Christ. It goes from "born of the virgin Mary" to "suffered under Pontius Pilate, died and was buried," missing what is most central for a disciple—the earthly life of Jesus, his way of nonviolent resistance to evil, his way of all inclusive embrace—even of the enemy, his way of building an alternative community of nonviolent, loving practice.

---

[52]Joseph Lelyveld, *Great Soul: Mahatma Gandhi and His Struggle with India* (New York: Alfred A. Knopf, 2011), 247.

The cross, the way Jesus died, only makes sense as a culmination of the way he lived.

A new theology of peace starts with the gospel portraits of Jesus. It does not look elsewhere for the foundation of an ethic of peace. It does not look to Cicero or the Greek philosophers. As we will see, the early Christians did not look elsewhere either. They followed the way of nonviolent resistance to evil and love for enemies—even in the teeth of overwhelming violence.

3

The Early Church's Stance on Peace and War

The early Church Fathers are those whose writings come down to us from the late first century to the beginning of the fourth century and who are respected for carrying forward the message of Jesus into a time of growth and development of Christianity and into times of persecution for the faith. They are writers marked by holiness of life and orthodoxy. Among the writings that come down to us from the first century are the Didache, the earliest document we have after the writings of the New Testament. The Didache was evidently used in the instruction of new converts into Christianity. It lays out the principal teachings of Christianity and dates from circa 80–90 CE. Also from this earliest period are writings of church leaders who personally knew the first apostles, such as Ignatius of Antioch and Polycarp, the Bishop of Smyrna, who personally knew the apostle John. Both of them were martyred for their faith. Clement, traditionally thought to be the third bishop of Rome, wrote a pastoral letter to the Christian community of Corinth at the end of the first century.

Among the Fathers of the second century are Justin, who was martyred for the faith, Athenagoras, Clement of Alexandria (c. 150–c. 215), and Tertullian (c. 160–c. 220). Notable writers from the third century who expressed their ideas on peace, violence, war, and the Christian's role in building a society of peace were Origen, (c. 185–c. 254), Arnobius (died c. 330), and Lactantius (c. 240—c. 320).

The early Fathers' importance lies first in their closeness in time to Jesus and the Apostles, their fidelity to the traditions handed down to them, often proven by their willingness to suffer even to the point of martyrdom, and the way they speak for their fellow Christians. Rarely do they say "I" think such and such. It is usually "we." Through them we see into the life and practice of the early church.

In addition, these early Fathers are perceived as especially qualified to interpret the meanings of the New Testament, not just because of their closeness in time, but also because they thought almost exclusively with New Testament concepts—"without drawing as heavily as did later generations on classical and Old Testament themes," as Roland Bainton writes.[1]

The Early Fathers' Vision: The End of War and a Full, Positive Peace

The early Fathers' vision of peace and the end of war was formed primarily, as we will see, by the teachings and practice of Jesus. However, the Fathers understood that Jesus was a Jew and was formed by the Jewish tradition, which he came not to eliminate but to fulfill. Consequently, the early Church Fathers read the Jewish scriptures avidly, but as Jesus did, selectively. They found in the Jewish scriptures a very positive, full understanding of peace that helped them appreciate and practice the teachings of Jesus all the more faithfully.

The early Fathers of the Church had a very positive, full understanding of peace, the peace of *shalom*. Peace for them was not just the absence of violence. Nor was it just inner, personal peace. As they read the Jewish tradition, they followed, just as Jesus did, the bright thread of hope and nonviolence. They did not adopt the strand of the Jewish tradition that focused on the warrior God. They did not embrace the idea of the "ban"—that people conquered by Israel belonged to God and should be sacrificed to him. They did not justify violence by referring to the stirring military victories and the military leaders of the Old Testament as would Christian teachers who came after them. Instead they picked out the teachings in the Old Testament that illustrated and gave depth to the teachings and practice of the Suffering Servant, Jesus. The early Fathers of the Church deeply appreciated the beautiful, stirring prophecies of Isaiah 2 and Micah 4 in particular. These prophecies proclaimed that peace would come to all nations through the spread of God's word and justice—without the need for kings and wars. War would be coming to an end. The prophecies represented a high, confident note in the Jewish scriptures.

---

[1] Roland Bainton, *Christian Attitudes toward War and Peace* (Eugene, OR: Wipf and Stock, 1960), 67.

Isaiah 2:3–4 reads:

And many peoples shall go and say, Come ye, and let us go up to the mountains of the Lord, to the house of God of Jacob, and he will teach us of His ways, and we will walk in His paths: for out of Zion shall go forth the law, and the word of the Lord from Jerusalem. And He shall judge among the nations, and convict many peoples; and they shall beat their swords into plowshares, and their spears into pruning hooks; nation shall not lift sword against nation, neither shall they learn war any more.

In the slightly more elaborated version of Micah 4:1–5:

In days to come the mountain of the Lord's house shall be established as the highest of the mountains, and shall be raised up above the hills. People shall stream to it, and many nations shall come and say: "Come, let us go up to the mountain of the Lord, to the house of the God of Jacob; that he may teach us his ways and that we may walk in his paths." For out of Zion shall go forth instruction, and the word of the Lord from Jerusalem. He shall judge between many peoples, and shall arbitrate between strong nations far away; they shall beat their swords into plowshares, and their spears into pruning hooks; nation shall not lift up sword against nation, neither shall they learn war any more; but they shall all sit under their own vines and under their own fig trees, and no one shall make them afraid; for the mouth of the Lord of hosts has spoken. For all the peoples walk, each in the name of its god, but we will walk in the name of the Lord our God forever and ever.

The fact that both Isaiah and Micah articulated such a clear message concerning the end of war stands in marked contrast to the other themes in the Jewish scriptures. They stand in marked contrast also to other writings on war from the ancient world. How did Isaiah and Micah come to see the world so differently and so hopefully? Scholars note that these prophecies were written much later in the history of Israel, in a time of peace under the beneficent rule of the Persians. Thomas Kruger writes, "The positive experience of Persian rule and the concept of a 'Persian peace' propagated by the Achaemenid rulers probably supported the hope for a peaceful coexistence of peoples on the basis of a common ethos and a judicial settlement of conflicts."[2] In addition, conviction in Israel had been growing that observance of the laws of Israel would guarantee the protection of Yahweh's strong right arm—that in itself would do away with the need for kings or war. Finally, the experience of the positive effect that the rule of law was having in their more proximate dealings with one another gave them a glimpse of what could happen if justice and the teachings of the Jewish law could continue to spread to other nations. Kruger continues, "Isaiah 2 and Micah 4, however, go one step further, envisioning a state of peace that is based on a judicial settling of conflict. In this development two other strands of Israelite tradition seem to play a part: the idea of connecting war with justice, and the expectation that law will spread so widely as to become universal."[3] These prophecies also grew out of the day-to-day experience the people had of overcoming revenge through the rule of law, an achievement that did not eliminate violence from society but gradually reduced its virulence.

The images in these two prophecies are very powerful—beating swords into plowshares, all sitting under their own vines and fig trees. It is an eminently positive vision of peace—war has given way to food production and relief of hunger; the distribution of wealth is such that all are prosperous and all are cooperating in positive social relationships. As Kruger writes, "Instead of preparing tools for hunting and killing one another, people will devote themselves to the production of food. Contrasting swords = war = death with plowshares = food production = life, the image of beating swords into plowshares reduces the complexity of reality into one simple and clear opposite."[4]

It is this vision of positive peace achieved through justice that the early Fathers of the Church embraced. The Fathers not only shared this vision of the future; they added to that picture an understanding of how that vision will be brought to practical reality—namely, through discipleship of the Crucified One, through responding to violence with love and the willingness to suffer.

It is striking how many early Christian writers quote these passages.

---

[2]Thomas Kruger, "'They Shall Beat Their Swords into Plowshares': A Vision of Peace through Justice and Its Background in the Hebrew Bible," in *War and Peace in the Ancient World*, ed. Kurt A. Raaflaub (Malden, MA: Blackwell, 2007), 164.

[3]Ibid., 168.

[4]Ibid., 161.

In their quotations they are saying that positive peace, that is, peace that is political as well as personal, peace that embraces the whole of human life—economic, social, and political—has indeed come to the nations through Jesus and the Christian people who do not make war and model how to build peaceful relations between people.

Justin Martyr writes in his *Apology* in about 150 CE that swords have been beaten into plowshares and goes on:

> And that this has happened, you can be persuaded. For from Jerusalem twelve men went out into the world, and these were unlearned, unable to speak, but by the power of God they told every race of men that they had been sent by Christ to teach all men the word of God. And we, who were former slayers of one another, not only do not war upon our enemies, but, for the sake of neither lying, nor deceiving those who examine us, gladly die confessing Christ.[5]

Justin identifies the justice that goes out from Jerusalem in the prophecy with the words the twelve uttered as they came out from Jerusalem. Moreover, he explains that the vision of peace without war is fulfilled through the nonviolent practice of Christians who not only refrain from war but who respond to persecution and violence with a straightforward willingness to suffer.

In his *Dialogue with Trypho*, Justin announces that the time of beating swords into plowshares has already arrived, that as Christianity has spread throughout the world, the world is increasingly at peace. The crucified one, Jesus, has shown the way:

> And we, who were filled with war, and mutual slaughter and every wickedness, have each through the whole earth—changed our warlike weapons,—our swords into ploughshares, our spears into instruments of tillage,—and we cultivate piety, righteousness, philanthropy, faith and hope which we have from the Father Himself through Him who was crucified.[6]

---

[5]Justin, *The First Apology of Justin, the Martyr* (Christian Classics Ethereal Library, www.ccel.org), Chapter 39.

[6]Justin, *Dialogue with Trypho* (www.earlychristianwritings.com.) 110.

Irenaeus comments on the Isaiah and Micah prophecies that the word of the Lord has spread through the world because of the practice of Christians demonstrating how to answer violence with love. As a result, the world is changing from war to peace:

> But if the law of liberty, that is, the word of God, preached by the apostles (who went forth from Jerusalem,) throughout all the earth, caused such a change in the state of things, that these nations did form the swords and war-lances into ploughshares, and changed them into pruning hooks for reaping the corn, that is into instruments used for peaceful purposes, and that they are now unaccustomed to fighting, but when smitten, offer also the other cheek, then the prophets have not spoken these things of any other person, but of Him who effected them. This person is our Lord.[7]

Tertullian quotes the prophecies of Isaiah and Micah and says:

> For the old law vindicated itself by the vengeance of the sword, and plucked out eye for eye, and requited injury with punishment; but the new law pointed to clemency, and changed the former savagery of swords and lances into tranquility, and refashioned the former infliction of war upon rivals and foes of the law into peaceful acts of ploughing and cultivating the earth.[8]

Origen, around 250 CE, also finds that the prophecies of Isaiah and Micah are graphically coming true in their midst and holds up the behavior of Christians as proof of the divinely inspired message of Jesus:

> And to those who inquire of us whence we come, or who is our founder, we reply that we are come, agreeably to the counsels of Jesus, to "cut down our hostile and insolent wordy swords into ploughshares, and to convert into pruning-hooks the spears formerly employed in war." For we no longer take up "sword against nation," nor do we "learn war anymore," having become

---

[7]Irenaeus, *Against the Heresies* (www.earlychristian writings.com), Book 4, Chapter 34.
[8]Tertullian, *An Answer to the Jews* (www.earlychristianwritings.com), Chapter 3.

children of peace, for the sake of Jesus, who is our leader, instead of those whom our fathers followed, among whom we were "strangers to the covenant.[9]

As we review these many quotations of the early Fathers we see, through their confirmation of the prophecy of Isaiah and Micah, that they believed the world the prophets had envisioned had come true in their midst. Through the practice of Christians following Jesus' message of love of enemy, renouncing the instruments of violence and war, they were seeing a great reduction of violence and hate. Enemies were changing into friends. Persecutors were standing back impressed by the way Christians handled their affairs—especially how they handled violence against them. Tertullian described the magnetic attraction of the Christian way to their fellow citizens: "But our sect will never be destroyed. You know that it builds up the more it seems defeated. Indeed everyone, seeing such endurance, is drawn as if by a magnet to look into what it is all about. And when he knows the truth, he too follows it."[10]

The Early Fathers' Abhorrence of War

The flip side of the early Fathers' vision of peace was their abhorrence for war. Living in the Roman Empire, they were embedded in a culture of conquest and war, a culture that rewarded success in battle above everything else, a culture that raised successful generals to the emperor's throne, a culture that, if armies were especially effective in slaughter and conquest, their leader could be not only made emperor but declared a god. In contrast, as the early Fathers read the gospels, they understood that Jesus had offered an alternative way of dealing with violence and injustice—the way of assertive, loving, nonviolent resistance—returning good for evil. They also could read what pain it gave Jesus to think that his people would launch a bloody revolution against the Roman occupiers, a campaign that Jesus could see would lead to their destruction, as indeed it did in the year 70 CE.

---

[9]Origen, *Contra Celsum* (www.earlychristianwritings.com), Book 5, Chapter 33.
[10]Tertullian, *Ad Scapulam* (www.earlychristianwritings.com, translation by Rev. S. Thelwall), Chapter 5.

The early Fathers were not caught up in the culture of death that reigned in their time. By studying war, they could see it for what it was, and they mocked and reviled it.

Again, it is striking how strong were their statements against war and how many of them spoke out in condemnation.

Athenagoras listed some of the horrors of wars: "the tyrant who has unjustly put to death myriads on myriads, could not by one death make restitution for these deeds; and the man who holds no true opinion concerning God, but lives in all outrage and blasphemy, despises divine things, breaks the laws, commits outrage against boys and women alike, razes cities unjustly, burns houses with their inhabitants, and devastates a country, and at the same time destroys inhabitants of cities and peoples and even an entire nation."[11]

Tertullian: When Peter cut off Malchus's ear, Jesus "cursed the works of the sword for ever after."[12] Speaking about the crown of laurel that was placed on the head of a soldier after a successful battle, he wrote: "Is the laurel of triumph crown made of leaves or corpses? Is it adorned with ribbons or tombs? Is it besmeared with ointments or with the tears of wives and mothers?"[13]

Cyprian noted with great irony that killing an individual is called murder, but mass murder in war is lauded: "The whole world is wet with mutual blood: and murder, which in the case of an individual is admitted to be a crime, is called a virtue when it is committed wholesale. Impunity is claimed for the wicked deeds, not on the plea that they are guiltless, but because the cruelty is perpetrated on a grand scale."[14]

Arnobius: Contrasting Christ with the rulers of the Roman Empire, he asks: "Did he, claiming royal power for himself, occupy the whole world with fierce legions, and of nations at peace from the beginning, destroy and remove some, and compel others to put their necks beneath his yoke and obey him? What use is it to the world that there should be . . . generals of the greatest experience in warfare, skilled in the capture of cities, and soldiers immovable and invincible in cavalry battles or in a fight on foot?"[15]

---

[11]Athenagoras, *On the Resurrection of the Dead* (www.earlychristianwritings.com, Roberts-Donalson English translation), Chapter 19.

[12]Tertullian, *On Idolatry* (www.earlychristianwritings.com, Thelwall translation), 19.

[13]Tertullian, *De Corona* (newadvent.org) Chapter 12.

[14]Cyprian, *Ad Donatum* (Christian Classics Ethereal Library, www.ccel.org.) 6.

[15]Arnobius, *Adversus Nationes* ii. 2.

He sees the contradiction of war—that even though all men are really from the same source, they nonetheless slay one another:

Forgetting that they are from one source, one parent and head, they tear up and break down the rights of kinship, overturn their cities, devastate land in enmity, make slaves of freemen, violate maidens and other men's wives, hate one another, envy the joys and good fortune of others, in a word all curse, carp at, and rend one another with the biting of savage teeth.[16]

He fervently rejects the pagan notion that divine beings could patronize, or take pleasure in human wars. Referring to Mars, for example, he says:

If he is one who allays the madness of wars, why do wars never cease for a day? But if he is the author of them, we shall say that a god, for the indulgence of his own pleasure, brings the whole world into collision, sows causes of dissension and strife among nations separated by distance of lands and brings together from different quarters so many thousands of mortals and speedily heaps the fields with corpses, makes blood flow in torrents, destroys the stablest empires, levels cities with the ground, takes away liberty from the freeborn and imposes on them the state of slavery, rejoices in civil broils, in the fratricidal death of brothers who die together and in the patricidal horror of mortal conflict between sons and fathers.[17]

Referring to the Romans, Lactantius says:

They despise indeed the excellence of the athlete, because there is no harm in it; but royal excellence, because it is wont to do harm extensively, they so admire that they think that brave war-like generals are placed in the assembly of the gods, and that there is no other way to immortality than by leading armies, devastating foreign countries, destroying cities, overthrowing towns, and either slaughtering or enslaving free people. Truly

---

[16]Ibid., Book 2.45.
[17]Ibid.

the more men they have afflicted, despoiled and slain, the more noble and renowned do they think themselves.[18]

These passages indicate just how strongly the early Christian fathers rejected war—because it fractured human relationships, led to a continuing spiral of violence, and caused such senseless destruction and death. They could see, through Jesus' teaching and practice and the witness of their fellow Christians, that war, which their culture assumed was the way the world ran, could be rejected at its root through love of enemy. To that understanding we now turn.

The Early Fathers on the Christian Response to Violence and Enemies

The early Fathers wholeheartedly embraced the teaching of Jesus on how to respond to violence and evil. They continually referred to the Sermon on the Mount and especially Jesus' teachings on how to respond to oppressive violence and enemy antipathy. They not only quoted the words; they also, as we shall see, walked the words.

It is important to review their testimony concerning the practicality and effectiveness of Jesus' way of responding with nonviolence to hate and violence because many will say dismissively that the message is a noble one but, as G. K. Chesterton writes, "too bad it has never been tried." In reviewing this written record it will be obvious to the reader that in the early church it *was* tried, and it "worked." Many pagans came to believe because of the witness of these courageous Christians. In fact, by early in the fourth century, the time of Constantine, Christians had become so numerous that Constantine saw fit to legitimate the Christian religion for the Roman Empire, thereby gaining the political support of a large, and increasingly important constituency, Christians, against his adversaries. In fact, the final war between Constantine and his rival Licinius was perceived as a war between paganism and Christianity and ended in a decisive triumph for Constantine.

The early church did not embrace a new legalism; they attempted to live out what they understood to be the mind of Christ. As Bainton puts it, "Christianity brought to social problems, not a detailed code of ethics or a new political theory, but a new scale of values. . . . He

---

[18]Lactantius, *The Divine Institutes* (newadvent.org/fathers/0701.htm), Chapter 18.

who was at peace was able to bestow peace. The Christian peace was creative and dynamic."[19]

The earliest written Christian document that we possess, after the writings of the New Testament, the Didache, lays out the "hard sayings" of Jesus as central to the life of a Christian:

> The teaching of these words is this: Bless those who curse you, and pray for your enemies, and fast on behalf of those who persecute you: for what thanks will be due to you, if you love only those who love you? Do not the gentiles also do the same? But love you those who hate you, and you will not have an enemy. . . . If anyone give you a blow upon the right cheek, turn the other also to him, and you will be perfect; if anyone impresses you to go one mile, go two with him; if anyone take away your cloak, give him your coat also; if anyone take from you what is yours, do not demand it back nor try to use force.

> You shall not be greedy or rapacious or hypocritical or malicious or arrogant. . . . Do not be wrathful, for wrath leads to murder, nor jealous nor contentious nor quarrelsome, for from all these murder ensues.[20]

Ignatius, the bishop of Antioch, at that time the third largest city in the ancient world, was arrested and led to Rome for his eventual martyrdom c. 110 CE. On the way he was led by ten Roman soldiers. He wrote six letters; one of them was to the community of the Ephesians:

> And on behalf of the rest of men, pray unceasingly. For there is in them a hope of repentance, that they may attain to God. See then, that they be instructed by your works, if in no other way. Be meek in response to their wrath, humble in opposition to their boasting: to their blasphemies return your prayers; in contrast to their error, be steadfast in the faith; and for their cruelty, manifest your gentleness. While we take care not to imitate their conduct, let us be found their brethren in all true

[19]Bainton, *Christian Attitudes toward War and Peace*, 54–55.
[20]*Didache* (www.earlychristianwritings.com, translation by Ben H. Swett, 1998), Chapter 1, 3-4; Chapter 2, 4; Chapter 3, 2.

kindness; and let us seek to be followers of the Lord (who ever
more unjustly treated, more destitute, more condemned?), that
so no plant of the devil be found in you, but you may remain
in all holiness and sobriety in Jesus Christ, both respect to the
flesh and the spirit.[21]

He wrote these words as he was being marched to Rome where he
would be thrown to wild beasts. He wrote another letter to the faithful
in Rome asking them not to try to interfere in the proceedings against
him. "I am the wheat of God, and let me be ground by the teeth of the
wild beasts, that I may be found the pure bread of Christ."[22]

One of the other letters he wrote was to Polycarp, the young bishop
of Smyrna, who would fifty years later also be martyred, burned at
the stake for his faith. To Polycarp, Ignatius wrote: "Suffer all men in
love, as indeed you do."[23]

Polycarp in turn tells the Philippians that "God will raise us from
the dead if we do His will and walk in His commandments and love
what He loved, . . . not rendering evil in return for evil, or railing for
railing, or blow for blow, or cursing for cursing."[24] "Pray also for kings
and potentates and princes, and for those who persecute you and hate
you, and for enemies of the cross, that your fruit may be manifest to
all, and that you may be perfect in Him."[25]

The author of the second Epistle of Clement (c. 150) bemoaned the
fact that some of his readers were not living out the nobility of the
words of Jesus. He recognized that when the gentiles heard the message
concerning loving one's enemies, "they are impressed by the overplus
[*perisson*] of goodness,"[26] but when they don't see the message lived
out, the Name of Jesus is blasphemed.

Justin, an early Christian apologist for the faith, was well trained
in Greek philosophy and wrote his *Apology* (c. 153 CE) as an attempt

---

[21]Ignatius, *Epistle to the Ephesians* (www.earlychristianwritings.com, Roberts-Donaldson
English translation) Chapter 10.

[22]Ignatius, *Epistle to the Romans* (www.earlychristianwritings.com, Roberts-Donaldson
translation) Chapter 4.

[23]Ignatius, *Epistle to Polycarp* (www.earlychristianwritings.com; Lightfoot translation,
1891), Chapter 1, verse 2.

[24]Polycarp, *The Epistle to the Philippians* (www.earlychristianwritings.com; Lightfoot
translation), Chapter 2, verse 2.

[25]Ibid., Chapter 12, verse 3.

[26]*2 Clement* (www.earlychristianwritings.com; Hoole translation, 1885), Chapter 13,
verse 4.

to engage the minds of the Romans, to help them appreciate on an intellectual level how appealing was the message of Christianity. He started a school in Rome to train others in this scheme of thought. He and a number of his students, including some young women, were eventually martyred for the faith (c. 153–57 CE). Justin wrote:

> We who hated and destroyed one another, and on account of their different manners would not live with men of a different tribe, now, since the coming of Christ, live familiarly with them, and pray for our enemies, and endeavor to persuade those who hate us unjustly to live comformably to the good precepts of Christ, to the end that they may become partakers with us of the same joyful hope of a reward from God the ruler of all.[27]

Justin recognized that this kind of behavior had a powerful effect on others in their society, and that was key in changing people from adversaries to sympathizers and then to converts to Christianity. In the *Apology* he comments:

> And concerning our being patient of injuries, and ready to serve all, and free from anger, this is what he says: "To him that smites your cheek, offer the other as well, and him who takes away your cloak or coat, forbid not. And whosoever shall be angry is in danger of fire. And everyone that compels you to go with him a mile, follow him two. And let your good works shine before men, that they, seeing them, may glorify your Father which is in heaven." For we ought not to strive; neither has he desired us to be imitators of wicked men, but He has exhorted us to lead all men, by patience and gentleness, from shame and the love of evil. And this indeed is proved in the case of many who one were of your way of thinking, but have changed their violent and tyrannical disposition, being overcome either by the constancy which they have witnessed in their neighbors' lives, or by the extraordinary (perisson) forbearance they have observed in their fellow-travellers when defrauded, or by the honesty of those with whom they have transacted business.

---

[27]Justin, *Apology*, xiv.14.

The objection that will be made in later centuries that Jesus' message of nonviolent resistance and love of enemy is noble but that it is meant as advice only for interpersonal relationships, relationships between individuals, not political relationships, is clearly answered in some of these early examples of witness for the faith. The message is being witnessed as central to the faith in the most public and political way—as these early fathers are put through the public spectacle of Roman law courts and are condemned to a public spectacle of martyrdom. Ignatius and Polycarp and Justin Martyr recognized that Jesus' hard sayings had everything to do with living the faith in public, in this world. They did not wait for the "perfect society" to arrive. They were not playacting. They were being faithful to their Master, enduring excruciating suffering, continuing to show bravery, staying within the zone of grace they had been given. Moreover, they not only did not turn on their persecutors; they also continued to try to reach them, change them, bring them into the faith, and influence their society to diminish its commitment to violence. They were trying to create a more perfect society.

Irenaeus (c. 190 CE) had a good sense of how the actions recommended by Jesus actually worked, the inner dynamics that gave them their power. He appreciated that by acting in a way that the oppressor does not expect, one is a free person, taking an unexpected initiative. His exegesis of the passage is similar to the contemporary exegesis presented in chapter 2 above. For example, Irenaeus wrote:

> The Lord bade us, he says later, "love not neighbors only, but even enemies, and be not only liberal givers and bestowers, but even that we should present a gratuitous gift to those who take away our goods." For "to him that takes away thy coat," He says, "give to him thy cloak also; and from him who takes away thy goods, ask them not again; and as you would that men should do unto you, do unto them:" so that we may not grieve as those who are unwilling to be defrauded, but may rejoice as those who have given willingly, and as rather conferring a favor upon our neighbors than yielding to necessity. "And if any one,'" He says, "shall compel you to go a mile, go with him two;" so that you may not follow him as a slave, but may as a free man go before him, showing thyself in all things kindly disposed and useful to your neighbor, not regarding their evil intentions, but perform-

ing your kind offices, assimilating yourself to the Father, "who makes His sun to rise upon the evil and the good, and sends the rain on the just and unjust."[28]

Clement of Alexandria enunciated an important principle concerning what violence can and cannot do. Violence can change someone's behavior for a time, but violent compulsion does not work half as well as nonviolent persuasion—which leads people to change their behavior by choice and for good. That truth will be forgotten later in the history of Christianity when the church turned to the state to use the power of the sword against heretics. Clement wrote:

> Above all, Christians are not allowed to correct with violence the delinquencies of sins. For it is not those who abstain from wickedness by compulsion, but those who abstain by choice, that God crowns. For it is not possible for a man to be good steadily except by his own choice.[29]

Tertullian (c. 197 CE) was himself converted to Christianity through witnessing the incredible courage and forbearance of Christians who were persecuted, who endured death in horrible ways but still managed to treat their persecutors with love and respect. "He was a Berber African converted by watching Christian slaves courageously facing death in the amphitheater, who has been called the father of Latin Christianity."[30] He challenged his readers to reflect on the way Christians responded to the violence inflicted upon them not only by the judges of the empire but by the mobs unrestrained by the authorities? Christians continued to follow the teachings of the Master even in the midst of horrendous violence against them.

> We Christians are expressly commanded by our Master to love our enemies. . . . How well we practice this command of our Master, you yourselves can tell with a witness; for how many times . . . have you judges shown a most savage cruelty to Christians! How often without your authority has the hostile mob

---

[28]Irenaeus, *Adversus Haereses* (www.earlychristianwritings.com), Chapter 4, verse 3.
[29]Clement of Alexandria, *Fragment in Maximus Confessor, Sermon 55* (www.newadvent.org), 661.
[30]John Gittings, *The Glorious Art of Peace* (New York: Oxford University Press, 2012) 76.

... invaded us with showers of stones and fire? The mob with the furies of a Bacchanal spare not even a dead Christian, but tear him from the quiet of a tomb . . . and mangle the body . . . and in this rueful condition drag it about the streets. But now in all this conspiracy of evils against us . . . what one evil have you observed to have been returned by Christians?[31]

Not only did the early Fathers consistently quote the Sermon on the Mount—the fifth chapter of Matthew, which includes "turning the other cheek," was their most frequently quoted passage of Sacred Scripture—and apply it to their lives and the lives of their readers, some of them developed additional theological reflections on the sayings. A number of them wrote treatises on the virtue of what they called "patience," deriving from the Latin verb, patior, meaning, "I suffer." The meaning of the term, patience, as they use it is very close to the term "nonviolent action" that we would use in our time.

Tertullian wrote a treatise on patience (c. 198-203 CE) that describes what happens when someone injures a Christian who exercises the virtue of patience.

We shall speak now of the joy which comes from patience. For every injury, whether occasioned by the tongue or hand, coming in contact with patience, will meet the same end as a weapon which is flung and dashed upon a hard and unyielding rock. An ineffectual and fruitless action will lose its force and will sometimes vent its passion and strike with the force of a boomerang upon him who sent it forth.[32]

It is clear from the passages quoted that the early Fathers did not think Jesus' teachings on love of enemy and nonviolent resistance were dreamy idealism or impractical advice in a world that was steaming with sin and violence. Rather they thought the teachings were eminently practical and when practiced produced amazing results. They practiced the teaching themselves—even, some of them, to the point of martyrdom. Note, however, that they expected love of enemy to

---

[31] Tertullian, *The Apology* (Tertullian.org/articles/reeve_apology.htm, translation by William Reeve, 1709), Chapter 37.
[32] Tertullian, *De Patientia* (pseudepigrapha.com), Chapter 8.

be practiced by *Christians,* those who believed in Jesus and who were filled with the Holy Spirit. They did not expect the pagan society as a whole to act in this way—until and unless pagan society as a whole had embraced the faith. Such a pattern of life was behavior that all believing Christians, caught up in the love and witness of the Christian community, could and should practice. It is not for an elite cadre of Christians. It is for all. It is not a law. It is a call.

C. John Cadoux, in his book *The Early Christian Attitude to War,* after reviewing this remarkable set of writings from the early Fathers points out that nowhere in these writings is there any treatment of the question of *defense of others.* In fact, as Cadoux points out: "Tertullianus even takes it for granted that, if a man will not avenge his own wrongs, a fortiori he will not avenge those of others."[33]

Ambrose, as we will see, is the one who turns the teaching around and makes defense of others, especially those weaker than ourselves, an obligation for a Christian. Augustine will underline that, and right up to recent times, the popes and the councils will be making defense of others an obligation. It is on that turning that the whole defense of Christian involvement in war will hinge.

Cadoux answers that the whole life of a Christian is a check on sin and consequently a defense of others. He gets right to the heart of the matter however, when he says: "The question is, Which is the right method for a Christian to use—the gentle moral appeal or violent physical coercion?" Notice too, that Ambrose, Augustine and typically the popes and the councils mean *violent* defense—assuming that there is no other kind. Not until the twentieth century will humankind witness once again the strength and power of another kind of defense, nonviolent action, played out on a large political stage—over and over again. We will return to the issue of "defense of others" in the final chapter.

In summary, the early Christian fathers taught faithfulness to the teachings of Jesus concerning love of enemy and nonviolent action. Toward the end of the period marked by the early Fathers, approaching the time of Constantine (c. 313 CE), drastic changes in the relations between the church and the state will begin to develop. The change resulting in the positive attitude of the state toward the church can be

---

[33]C. John Cadoux, *The Early Christian Attitude to War* (London: Headley Bros., 1919), 51.

seen as a victory over the persecutors. That victory "was in no small measure due to the power of the Christian spirit operating against tremendous odds without the use of any sort of violent resistance . . . a strenuous adherence to the Master's teaching—an adherence based on a simple sense of obedience to him, but issuing, as posterity can see, in the exertion of immense moral power," as Cadoux phrases it.[34]

The practice of Christians in the early centuries shows that the church can put Jesus' teaching on nonviolence into practice pervasively and persuasively. Thomas Merton put it simply: "Christianity overcame pagan Rome by nonviolence."[35]

Those who want to cling to the tradition that allows Christian participation in war for a just cause dismiss the practice of the early church in another way. They say that the early Christians did not bear any responsibility for the political affairs of the empire. Once they had such responsibility they realized they had to use the sword to keep order and to protect the empire. They then dropped their scruples and began to compromise their principles, accepting that with statecraft inevitably came the use of the power of the sword. That claim is a very old one. A similar accusation was leveled against Christianity toward the end of the second century by the pagan writer Celsus in the *True Discourse* (c. 178 CE). His original treatise has not survived, but much of what he wrote was repeated in Origen's work *Against Celsus* (c. 248 CE) written some seventy years after Celsus wrote. Celsus criticized Christianity for not taking political responsibility for the defense of the Roman Empire. Christians would not join the army and would not fight to defend the empire. Celsus asked, "What if everyone took that stance?—the Emperor would be left alone and the Empire overrun by the barbarians." Origen did not deny Celsus's accusation that Christians refused to join the army and fight to defend the empire. He did, however, deny that Christians refused to take political responsibility for the well-being and defense of the empire. He answered:

> To this our answer is that we do, when occasion requires, give help to kings, and that, so to say, a divine help, "putting on

---

[34]Ibid., 54.

[35]Thomas Merton, *The Conjectures of a Guilty Bystander* (Garden City, NY: Image Books, Doubleday, 1966), 101.

the whole armor of God." And this we do in obedience to the injunction of the apostle, "I exhort, therefore, that first of all, supplications, prayers and intercession, and giving of thanks, be made for all men; for kings and for all that are in authority;" and the more anyone excels in piety, the more effective help does he render to kings, even more than is given by soldiers, who go forth to fight and slay as many of the enemy as they can. . . . And as we by our prayers vanquish all demons who stir up war, and lead to the violation of oaths, and disturb the peace, we in this way are much more helpful to the kings than those who go into the field to fight for them. . . . We do no indeed fight under him, although he require it; but we fight on his behalf, forming a special army—an army of piety—by offering our prayers to God.[36]

Origen goes on to point out that the Roman priests who are guardians of temples are not enlisted in wartime so as to keep their hands undefiled by blood and murder when offering their sacrifices. As Louis Swift commented: "The Christians' battle is against the power of evil both within and outside man that stir up conflicts and prevent a lasting peace. . . . Origen shows that for himself at least Christian pacifism is based not on the issue of idolatry or the moral excesses of military life but quite simply on Christ's prohibition on killing."[37]

Origen also said: "It is clear that barbarians themselves, once converted to God's word, would become most law-abiding and civilized." The Christian's defense of the empire is therefore two-pronged—enlist the invincible power of prayer and, through witnessing to the gospel, work to convert barbarians—to change them from enemies into fellow Christians and loyal members of the empire.

Some contemporary writers find Origen's response to Celsus inadequate, and others find it to be quite persuasive. For example, Robert J. Daly writes, "From the understanding that modern Christians have of human nature, society, and the world, from our experience of the way salvation is worked out in this world, we can only conclude that

---

[36]Origen, *Against Celsus* (www.earlychristianwritings.com, Roberts-Donaldson translation), Book 8, Chapter 73.

[37]Louis Swift, *The Early Fathers on War and Military Service* (Wilmington, DE: Michael Glazier, 1983).

Origen's vision, for all its beauty, was unrealistic. . . . He locates this responsibility [for maintaining order and peace] entirely in the internal and spiritual realm of being."[38]

In contrast, Cadoux finds that Origen, the finest thinker of his era, presents a compelling defense of Christian pacifism. Staying faithful to the gospel teaching and building up the church can have a profound, practical impact on the state. Origen recommends not just prayer. It is not just an internal and spiritual response. Cadoux writes: "[Origen's] program thus consists of two gradual processes going on side by side as the result of the spread of Christianity: firstly, the gradual diminution of crime and the risk of foreign aggression, and secondly, the gradual substitution of spiritual influence for physical coercion—a more effective remedy for crime and aggression."[39]

Daly responded: "[Origen's] theory of an increasing Christianization carrying with it a decreasing need for military force is indeed a beautiful and hopeful conception. But, alas, it did not work out that way. . . . The theory was flawed at the outset."[40] To that Cadoux would say: but it had been working that way in the first centuries. People were being converted and changed as the early Christians practiced nonviolence and love of enemy. Cadoux wrote:

> Some modern writers have pointed to the attacks later made on the Empire by Christianized barbarians as if they proved the shortsightedness of Origen: but they do nothing of the sort, for the Christianity given to these barbarians was not the same article as that for which Origen was bargaining; it was the Christianity of a Church that had made a compact with the powers that be and was accordingly obliged to sanction for its adherents the use of the sword at a ruler's bidding.[41]

In other words if the Christian church had not abandoned the teaching of Jesus in regard to hate and violence, the way that Christians had been following for the first three centuries, barbarians would have continued to be impressed and converted. The empire would not have

---

[38]John Helgeland, Robert J. Daly, and J. Patout Burns, *Christians and the Military: The Early Experience* (Philadelphia: Fortress Press, 1985), 43.

[39]Cadoux, *Early Christian Attitude to War*, 89.

[40]Helgeland, Daly, and Burns, *Christians and the Military*, 42.

[41]Cadoux, *Early Christian Attitude to War*, 90.

been under violent attack. The prophecies of Isaiah and Micah would have continued to be fulfilled.

A final component of the teaching of the early Fathers of the Church concerns whether or not Christians were permitted to serve in the Roman army.

The Early Fathers on Military Service

In the first hundred years of the church's existence there is no indication that Christians served in the military. Rome was able to attract enough recruits to serve in its army without resorting to conscription. As Swift commented: "At least during the first hundred years of Christianity the social status of many believers, as well as the issues of violence and idolatry, would seem to have posed serious barriers to enlistment, and since there was no involuntary conscription during this period, Christians could easily avoid military service if they chose to do so."[42]

By the end of the second century, according to the criticism of Christianity of Celsus (c. 178 CE), which we reviewed earlier, Christians were still rejecting military service on a large scale. About this time, however, there is some indication that Christians were beginning to join the army. Toward the end of the reign of Marcus Aurelius (161–80) there are references to the miracle of the rain that saved a Roman legion (Legio XII Fulminata) from defeat in a battle with the Germans and Sarmatians. Tertullian and, later, Eusebius attributed the miracle to the prayers of Christians in the legion, whereas pagan sources (Dio Cassius 72.14) recount the miracle but do not mention Christians. Whatever the true story, there must have been enough Christians in the legion to warrant acceptance of the Christian version by the community.

It is through the writings of Tertullian that we begin to see traces of Christian involvement in the army. In his *Apology*, which was probably composed at the end of the second century, Tertullian takes pride in the spread of Christianity to all segments of Roman society. He wrote: "We are of yesterday, and yet we have filled all your places, your cities, islands, villages, townships, your very camp, tribes, companies, palace, senate, forum; we leave you only your temples. We can count

---

[42]Louis Swift, "Early Christian Views on Violence, War, and Peace," in *War and Peace in the Ancient World*, ed. Kurt A. Raaflaub (Malden, MA: Blackwell, 2007), 281.

your armies; the Christians of one province are more numerous."[43]

When, however, Tertullian takes on the issue of permissibility of Christians serving in the Roman army directly, he is sternly negative. After dismissing arguments for serving in the military on the basis of scriptural models like Moses, Joshua, and the centurion in the gospels (which some must have been using to justify their service), he argues that "the Lord, in disarming Peter, unbelted every soldier."[44] For those converted while already serving he recommends that they abandon their commitment as many have already done. In his message to those Christians considering entering the service he argues that all military service, involving as it does issues of bloodshed and idolatry, is out of the question.

Origen is no less clear on the issue of Christians serving in the army. The meaning of Christ's words about perishing by the sword is very clear. Origen writes: "We must beware of unsheathing the sword simply because we are in the army or for the sake of avenging private injuries or under any other pretext because Christ's teaching in the Gospels considers all of these uses an abomination."[45]

How one interprets the Old Testament was and remains a very important issue—determining whether or not one will be faithful to the peacemaking message of Jesus or turn to some other ethic as one's stance toward war and violence. For example, the violence depicted in the Old Testament led Marcion and the Manichees to totally reject the Old Testament. Marcion found the gap between Yahweh, a warrior God, and Jesus' description of his loving Father to be so great that Christians should have nothing to do with the Old Testament. Although there was sympathy for Marcion's opinion—the gap is great between the description of Yahweh in the Old Testament and Jesus' description of God as a loving Father. Nonetheless the early church prized its Jewish roots and heritage, recognizing that Jesus came to fulfill, not reject, the religion of his forebears. Marcion was therefore perceived to be outside the circle of true faith.

Tertullian rejected the appeal to the Old Testament that people in his time were using to justify joining the army. Tertullian emphasized the difference between the old covenant and the new but he did not go

---

[43]Tertullian, *Apology* (Oxford: Clarendon Press, translated by T. H. Bindley, 1890), Chapter 37.

[44]Tertullian, *On Idolatry* (newadvent.org.), Chapter 19.

[45]Origen, *Commentaries and Homilies*, 102.

as far as Marcion. He said that what had been permissible under the law was unthinkable in the new era of grace and the Spirit, thereby relegating the old covenant to the past.

Origen also rejected using the figures of the Old Testament as models of behavior to justify joining the army—without thereby rejecting the Old Testament. He interpreted the stories of war and the warriors blessed by God allegorically, meaning they stood for the Christian's interior struggle with the inner demons of domination and violence. Wars of the Old Testament must have a spiritual sense if they are to be incorporated into Christian thought. He wrote, "Unless the carnal wars [i.e., of the Old Testament] were a symbol of spiritual wars, I do not think that the Jewish historical books would ever have been passed down by the Apostles to be read by Christ's followers in their churches."[46]

Origen's hermeneutic is similar to the one Gandhi used to interpret the Bhagavad Gita. The Gita tells the story of a young man commanded by God to enter into battle—even with his own relatives. Gandhi found the Gita to be a constant source of inspiration. He read parts of it every day of his adult life. He interpreted it, however, allegorically—as the story of how a young man struggled with and resisted his inner compulsions, attachments, and instincts for domination.

Another early writer, Adamantius, in *Dialogus de recta in Deum Fide,* read the various sections of the Old Testament and found still another way to preserve the Christian relationship to the Old Covenant while not accepting the war practices of the Old Testament as exemplary for Christians. The hermeneutical key for him was the notion that the Old Testament unfolded in a progressive revelation. The early stories of war and conquest corresponded to the relative immaturity of the Israelite people—stuck at the same stage of development as the peoples that surrounded them. Gradually the Old Testament began to scorn the desire for a king and attributed success in armed struggle to the power of God alone. Still later Isaiah began to celebrate the coming "suffering servant." Adamantius wrote: "Does not a woman, after she has borne a son, first nourish him on milk, and only later, after he has grown up, give him more solid foods? . . . In the same way God has given laws to men according to the stage of their intellectual

---

[46]Origen, *Ephesians* 6.11.

development."[47] So also God's progressive revelation proceeds through the stages of human development. Only when humanity is able to handle the full truth does God reveal his Son, ready to nonviolently fight for and even suffer for humanity. As Jesus read his tradition selectively, choosing the passages in Isaiah and Daniel that could best embody what he had come to know about his role and his Father, so also did the early Church Fathers, as we have seen, read the tradition selectively—especially appreciating and reflecting on the prophecies of Isaiah and Micah.

Scholars underscore the fact that Origen, as well as the other early Church Fathers, consistent with Paul's teachings in Romans 13, showed loyalty and respect to the emperor, paid taxes, and perceived the Pax Romana as a blessing to Christianity, facilitating its spread across the ancient world. They point out that Origen prayed for the success of the Roman armies and even called the wars fought by the Roman armies just. Robert Daly goes so far as to say that Origen, by declaring that some of the wars of Rome are just, is therefore the real source for the "two swords theory,"[48] implying that Origen is trying to have it both ways—calling the wars just while forbidding Christians to participate in them. Daly overlooks the fact that Origen is referring to Christians precisely as believing Christians—as distinct from their role as citizens of a pagan empire. He respects the Roman Empire and understands the purposes of the empire's wars but sees the empire's practices, including its wars, as sub-Christian. For Origen, a Christian, who has learned the ways of Jesus, practices according to a much higher standard.

This again is similar to Gandhi's response when asked if he thought the Second World War was a just war. Gandhi answered that if there ever was a just war, he would have to say that the fight to save the Jews from the Holocaust was just. But he could never fight in a war because he believed that war by its very nature led not to peace but to more war and that there was another even more powerful way of fighting evil without becoming what you were fighting against—nonviolent action, satyagraha.

Despite the clear condemnation of Christians serving in the Ro-

---

[47]Adamantius, *Dialogus de recta in Deum Fide*, I, 9–16, as quoted in John-Michel Hornus, *It Is Not Lawful for Me to Fight* (Eugene, OR: Wipf and Stock, 1980), 53.

[48]Helgeland, Daly, and Burns, *Christians and the Military*, 40.

man army by the early Fathers, evidently Christians were beginning to volunteer to serve in the army. That is clear from the persecution of Christians by Diocletian in 303 CE. He ordered that the Christians serving in the army be the first to be put to death if they refused to sacrifice to the Roman gods.

Scholars give various reasons for this apparent gap between the unanimous teaching of the Fathers against participating in war and this emerging practice. Some explain it by saying that in this period, just before Diocletian, a time of peace in the empire, soldiers could serve without ever having to shed blood. Their roles were those of policemen, whose role was to protect and not to conquer and kill, and if they did not rise too high in the legions, they would not have to sacrifice to the Roman gods. Others point out that some were using the Old Testament and the stories that featured God commanding the Israelites to conquer and kill their enemies as their justification for entering the army—ignoring the teaching of the New Covenant.

James Turner Johnson describes quite clearly the changes that were happening in the Roman Empire all during the third century when there is evidence that Christians are beginning to join the army. He points out that the army and governmental leadership of the empire on all levels came increasingly not to be restricted to those of aristocratic birth but was opened to people with modest backgrounds; the army rewarded merit and achievement as never before. He writes, "Achievement in military service could lead to high civilian status and power. . . . The avenue of social advancement offered by the army represented a kind of vacuum into which Christians were drawn by reason of their social aspiration."[49] For purely human reasons, despite the clear teaching of the Early Fathers, Christians began to be drawn into the army.

To conclude this survey of the Early Fathers' practices and teachings, a number of things stand out:

The early church and the early Church Fathers tried to be faithful disciples of Jesus' teaching on "love your enemies" not just because they rejected violence as a dead end but more positively because they understood that this was the way Jesus behaved. Matthew 5:28–32 was their primary guide. This is the passage that inlcudes the hard sayings about "turning the other cheek and going the second mile."

---

[49] James Turner Johnson, *The Quest for Peace* (Princeton, NJ: Princeton University Press, 1987), 37, 41.

Under persecution, they found plenty of opportunities to practice love for hate.

There is a confidence and even a joy in the way they write about their experiences. In practicing nonviolence, they seem to exult in the power that it gives them. Even while being dragged to Rome by soldiers, Ignatius writes six letters encouraging other Christians to not be afraid—even as he knows that lions await him. Over time, they seem to find power because they see that against all odds, Jesus' way seems to work. Enemies are changed into friends. Pagans come to believe. The church grows. Even a hard-nosed, no-nonsense person like the lawyer Tertullian is so impressed by their way of life that he joins them and is baptized.

Their way of life was clearly not "passive resistance." They were actively nonviolent. They understood Jesus' statement in the Sermon on the Mount asking his disciples: What *more* do you do . . . don't even the pagans love their friends? What is the *perisson* that you do? What is the overplus, the beyond what people might expect that you do? That way of *perisson* also seemed to be quietly effective. As Justin wrote: "And this we are able to show in the case of many who were formerly violent and tyrannical, conquered whether through having followed the constancy of their [Christian] neighbors' lives, or through having noticed the strange patience of their fellow-travelers when they were overreached. " Just through their constancy and through their "strange patience," they realized they were having an impact on those around them. Their gospel-based nonviolence made them reach out to others as when they helped pagans afflicted with the plague after pagan friends had fled the scene, as described by Cyprian in his essay *On Patience*. Gospel-based nonviolence is the reverse of passivity—it demands active outreach.

The early Fathers had a deep distaste for war. Their distaste is not simply because Jesus rejected violence for himself and for his followers. It also seems to result from their own critique of the practices of their culture. To them it was absurd that those who receive the most glory in the Roman culture are those who have slaughtered the greatest numbers in "successful" wars. They are named emperors. They are proclaimed "gods." Tertullian sounds like an Erich Maria Remarque or a Philip Caputo when he writes: "The laurel, is it besmeared with ointments or the tears of wives and mothers?"

This way of life is not adequately described by the word "pacifism."

It was far more than an unwillingness to participate in war. It was *active peacemaking*—on a number of levels.

First, the early Christians faced up to violence. They did not turn away from the real world. They met the pagan world on its terms and worked to convince that world that there was a better way to oppose violence—the way of Jesus.

Second, they worked to build a positive peace, a society where the poor and the outcasts would be welcomed and shown care, where the sick would be nursed back to health. Julian, the nephew of Constantine who became emperor after Constantine's son Constantius II, and known to history as the "Apostate," because he rejected Christianity and tried to reinstate paganism as the official Roman religion, recognized quite clearly how thoroughly the early church had embraced its mission to build a social order of care and justice for the poor. Julian wrote: "It is disgraceful that no Jew ever has to beg and the impious Galileans [his preferred term for Christians] support not only their own poor but ours as well."[50]

Third, they built structures and nurtured practices that would allow the larger society to see an alternative in the concrete. It is hard to understand why some authors, even after reading the writings of the early Fathers, dismiss the early church as a sect, separating itself from the world and taking no responsibility for it. For example, James Turner Johnson, in his book *Quest for Peace,* describes the early church as having "a desire to separate themselves from the world so as to live the morally pure life of the 'new age' that they expected soon to dawn."[51]

On the contrary, the Early Fathers such as Justin and Tertullian, Ignatius and Origen understood their mission to reach out to the world and preach the good news to all people. They were not interested in separating from the world. They were on for changing the world. Justin and Origen established schools dedicated to entering into dialogue with Roman and Greek culture so they could more effectively build common bonds of understanding between paganism and Christianity and develop the rational skills needed to articulate the theology of a world faith. As we have seen, all the early Fathers took pride that the prophecies of Isaiah and Micah were coming true in their midst, in the very world in which they lived. The world was turning to *shalom*

---

[50]Julian, *Ep.* 22, 430D–431A.
[51]Johnson, *Quest for Peace*, 13.

through their efforts. Swords were being beaten into plowshares. The early Christian church did not separate itself from the world—instead it tried to be both a model and a leaven for the world.

As H. A. Drake put it:

> Organizationally, Christianity was a "movement," that is, an organization devoted to effecting change in the public sphere. Because there is something that movements want to change, they are driven by a sense of purpose; they have an agenda. Christianity clearly was a social movement, not a protest movement. . . . Social movements are in it for the long haul. They advance their goals by building their own alternative institutions, coexisting with the current political order rather than seeking to dismantle it.[52]

Given the strong continuity between the teaching and nonviolent practice of Jesus in his lifetime and the teaching and nonviolent practice of the early church for the first three plus centuries, what happened? How did the church go, in a little more than a century (Diocletian to Theodosius) from being a persecuted minority to being the established religion of the empire? How did the church go, in a little more than a century, from being persecuted by the pagan Roman Empire to being the persecutor of pagans using the sword of the Roman Empire? How did the church change, in a little more than a century from a situation in which Christians were forbidden to join the Roman army to a situation in which *only* Christians could belong to the Roman army? How did the church, which steadfastly maintained for the first three plus centuries that faith and belief should not be coerced become the institution that used force and coercion to compel belief from unbelievers? How did the church that prided itself on its commitment to love one's enemy and follow Jesus' way of nonviolent returning love for hate come to justify and participate in all manner of violence, including mass-organized state violence or war? Part of the answer to what happened will be found in the life and practice of the Emperor Constantine.

---

[52]H. A. Drake, *Constantine and the Bishops* (Baltimore: Johns Hopkins University Press, 2000), 76.

4

Constantine

In Constantine's youth, around the year 290, the Emperor Diocletian elevated another general, Maximian, to virtually equal status, assigning him to be Augustus of the western half of the empire while he himself stayed Augustus of the east. In 293, understanding that the empire was vulnerable at its borders, Diocletian ordered additional political reforms. He named junior colleagues for himself and Maximian. Each of the new appointees would have the title caesar and would govern a fourth of the empire. Together they were known as the tetrarchy. This arrangement was designed to strengthen the administration and control of the borders and put decision making closer to the action. Galerius was named caesar of the east under Diocletian and Constantius, Constantine's father, was named caesar of the west under Maximian. This arrangement in Diocletian's thinking also provided a way of peaceful succession, avoiding the method by which Diocletian himself and other recent emperors had come to the throne—through acclamation by the army.

How Constantine Came to Power

In his youth Constantine lived at and served in Diocletian's court in Nicomedia, but when news came that his father, who was fighting the Picts in Britain, was in a precarious position, Constantine rushed to his father's aid. In 305, Constantine was with his father when Diocletian surprised everyone with another innovation—he resigned his position as emperor and insisted that Maximian resign his post as well, with Galerius and Constantius stepping up to the posts of augusti for the east and west, respectively. Diocletian then surprised everyone with his appointments of the two new caesars. Lactantius described the scene:

The gaze of all was upon Constantine, no one had any doubt; the soldiers who were present, the military officers who had been chosen and summoned from the legions, had eyes only for him; they were delighted with him, they wanted him, they were making their prayers for him. . . .Then suddenly Diocletian proclaimed Severus and Maximin Daza as Caesars. Everyone was thunderstruck. Constantine was standing up on the platform, and people hesitated, wondering whether his name had been changed. But then in view of everybody Maximian stretched his hand back and drew Daza out from behind him, pushing Constantine away.[1]

Both Constantius and Maximian had capable sons in the prime of life, Constantine and Maxentius. Both had been passed over. Both decided to bide their time and find another way to power. In 306 Constantius died, and his army acclaimed Constantine as the successor to the purple and Galerius, the remaining augustus, agreed that Constantine was officially a caesar. He ruled from a palace in Trier, Germany. In 307 Constantine married Maximian's daughter to tighten his links with the recognized powers. In the meantime Maxentius, now his brother-in-law, had won the support of the people of Rome and the praetorian guard in Rome and took up residence there, taking full advantage of the symbolic importance of Rome as the capital of the empire and engaging in large public works—acting as if he was the new augustus of the west. Constantine was tied down in campaigns against the barbarians on his northern frontier. It was only in 312 that Constantine was able to invade Italy, take on Maxentius, and secure his position as the augustus of the west.

As he approached Rome, according to the story that he told Eusebius, the bishop of Caesarea, many years later, he saw a sign in the heavens in the shape of the cross and heard the words "*In hoc signo, vinces*," translated as "In this sign you will conquer." He was puzzled. Eusebius wrote:

And while he continued to ponder and reason on its meaning, night suddenly came on; then in his sleep the Christ of God

---

[1]Lactantius, *De Mortibus Persecutorum* (Oxford: Oxford Early Christian Texts, 1984), 19.1–5.

appeared to him with the same sign which he had seen in the heavens, and commanded him to make a likeness of that sign which he had seen in the heavens, and to use it as a safeguard in all his engagements with the enemy . . . sending for those who were acquainted with the mysteries of His doctrines.[2]

He learned of the significance of the cross and began a course of religious instruction.

Constantine did as he was told in the dream, approached the Milvian Bridge over the Tiber, encountered Maxentius, and threw him off the bridge. His army conquered. As Jacob Burckhardt writes, "With this battle the entire west found its master; Africa and the islands fell to the conqueror. . . . Now the problem was to base his power, wherever possible on foundations other than mere strength."[3]

In that very year, 312, Constantine and Licinius, who had come to power after Galerius, as the augustus of the east, jointly issued the Edict of Milan. The edict was in effect an admission that an entirely different response to Christianity was required from the one that Diocletian had taken just a decade earlier in 303—the first empire-wide persecution of Christians. That persecution had failed. Many in the empire who were not Christians found the actions against Christians to be unjust, and many refused to actively support the persecution. Constantine and Licinius came up with an entirely different approach. They defined state security in terms of a general monotheism. The edict made legitimate any form of worship and granted freedom of belief to all citizens. The edict did indeed give legal standing to Christianity—because it was Christianity that had been persecuted—but it did more. It gave, in the words of the edict—"all men freedom to follow whatever religion each one wished, in order that whatever divinity there is in the seat of heaven may be appeased and made propitious."

On the one hand, the edict was quite traditional. It recognized the tradition that reverence for the divinity was important for the survival and success of the empire. People believed that the gods or god could and did intervene in the affairs of history, and it made sense to stay

[2]Eusebius, *The Life of Constantine*, trans. E. C. Richardson, in *A Select Library of Nicene and post-Nicene Fathers of the Christian Church*, ed. P. Schaff and H. Wace (New York, 1890), 1:29–30.

[3]Jacob Burckhardt, *The Age of Constantine the Great* (Berkeley: University of California Press, 1949), 271–72.

on their good side. Moreover, the edict followed the ancient Roman tradition that the emperor needed to be a faithful servant of god. Divine approval served as the foundation for the legitimacy and the success of an emperor's reign. That is why through the years the emperor had become increasingly remote and above the rest of his subjects, inspiring awe and virtual worship himself. The emperor needed to be perceived by the people as a *"comes"* or a friend of god for legitimacy's sake. On the other hand, the edict did not specify that "god" was the traditional pantheon of the Roman gods. Increasingly, paganism had been moving from polytheism to a general monotheism. Increasingly, there was a desire for a personal relationship with the divinity, and concerns about salvation had become more important. Pagan scholars and Christian apologists in this era were in continuing dialogue.

This was a policy that meant a win for all the parties involved. Its effect was to add the Christian God to the pantheon that had traditionally been considered responsible for the success of the Roman Empire. It not only proclaimed that all had the freedom to follow the religion of their choice, it implied that there is more than one path to supreme truth. The god invoked as the protector of Rome's well-being was vaguely described as "the supreme divinity," an umbrella designation all could accept. The edict was designed to produce peaceful relations within the empire.

Perhaps what was even more important was that the edict gave official recognition to the principle that religion cannot be coerced. As H. A. Drake comments: "The edict constitutes a landmark in the evolution of Western thought—not because it gives legal standing to Christianity, which it does, but because it is the first official government document in the Western world to recognize the principle of freedom of belief."[4] As we will see, Constantine throughout his reign was tempted to depart from this principle—that belief cannot be coerced through the sword—but consistently acted instead in a manner that reflected the Christian belief in returning mildness for hate. Instead of violence, he used "soft" power to mediate and resolve conflicts within and between religious faiths.

In the year 324, after years of struggles with Licinius, Constantine

---

[4]H. A. Drake, *Constantine and the Bishops* (Baltimore: Johns Hopkins University Press, 2000), 194.

invaded the territories of his former ally and defeated him on land. Constantine's son Crispus defeated Licinius in a naval battle, and Licinius was sent into exile and then put to death on the grounds that he was attempting a coup and was planning a persecution of Christians in the east. At long last Constantine was the undisputed sole emperor of the Roman Empire. His reign lasted from 306 to 337.

What Constantine Did for the Church

Not only did the Edict of Milan acknowledge Christianity as an acceptable religion in the empire—which meant an end to fearsome persecutions—the edict also restored seized property and provided for the recall of exiles. Before Constantine, in order to serve in an official capacity in the empire—magistrate, legate or consul, etc.—one had to offer sacrifice to the Roman pantheon. Constantine eliminated that requirement, thereby opening up the field to Christians for advancement to positions of power and influence within the empire.

Shortly after his defeat of Licinius and his taking control of the eastern empire, Constantine issued two more edicts to all the provinces of the empire. In the first, known as the Edict of Piety, Constantine spelled out the details of the restitution to be made to Christians, proclaimed that civil law would protect the personal property of Christians and church property, and expressed sorrow for the sufferings that had been inflicted on them by Diocletian's persecutions; he invoked the "Divinity, alone and truly God, possessor of almighty and eternal power" language that expressed his political objective of forging unity across the empire through a monotheistic common denominator. The second edict, the Edict to the Eastern Provincials, underlined the policy of noncoercion of belief. Debate and exhortation will show the way to God; coercion will not.

Constantine recognized the political importance of the Christian community in the empire—estimated at this time to be 10 percent of the 60 million total population, or 6 million people—because of their dedication, strong community ties, and their coherent agenda. They had shown the ability to endure suffering and privation and through numerous apologists they had reached out across the divides of theory and practice to leading pagan thinkers and philosophers. They had shown a willingness to be "players" in the empire. Moreover, they had strong organizational leadership. Their bishops were respected leaders in diverse communities across the empire. Bishops were chosen for reasons of personal merit, not as the empire's traditional elites were chosen for their ties to powerful families or because they enjoyed extensive networks of patronage. The bishops were revered to the degree that they embodied the teaching and practice of Jesus in their lives. As a result, Constantine manifested great confidence in the bishops. He took major resources from the state and distributed them to the bishops to use for works of charity for the poor and needy in their respective dioceses. That in turn magnified the importance of the local bishops in the eyes of their constituents.

He gave the bishops unusually great legal and juridical privileges. For example, in 316 a law was passed that bishops could sanction the manumission of slaves by their owners even if other witnesses were not present. In 316, a law was passed that allowed a case to be switched from a civil court to a religious court. If the bishop made a ruling, it was not subject to appeal, and judges could accept testimony from a single bishop and not have need for any other witnesses. Constantine had complete trust in the probity and independence of the Christian bishops. H. A. Drake analyzes these cases and their background. Evidently, Constantine was trying to offset the built-in bias in the law courts against the poor. By involving the bishops and giving them such a strong hand he was attempting to redress that bias. Drake writes:

> If Constantine's purpose was to supplant a corrupt bureaucracy, then the bishops were a logical, indeed a brilliant, choice. In number and distribution, there were enough of them in place for the reform to take effect immediately, at virtually no cost to the state. More important, the bishops were far more independent and more likely to identify with the problems of the poor than were secular officials.[5]

Constantine built magnificent churches—including a church of Saint Peter's in Rome, Santa Sophia in Constantinople, and the Church of the Holy Sepulchre in Jerusalem.

Finally, Constantine intervened in and mediated the important,

---

[5]Ibid., 340.

theological/polity disputes that divided the church in his time—the Donatist controversy and the Arian heresy.

The Donatist Dispute

During the persecution of Diocletian in the years 303–5, some bishops handed over to authorities, under threat of torture or death, copies of the Sacred Scriptures and or the sacred vessels of the liturgy. They were the *traditores* (traitors), "the ones who handed over." A large contingent in North Africa, led by the bishop of Carthage, Donatus, believed that the subsequent actions of the tainted clergy were not valid. Tainted bishops had ordained others who in turn had administered sacraments. None of it was valid. Those in that line had to be expelled from the church to keep the church pure. The Donatists appealed to the emperor. Constantine took very seriously his duty to provide justice to his subjects and believed that proper regard for religion was vital to the security of the state, so he agreed to intervene. He appointed a commission headed by the bishop of Rome, Miltiades, and included three bishops Constantine summoned from Gaul. (Gaul, under Constantine's father, Constantius, had not agreed to participate in Diocletian's persecution, so clergy from Gaul were not implicated in the *traditores* accusations.) Miltiades invited, on his own initiative, fifteen additional bishops, all from Italy. When the Donatist delegation arrived and saw that it was to be a full-fledged court case, they left and appealed again to the emperor. Constantine then summoned a new council composed of bishops from all the provinces under his rule to meet in Arles, Gaul. The council confirmed the decision of the Roman commission. The Donatists appealed to Constantine to personally decide the case. He found in the Donatists' opponents' favor. The Donatists refused to accept the decision. After a time, he became very upset with the leadership of the Donatists because they refused to compromise or to abide by the even-handed decisions made by their peers. He unleashed all the tactics of persuasion available to him, short of the death penalty. The Donatists still refused to yield. After several years, he wrote to the Catholic bishops of North Africa that the only thing left to do was to cultivate patience and let the judgment of God take care of vengeance. While promising to build a new basilica in place of one that had been seized by the Donatists, he repeated that "God indeed promises to be avenger of all and thus when vengeance is left to God a harsher penalty is exacted from one's enemies."[6]

The Donatist controversy would continue to roil the church for another century—to be addressed by another emperor, and this time with violence, the sword. Constantine did not choose that method. As Drake wrote, "It remains significant that the face he chose was that of Christian love and endurance, that the principle he chose was one compatible with the Edict of Milan."[7]

The Arian Controversy

Arius, a priest of Alexandria, began to teach that if, according to the scriptures, the Son in some way came from the Father, the Father therefore must be in some way greater than the Son and there must have been a time when the Son did not exist. The sense of the faithful was that Jesus Christ was fully God and fully man. Arius's teaching was condemned by his bishop Alexander for undermining a central teaching of Christianity. Arius appealed to other bishops. Constantine intervened by writing a letter to both parties, counseling that they come together and settle their differences through dialogue. That did not work, so Constantine, having learned his lesson during the Donatist controversy, convened an ecumenical council of all the bishops of the empire. The council took place at Nicaea. The bishops took their places according to their rank, and a hush came over the assembly as the emperor made his entrance. Eusebius in his *Life of Constantine* described the entrance of the emperor to the council.

> And first of all, three of his immediate family entered in succession, then others also preceded his approach, not of the soldiers and guards who usually accompanied him, but only friends in the faith. And now, all rising at the signal which indicated the emperor's entrance, at last he himself proceeded through the midst of the assembly, like some heavenly messenger of God, clothed in raiment which glittered as it were with rays of light,

---

[6]Constantine Augustus to all the bishops throughout Africa and to the people of the Catholic Church, S. Optati Milevitani, Libri VII. Ed. J.L. Maier, *Le Dossier du Donatisme*, 2 vols. TU 134, 135 Berlin, 1987–89, Appendix 9. As quoted in Drake, *Constantine and the Bishops*, 221.

[7]Drake, *Constantine and the Bishops*, 221.

reflecting the glowing radiance of a purple robe, and adorned with the brilliant splendor of gold and precious stones.[8]

Constantine made sure that a way was found to clarify and settle the dispute once and for all. Out of a long process of theorizing and debate, the Greek term *homoousion,* "of the same substance," was developed to express the Son's relationship with the Father. Arius was able to agree to *homoiousion,* "similar to the Father" and that one letter, *iota,* made all the difference. All but two bishops subscribed to the formula. Arius could not and was banished. Once again, conversation, argumentation, and councils were chosen as the way to resolve conflicts within the church—not violence. Once again, Constantine behaved in a way consistent with the approach of the early Fathers who insisted that belief could not be coerced. Once again he stayed consistent with the Edict of Milan.

Three Widely Divergent Views of Constantine

The first view of Constantine is that of Eusebius, bishop of Caesarea, the first historian of early Christianity and a contemporary of Constantine. In his church history Eusebius chronicled the first three centuries of the church's existence up to and including an account of Diocletian's worldwide persecution up to the year 324 when Constantine defeated Licinius. Eusebius's account of Constantine's life was written from the standpoint of a loyal booster of the church. From Eusebius comes the story of Constantine's vision of the cross in the sky before the Battle of Milvian Bridge. He portrays Constantine as a deeply committed Christian from that moment on, one who did all he could to further the church's interests. Eusebius saw Constantine as a man sent by God to help fulfill God's plan, a plan that had a dual mission for Rome and Christianity—Rome was to subdue the multiple governments and bring them into one empire, and the church was to destroy polytheism and bring all into the one kingdom of God. Constantine for Eusebius was the "bishop of the outside," taking care of all the things outside the church that made difficult the life of the church.

The second view is that of the famous historian Jacob Burckhardt, who dismisses Eusebius's account of Constantine as a pack of lies.

---

[8]Eusebius, *Life of Constantine,* 3.6.

Burckhardt says that Constantine was not the perfect Christian. Constantine was not baptized until on his deathbed. His only interest, according to Burckhardt, was power, how to gain it and how to keep it. He murdered his son Crispus and his wife, Fausta, because he saw threats to his power. He used the church. He never gave up his position as head of the pagan church and kept his title "pontifex maximus," the title of the leader of the pagan church. He produced coins showing himself as the "*comes,*" "friend" of the sun God and a kinsman of Apollo.

Historians of the early Church Fathers with a particularly "pacifist" bent underline Burckhardt's findings—not wanting Christians to be too sanguine about the relationship the church began to forge with the empire under Constantine. For example, Jean-Michel Hornus writes: "After his conversion, Constantine—at the same time he was extending benevolence to Christianity—continued to protect and patronize pagan cults. . . . On his deathbed his last wishes to his surviving sons were that they kill all of his brothers to simplify questions of succession."[9]

The third perspective is that of H. A. Drake, who proposes that Eusebius wrote more of a classic panegyric rather than a historical account as we have come to understand history. Drake recognizes that Eusebius brought his strong commitment to the church to his writing and interpreted Constantine in the most favorable light for the church's well-being. Drake's account, in his very fine book, *Constantine and the Bishops*, portrays Constantine as a master political operative who at one and the same time brought peace between paganism and Christianity for the sake of his own successful reign and made sure he enjoyed immense *auctoritas*, legitimacy, for his reign—not just *potestas*, armed might. He accomplished that by portraying himself to the people as not only a protector of Christianity but also of the traditional pagan pantheon, He had the bona fides of one who was approved by a group with unquestioned integrity—the Christian bishops—as the senate used to provide legitimacy to emperors in the early days of the empire. Drake also makes clear how sparingly Constantine used his *potestas*, armed might—*auctoritas* was usually enough to settle matters—and how in one internal religious conflict after another, he refrained from using the sword to coerce belief.

---

[9]Jean-Michel Hornus, *It Is Not Lawful for Me to Fight* (Eugene, OR: Wipf and Stock, 2009), 201.

How the Church Responded to Constantine

For four centuries Christians had lived under the constant threat of persecution and death from the Roman Empire. Periodically, individual emperors followed through on the threat—the most recent, Diocletian's in 301–3, occurred only a decade before Constantine began his march to complete power. Roland Bainton writes: "Constantine attained sway over the entire empire only after twenty years of civil war in which Christianity was itself an issue. There were at one time seven contestants for the purple, each with a policy of persecution or toleration. Inevitably the hopes, prayers, and frequently also the arms of Christians gravitated to their champion."[10]

Throughout the third century the makeup of the Roman legions had become less and less Roman, and barbarians of the provinces gradually made up the ranks of the army and eventually the officer corps. James Carroll writes, "The third century was a period of civil war, barbarian invasion and general breakdown throughout the empire. As chaos mounted, so did the power of the military, which successfully asserted authority over the Roman Senate and even over the seat of the emperors."[11] The great persecutors of the third and fourth centuries —Maximus Thrax, Decius, Diocletian, and Galerius—had come from the half-barbarian provinces in the Danube area. If the barbarian emperors had been the persecutors of Christianity and Constantine had befriended Christianity, the connection began to be made that paganism and barbarians go together, whereas Rome and Christianity go together. Constantine was hailed not only as the protector of Christianity but also as the restorer of Rome.

One can only imagine the relief and gratitude Christians felt for the emperor who had declared their religion acceptable to the empire. Christians were not only freed from the threat of persecution, they were also free to choose life paths that meant upward mobility in the empire—because Constantine had removed the obligation of sacrificing to the Roman gods as a prerequisite for serving as an official in the empire. Christians became full members of civil society and could

---

[10]Roland Bainton, *Christian Attitudes toward War and Peace* (Eugene, OR: Wipf and Stock, 1960), 85.

[11]James Carroll, *Constantine's Sword* (New York: Houghton Mifflin, 2001), 165.

practice their religion without fear of reprisals; civil law protected their personal property as well as the property of the church.

Moreover, with the restoration of peace to the empire, the way was open for Christianity to spread even further—using the good Roman roads—without encountering opposition from local rulers. Eusebius's enthusiasm for Constantine jumps off the page of his *History of the Church*:

> Men had now lost all fear of their former oppressors; day after day they kept dazzling festival; light was everywhere, and men who once dared not look up greeted each other with shining faces and smiling eyes. They danced and sang in city and country alike, giving honor first of all to our Sovereign Lord, as they had been instructed, and then to the pious emperor with his sons, so dear to God. Old troubles were forgotten, and all irreligion passed into oblivion: good things present were enjoyed; those yet to come eagerly awaited. In every city the victorious emperor published decrees full of humanity and laws that gave proof of munificence and true piety.[12]

Gradually, Christians could more easily look upon the empire and the church as partners. As Bainton writes, "The religion of the one God and the empire of one ruler were recognized as having been made for each other. Polytheism was a religion appropriate for a congeries of city-states perpetually in strife, but monotheism and universal monarchy were congruous, and to the confession of one faith, one Lord, and one baptism could now be added that of one empire and one emperor."[13]

Mass conversions began to take place. The growing number of Christians in the empire made it very difficult for Christians to leave it up to the pagans by themselves to defend the empire. Christians increasingly felt an obligation to the emperor and to the empire to help defend against the pagans/barbarians pressing on all sides. Christians were conscripted into the army.

Constantine's mother, Helena, had returned from a sojourn in the

---

[12]Eusebius, *The History of the Church from Christ to Constantine,* trans. G. A. Williamson (New York: Dorset Press, 1965), 413–14.

[13]Bainton, *Christian Attitudes toward War and Peace,* 87.

Holy Land where she claimed to have found a relic of the true cross and some of the nails that had been used to crucify Jesus. Constantine fashioned a standard for his army that was kept protected in its own private tent. Eusebius recounts that the standard consisted of a picture of the cross without a body. Carroll writes: "The cross, even apart from its association with the death of Jesus, is the perfect emblem of Constantine's program, with its joining of horizontal and vertical axes and with its evoking of the four directions: north, south, east and west. The cross of the compass unites the globe; a hand-held globe surmounted by a cross would be, with the crown and scepter, a symbol of the Christian king."[14]

Constantine had the nails fashioned into his war helmet and into the bits of his war horse's bridle.

The Church's Response to Constantine: Was It a "Fall"? or Was It a "Development"?

The responses to this question of whether the reign of Constantine was a "fall" or a "development" range all over the map and typically reflect the biases of the authors, depending on where they stand on pacifism or the theory of the just war. A sampling of assessments follows:

Kent Shifferd writes, "Christianity was captured by the state in the fourth century and has, for the most part, remained there ever since. A deal was struck between the Byzantine emperor and the bishops, in which the latter would sanction his wars in return for making Christianity the only legal religion."[15]

Thomas Schubeck writes, "The bad news was that Christians uncritically accepted the emperor and the many changes that his regime brought about, which significantly compromised the church and its mission. The church which had faithfully proclaimed good news to the poor in the first three centuries, came to accommodate the rich and to regard wealth and pomp as signs of God's favor."[16]

John Helgeland, Robert J. Daly, and J. Patout Burns write: "Rather than see this as the church selling its soul, our study shows that it makes far more sense to see it, polemic and apologetic excuses aside,

---

[14]Carroll, *Constantine's Sword*, 193.

[15]Kent Shifferd, *From War to Peace: A Guide for the Next Hundred Years* (Jefferson, NC: McFarland, 2011).

[16]Thomas Schubeck, *Love That Does Justice* (Maryknoll, NY: Orbis Books, 2007), 93.

as a fairly natural and logical development from the kind of experiences Christians were engaging throughout the previous century."[17]

C. John Cadoux writes: "It is generally thought that, with the accession of Constantine to power, the Church as a whole abandoned her anti-militarist leanings, abandoned all her scruples, finally adopted the imperial point of view, and treated the ethical problem as a closed question. Allowing for a little exaggeration, this is broadly speaking true. The sign of the cross was now a military emblem, bringing good fortune and victory. The supposed nails of the cross which the Emperor's mother found and sent to him, were made into bridle bits and a helmet which he used in his military expeditions. . . . The meek and peaceful Jesus became a God of battle."[18]

Louis J. Swift writes: "When the two periods are characterized as pacifist and non-pacifist, each full-blown in its own way, a false dichotomy is established, and the new attitude toward Christian participation in war that grew up in the fourth century appears as a kind of *volte-face*. We are then tempted to see this change as abandonment of principles and the adoption of expediency after the interests of the church and state had become synonymous. That kind of assessment is oversimplified. . . . By the end of the third century a significant number of the faithful were somehow finding it possible to reconcile the two things in their own minds. . . . Military duty was little more than a civic function. . . . The change that occurred represents a major shift rather than a reversal in Christian thinking."[19]

There is no doubt that the church was pulled in opposite directions during Constantine's reign. On the one hand, the church began to see the Roman Empire not as the enemy but as an asset. Rome provided the means for the spread of the gospel through the peace it had achieved throughout the civilized world, through its system of roads and its common language. In addition, by teaming up with the emperor, the church at the Council of Nicaea had been able to develop a formula (*homoousion*) found nowhere in scripture that allowed for a clear demarcation of orthodoxy and gave grounds for resolving the great

---

[17]John Helgeland, Robert J. Daly, and J. Patout Burns, *Christians and the Military* (Philadelphia: Fortress Press, 1985), 88.

[18]C. John Cadoux, *The Early Christian Attitude to War* (London: Headley Bros., 1919), 212.

[19]Louis J. Swift, *The Early Fathers on War and Military Service* (Wilmington, DE: Michael Glazier, 1983).

Arian heresy. Finally, the power of Rome maintained the borders that separated the civilized world from the hordes of "barbarians" and the forces of perceived anarchy. Should not Christians participate in the defense of this now beneficent empire? On the other hand, the church perceived that if it continued to partner with the state, it would be drawn into the violent power that the state wielded. How could the church be faithful to the martyrs of the faith who had been victims of the violent power of the state if the church now embraced and supported that same violent power?

With the acceptance that came to the church from Constantine, the church had to rethink its way of relating to the pagan, previously outside world. Should it embrace, for example, pagan literature and cultivate an interest in philosophy? Should Christians bear arms? Now that they were an integral part of the culture, how much of the culture should they accept? What should they try to influence and control? As the church took over wholesale the world and expanded its influence over more and more areas of its culture, the question arose: In what way was the church still in touch with its past? Robert Markus writes: "The great need felt by Christians of the post-Constantinian age was for restoration of a lost continuity with the age of persecutions. It was met by three developments: a huge extension of the cult of martyrs, a new interest in the Church's past, and especially, the growing appeal of asceticism. These were the principal means which helped the Christian community to convince itself that it was still identical with the Church of the martyrs."[20]

The church struggled to stay faithful to the memory of the martyrs: churches were built in which relics commemorating the martyrs could be housed, and faithful Christians imitated the martyrs by voluntarily enduring suffering in their own bodies through practices of asceticism. Nonetheless, when the church began to encourage its members to participate in the defense of the empire, something very basic was lost, and the fundamental tie back to the early Fathers and martyrs was cut. The early Fathers and martyrs met violence with love, and their suffering was voluntarily endured for the sake of those who were doing the persecuting. They demonstrated and embodied a new approach to wielding power—the Way that Jesus taught and embodied.

---

[20]Robert Markus, *Christianity and the Secular* (Notre Dame, IN: University of Notre Dame Press, 2006), 32.

When the church at the time of Constantine began to partner with the state, church members went right back to the concept of power that had perennially ruled humanity—power as the power of the sword, power as violence. They began to abandon the distinctive way that Jesus wielded power. The distance from the way of life of the early Fathers and martyrs was so great that within a hundred years *only* Christians could belong to the Roman army.

The turn to the power of the sword at the time of Constantine was not, however, complete. Constantine refused to use the power of the sword to compel belief. He maintained his principle that true faith could not be compelled—it had to be freely embraced. Over the course of the following century, that too would change. In 380 CE the Emperor Theodosius declared that Christianity was the official religion of the empire, that paganism was outlawed, and he took steps, using the power of the sword, to destroy pagan temples and punish those who did not comply with his edict. Then came Augustine who provided the theoretical basis for the use of the power of the sword to compel belief within the Christian family and to punish those deemed heretical. Augustine also developed the just war theory, the theory that has prevailed as the central teaching of the Christian churches on the question of war and peace for seventeen centuries. Augustine, not Constantine, is the real pivot point in the history of a gospel-based theology of peace. To Augustine's thought and place in history, therefore, we now turn.

5

Augustine

Augustine is a towering figure in the history of the church. His book *The Confessions of St. Augustine* has been read down through the ages. Augustine's painfully honest internal journey of self-discovery, his portrayal of his struggles against the chains of habit and sexual desire, his feelings of utter powerlessness and his eventual deliverance into the arms of grace and a God whom he recognizes as more intimate to him than he is to himself is told with such clarity and conviction that readers perennially have had light shed on their own struggles and their own intimations of grace and deliverance.

Nonetheless, it is remarkable how different and far from the early Church Fathers is Augustine when it comes to a whole range of important issues: the degree of human depravity—humans' ability to choose good and avoid evil; the meaning of original sin; the place of the state and its power of the sword; the relevance of the wars in the Old Testament for Christians; whether Christians had any hope of bringing about peace in the world; the inevitability of war; and the interpretation of the "hard sayings" of Jesus. This chapter describes those differences, attempts to explain how Augustine came to hold what he held, and tries to explain why the church has been enthralled with Augustine's theory of justifiable war through the centuries even as it has rejected many of his other teachings.

Augustine's Times

It is important to understand the times in which Augustine lived in order to understand his thought. Augustine came to maturity almost a hundred years after Constantine's and Licinius's Edict of Toleration. Christianity had been the preferred religion of the empire for decades. The emperors of Augustine's time, with the exception of Marcus Aurelius, had continued to not only favor the Catholic Church but had gone out of their way to root out vestiges of paganism from the empire, often using the power of the sword to do so. Events on the ground seemed to underline the rightness of the emperor's giving support to Christianity. For example, in 394, when Theodosius, the eastern emperor moved on Eugenius, the western emperor, who enjoyed the support of the pagan party in the senate, Theodosius was at first losing badly. On the second day of the battle, however, a strong wind suddenly came from the mountains in the face of Eugenius's forces. John Helgeland, Robert J. Daly, and J. Patout Burns write: "This gale propelled the arrows and javelins thrown by Theodosius's army and turned back those of his enemy. In addition, Gothic auxiliaries that had been sent to cut off Theodosius's retreat defected and joined battle on his side."[1] Many interpreted it as confirmation of divine favor for Christianity.

The man who welcomed Augustine into the church and who baptized him in 387, Ambrose (340-97 CE), was the bishop of Milan (proclaimed bishop by the people while still a catechumen) and a former governor of northern Italy. A strong personality—he was able to make the Emperor Theodosius kneel in repentance for his massacre of a rebellious community. Ambrose saw the Roman Empire and Christianity as conjoint agencies of salvation. John Mark Mattox writes: "For him the defense of the Empire coincided in his mind with the defense of the faith. . . . Wars fought by Rome champion the cause of Christians, the new chosen people. . . . [They] facilitate the spread of Christianity and serve as retribution against those who war against the Empire, which now appears to have received the divine commission to spread—by war, if necessary, the gospel of peace."[2]

At first, Augustine held a similar view on the conjoint nature of the Roman Empire and the church to that of his mentor, Ambrose. For example, in 404, in his early days as a bishop, Augustine gave a sermon in which he said:

---

[1] John Helgeland, Robert J. Daly, and J. Patout Burns, *Christians and the Military: The Early Experience* (Philadelphia: Fortress Press, 1985), 74.

[2] John Mark Mattox, *Saint Augustine and the Theory of Just War* (New York: Continuum, 2006), 20.

The promises and prophecies of the Scriptures are being fulfilled; it is wonderful; let them sit up and note the marvelous things that are happening before their eyes, the whole human race streaming together to honor the Crucified. Let the few who have so far remained aloof hear the *strepitus mundi*, the world's roar acclaiming the victory of Christianity.[3]

In addition to the fact that Christianity was so much in the ascendancy was the fact that Rome was in decline—not that people recognized it clearly at the time. It was hard to believe that there was much outside Rome—it was all they had ever known—even as it was being pressed on every side by great migrations of peoples from northern Europe and central Asia. Augustine lived at the time of the fall of Rome to Alaric and through the sacking of North Africa by the Vandals from Spain—including the wanton destruction of churches.

The instinct was strong, therefore, to defend the empire and for Christians to join in the fight. To defend the empire was to defend the faith. To defend the empire was to protect the known world from chaos. Ambrose did not believe in self-defense. He believed that if he was attacked personally he could not respond with violence—that would not be consistent with following Jesus' way. However, he thought that "he who does not keep harm off a friend, if he can, is as much in fault as he who causes it."[4] With that simple comment, Ambrose opened the door to all kinds of subsequent violence and justifications of the violence. Augustine later took up this idea.

Just war theory began to be articulated by Ambrose and then was elaborated by Augustine and developed in a number of varied writings. The origin of the thinking goes much deeper, however, than the spontaneous instinct to come to the aid and protection of their beloved Roman Empire. It is rooted, for Augustine, in his anthropology—what he thought was the nature and fate of humankind—a much different view of human nature than that of the early Church Fathers.

As we have seen, those in the early church relished practicing what

---

[3]Francois Dolbeau, ed., *Augustin d'Hippone: Vingt-six sermons au people d'Afrique,* Collection ds Etudes Augustiniennes, Serie Antiquite 146 Paris, 1996 as quoted in Robert Markus, *Christianity and the Secular* (Notre Dame, IN.: University of Notre Dame Press, 2006), 31.

[4]Ambrose, *Duties of the Clergy*, I.36, 179.

Jesus preached. They faced violence and persecution with patient endurance and loving outreach. They felt powerful in their united resistance and endurance. They saw the results of Jesus' approach with their own eyes as the empire began to come over to their side. As Adolf Harnack put it in his book *The Mission and Expansion of Christianity*, "But revolutions are not effected with rosewater, and it was a veritable revolution to overthrow polytheism and establish the majesty of God and goodness in the world. . . . It was set side by side with the message of the Savior and of salvation, of love and charity . . . a feeling of perfect confidence that God was *present,* and a conviction of his *care* and *providence*. . . . The more thoughtful were conscious that he reigned in their life with a might of his own."[5]

Augustine's View of Humanity

Compare that stance of confidence and strength with Augustine's portrait of humankind. He looks into himself and observes humans around him, and he sees three different lusts, the generic term for all earthly desires: avarice, *libido dominandi,* and sexual lust. In these lusts temporal goods are preferred over eternal goods. And, for Augustine, humans are incapable of overcoming these lusts through their own power.

Avarice, restless covetousness, has no bounds. There is no limit to human desires for earthly goods; life for citizens of the earthly city as opposed to citizens of the City of God is an endless pursuit of one object after another, none of which can ever bring real satisfaction. His description of this lust brings to mind Hobbes's portrait of *bellum omnium contra omnes,* the war of all against all—the consequences of the fierce competition for inevitably scarce goods. Society is divided against itself, and the strongest oppress the weaker. Augustine writes, "Thou dist at first desire a farm; then thou wouldst possess an estate . . . till thou has reached the shore: arriving at the shore, thou covetest the islands: having made the earth thine, thou wouldst happily seize upon heaven."[6]

---

[5] Adolf Harnack, *The Mission and Expansion of Christianity in the First Three Centuries* (New York: Harper Torchbooks, 1961), 98. Originally published in London by Williams & Norgate, 1908,

[6] Augustine, *En. In Ps. XXXIX*, 7, as quoted in Herbert A. Deane, *The Political and Social Ideas of St. Augustine* (New York: Columbia University Press, 1963), 45.

Libido dominandi. The second identifying characteristic of fallen humanity is the lust for domination over others or the lust for power, which is associated with the love of glory, honor, and fame. Augustine sees the price of this drive in the misery and suffering it produces and is aware that it can lead to atrocious crimes.

Sexual lust. Reflecting on his own experiences of bondage to sexual desire, Augustine thought humans helpless to control sexual desire, "this diabolical excitement of the genitals,"[7] which arises in everyone and is out of control. The inability of the will to control sexual passion is one of the primary proofs for him of the Fall of humankind in Adam's sin. He points to the fact that sexual passion arises unbidden; it is not in the control of the will; and at other times when the will wants to engage in sex, the organs rebel. Before the Fall, as he reads Genesis, Adam and Eve had their passions and their wills in harmony. No longer. Augustine wrote:

> At times, without intention, the body stirs on its own, insistent. At other times it leaves a straining lover in the lurch, and while desire sizzles in the imagination, it is frozen in the flesh; so that, strange to say, even when procreation is not at issue, just self-indulgence, desire cannot rally to desire's help—the force that normally wrestles against reason's control is pitted against itself, and an aroused imagination gets no support from the flesh.[8]

Augustine concludes that humans are helpless—witness their infancy, their sexuality, and their mortality. Even those who are baptized are caught in these nets of helplessness—and this is where he really parts company from the early Fathers. They reveled in their release from the bondage of sin that came with baptism. Augustine grants that some Christians can indeed be trying to live lives oriented to the eternal, but they are far outnumbered by those who are living in the city of man. In fact, he warns, no one can ever know who will be saved. Those who are currently living upright lives can fall and be damned. Those who seem to be on their way to damnation may turn and be saved. Like the story of the tares and wheat—all live together in mixed

---

[7]Augustine, *Opus Imperfectum*, 2.33, as quoted in Elaine Pagels, *Adam, Eve, and the Serpent* (New York: Vintage Books, 1988), 140.

[8]Augustine, *The City of God*, 14.17, as quoted in Gary Wills, *Saint Augustine* (New York: Penguin Putnam, 1999), 133.

company both in the church and in the *civitas,* the city. In that, there is no difference between the church and the state. Both the good and the damned coexist side by side. This mixture will last until the end of time. The tares and the wheat will not be separated out until the final judgment. Moreover, God has determined that only a few will be saved. Most will be damned. Human kind is a *massa damnata,* a damned mass.

The anthropology of Augustine revolves around two poles: the deep and painful awareness of the human condition as expressed in the three lusts and, at the other pole, the yearning expressed at the beginning of the *Confessions*: "groaning with inexpressible groaning in my pilgrimage, remembering Jerusalem with my heart stretching in yearning for it: Jerusalem, my homeland."[9]

To be fair, Augustine's description of humankind's sorry, hopeless state is not the end of his story. Although he refuses to accede any strength or hope for humankind on its own, and although he rejects the Neoplatonic view that humankind can climb the ladder of wisdom and gain union with the One using its own powers, that only sets the stage for his even more fundamental message about the grace of God. All is grace. Humans are powerless on their own, but the grace of God comes down and lifts them up.

A corollary of Augustine's anthropology is his vision of the role of the state. Because, as long as the world lasts, societies will be made up primarily of sinners, whose greed and desire for power and domination will continually produce conflict, violence, and chaos, there is a need for a countervailing power to keep the lid on. That power is the state. The state, with its power of the sword, is necessary to keep some semblance of order. Otherwise society would collapse into anarchy. As Augustine wrote:

> Surely, it is not without purpose that we have the institution of the power of kings, the death penalty of the judge, the barbed hooks of the executioner, the weapons of the soldier, the right of punishment of the overlord, even the severity of the good father. All those things have their methods, their causes, their reasons, their practical benefits. While these are feared, the wicked are

---

[9] Augustine, Confessions XII, 16.23, as quoted in Robert Markus, *Saeculum: History and Society in the Theology of Augustine* (London: Cambridge University Press, 1970), 83.

kept within bounds and the good live more peacefully among the wicked. . . . Even so, it is not without advantage that human recklessness should be confined by fear of the law so that innocence may be safe among evil-doers, and the evil-doers themselves may be cured by calling on God when their freedom of action is held in check by fear of punishment.[10]

Augustine had spent most of his young adult life pursuing a career in the classics and had been an avid student of Plotinus and Neoplatonism. That philosophy heavily influenced his thought all through his life. The Neoplatonic world is eternal—continually emanating from the One and returning to the One—and hierarchically structured: God occupies the top position, and all beings are arrayed beneath him in terms of their being and value. Right under God stands the king or emperor. All power flows from the top down. People need to heed the directives of the king. Not to obey is to introduce disorder into the universe. Fundamental to the notion of hierarchy is the notion of order. The centrality of order in Augustine's thought becomes even more apparent in his complete disdain for civil wars, which disrupt the hierarchy of being in the person of God's lieutenant on earth.

Another corollary of Augustine's anthropology is his teaching on war. Given humanity's propensity for domination and humanity's all-grasping avarice, war is inevitable, according to Augustine. Given humanity's pride, a longing for a perverse kind of exaltation, a deliberate turning from God, war is inevitable. It is in some way a necessary part of the order of things on earth.

How Augustine Differs from the Early Fathers

We have already reviewed how the early Fathers thought of war. They saw it as the scourge of humankind. They scorned the Roman propensity to declare heroic those who killed the greatest number. They also felt that Christianity, following in the footsteps of the nonviolent savior who taught love of enemy and who embraced suffering as a way to reach the hearts of enemies, was fulfilling the prophecies of Isaiah and Micah—that swords were being turned into pruning hooks and

---

[10]Augustine, *Ep.* CLIII, VI, 16, as quoted in Deane, *Political and Social Ideas of St. Augustine*, 138.

the world was finding *shalom* under various olive trees. Christians were gradually bringing peace to the empire and drying up the cesspools of enmity that produced wars.

Augustine, who had such a dark view of humanity, could not see it that way. Saints and sinners would always be mixed together, and there would always be just a few saints in the mix. Given the Fall and the sin that humankind inherited, war would be with humankind until the end of time.

His Neoplatonic view of the world also influenced his teaching on war. Disorder is the result of preferring something lower on the hierarchy of being to something higher. Those disordered objects of desire create conflicts and can lead to war. The state is the mechanism for restoring order in the world. If a state has been attacked or a state has its territory taken or its members are harmed, order is lost. The state uses war to restore order and bring peace. Mattox writes: "The Neoplatonic concept of order imposes on Augustine the necessity to view war as a phenomenon which, when unjustly pursued, tends to promote cosmic disorder, and when justly pursued, tends to promote the orderliness of the universe."[11]

Augustine also had Manichaeism in his past. He was a devotee for nine years as a young man. Manichaeism was strictly pacifist. Devotees believed in the essential oneness of humanity and that to kill or injure one person was to injure all—including oneself. They also rejected the Old Testament because, in their view, the warrior God of the Old Testament was totally at odds with the New Testament and the God—a loving Father—whom Jesus preached. We have already seen how the early Fathers insisted on maintaining continuity with Judaism and accepted the Old Testament but how they gingerly handled the issue of Old Testament wars, using a variety of approaches, from allegory to a hermeneutic of gradual revelation. Not so Augustine. He is careful to rebut charges that he is still Manichean. He therefore defends the heroes of the Old Testament, and he simply accepts as just the wars that Moses and David led, because God ordered them. If God ordered them, they had to be just. God's wisdom is beyond ours. If those wars were just, he continues, war is in itself not unjust.

Augustine goes on then to extend this way of thinking to justify the use of the sword, the state's weapon of choice for ensuring order,

---

[11]Mattox, *Saint Augustine and the Theory of the Just War*, 100.

to chastise, and change the minds of heretics. At first Augustine stuck to the way the early Fathers approached religious faith—that it had to be freely embraced and could not be forced. And he was faithful to the way. As we saw in the last chapter, Constantine handled the disputes within the church; he believed that matters of religious faith could not be coerced. At the beginning of Augustine's episcopacy he rejected using the sword of the state to force the Donatists back into the fold of the Catholic Church in North Africa. He said he did not want to produce a whole packet of people who came into the church under duress and who only pretended adherence to the faith. Gradually, however, he changed his mind because as he said, he learned that it "worked." His own congregation seemed to accept those who were forced, and those who were forced to come in seemed to be happy that they had been forced. In his letter to Boniface in the year 417 he invoked the idea of the *ordo temporum* to justify the use of coercive power against the Donatists—Christianity had come into a new age. It was no longer in the age of the Apostles but had come into the age of the state's collaboration with the church. Robert Markus writes:

> To the Donatists' plea that the Apostles would not have wished to resort to such powers, Augustine replies that the time of the Apostles reflected a very different stage in the gradual realization of the prophecies from the present time, now that the Church has acquired the power to coerce by means of the faith and devotion of kings; and everything is to be done in its season. In Apostolic times the wedding guests were invited; in these times they are rightly compelled to come in.[12]

Augustine began to quote the banquet passage in the New Testament to justify his stance in favor of using violent approaches to compel heretics back into the fold: "Let the heretics be drawn from the hedges, be extracted from the thorns. Stuck in the hedges, they do not want to be compelled: 'We will enter when we want to.' But that is not the Lord's command. He said, '*Compelle intrare*,' 'Compel them to come in.' Use compulsion outside, so freedom can arise once they are inside."[13]

Augustine became convinced that men needed such firm handling.

---

[12]Markus, *Saeculum: History and Society in the Theology of Augustine*, 35.
[13]Augustine, Sermons, 112, 8, as quoted in Wills, *Saint Augustine*, 103.

He summed up his attitude in one word: *disciplina*, discipline, an essentially active process of corrective punishment. As Peter Brown wrote: "The persecution of the Donatists was another 'controlled catastrophe' imposed by God, mediated on this occasion, by the laws of Christian emperors . . . the relationship of the human race to its stern father, who would whip the son he receives, and indiscriminately at that."[14]

We can look back and trace how and when Augustine became, in effect, "the theorist of the Inquisition," as Peter Brown, his biographer, wrote.[15] We can read just how often he justifies violence using this example of a father beating his son. It is his favorite way of demonstrating that a person can be violent, whipping his son, and still hold love in his heart. He will extend that example to soldiers killing others in war and insists that they can love even as they kill. We also know from the *Confessions* just how violent his father had been to him and how much he resented it and can speculate how much his image of God as the stern taskmaster and punishment dealer stems from these experiences. Augustine certainly was not a "Grand Inquisitor." He did not believe in capital punishment for heretics who would not bend. But he did countenance almost everything short of that, including fines, confiscations of property, physical coercion, and exile. He provided the rationale, and his authority gave cover for so much of the violence that would come later—from the Crusades to the Inquisition.

A final important way that Augustine parted company from the early Fathers was the way that he interpreted the so-called hard sayings of the New Testament that were so important to the Fathers and that gave them a new scale of values or a charter for how to resist the oppressions that came their way.

The first hard saying—"You have heard it said, an eye for an eye and a tooth for a tooth, but I say to you do not violently resist one who does you harm—if someone strikes you on the right cheek, turn to him the other, if someone takes your coat, give him your cloak as well. If someone presses you to carry his pack for a mile, go two" (Matt. 5:38–42). The early Fathers, from the Didache on, read those words as a charter of action—act in surprising, loving, creative nonviolent ways to those who harm you and aim to touch their hearts

---

[14]Peter Brown, *Augustine of Hippo* (Berkeley: University of California Press, 1967), 233.
[15]Ibid., 236.

and win them over. Augustine, on the other hand, interpreted them as simply counseling pure interior dispositions of the heart—the words had nothing to do with how you should act. In his Letter to Boniface for example, he wrote:

> Accordingly those commands [Matt: 5.29, about turning the other cheek] pertain more to the interior disposition of the heart than to external actions, the idea being that we should maintain an interior spirit of patience and benevolence but do what seems most beneficial for those whose welfare we are bound to look out for.[16]

For Augustine, the sayings of Jesus in the Sermon on the Mount about "turning the other cheek, and going the extra mile," said nothing about how a Christian should act. They referred only to the disposition one maintained in one's heart. One could turn to violent action, as long as it was for a just cause and one kept a loving disposition in one's heart. Doing "what seems most beneficial for those whose welfare we are bound to look out for," therefore, included and did not exclude acts of violence.

In chapter 2 we saw that current scripture scholarship understands the sayings in the Sermon on the Mount about turning the other cheek and going the extra mile to be vivid examples of ways to respond creatively to situations of oppression. Far from being passive, they are active responses designed to catch the oppressor by surprise, inviting the oppressor—a slave owner humiliating a slave by slapping him with a backhand, an occupying soldier pressing a Jew to carry his pack—to act differently and to recognize his or her human dignity. Moreover, we saw in chapter 4 that the early church found these sayings to be at the heart of the gospel of peacemaking. They found them to be eminently practical guides for behavior. Not so Augustine.

Augustine further justified his reading of the sayings to be merely exhortations to keep a strong interior loving attitude by pointing out that Jesus himself did not obey his own counsel. When he was brought before the Sanhedrin and was slapped in the face, Augustine says he did not turn the other cheek. He did however, keep his wits about him

---

[16]Augustine, *Letter to Boniface*,138.13.

and keep his composure and from his inner calmness reprimanded the soldier who struck him. In another letter Augustine writes:

> Finally those precepts refer rather to the interior disposition of the heart than to the act which appears exteriorly, and they enjoin us to preserve patience and kindly feeling in the hidden places of the soul, revealing them openly when it seems likely to be beneficial to those whose welfare we seek. This is clearly shown in the case of the Lord Christ Himself, a unique model of patience, who was struck on the face and answered: "If I have spoken evil, give testimony of the evil, but if well, why strikest thou me?" If we look at the words literally, He obviously did not fulfill His own precept, for He did not offer His other cheek to the striker; on the contrary He forbade the one who did it to augment the wrong.[17]

Current scholarship, in contrast, understands Jesus' response to the soldier who slapped him to be a classic example of a nonviolent, creative response. It is not literally a turning of the other cheek, but it is squarely in the spirit of Jesus' counsel to respond to violence assertively, creatively, and nonviolently. Jesus' sayings in the Sermon on the Mount are not prescriptive rules but examples of how to act in a whole range of situations of oppression. Jesus' response before the Sanhedrin to the soldier who slapped him fully embodied his teaching in the Sermon on the Mount.

The other key saying of Jesus that was important to the early Fathers was the command to "love your enemies and do good to those who persecute you." They understood that to act this way was to be like their heavenly Father who brings rain on the good and bad alike. As we saw, they practiced love of enemies and saw the world around them change. For Augustine, this teaching was transposed to refer to the interior attitudes of the Christian. One could participate in war and kill as long as one kept love in one's heart. War and even the killing in war, were justifiable if the war was to restore order or punish evildoers and keep them from doing even greater evils. One was faithful to the

---

[17]Augustine, *Letter to Marcellinus* 138 (translation from *Fathers of the Church* series, vol. 20).

gospel while killing in war—as long as one kept love in one's heart. Brown writes, "Augustine merely turned the Christian struggle inwards: its amphitheater was the 'heart'; it was an inner struggle against the forces in the soul; the Lord of this world becomes the Lord of desires."[18]

Augustine and the Just War Theory

As we have seen, war for Augustine was, given the corruption of humankind, inevitable. It was justified if it was ordered by God or if it was ordered by God's representative on earth, the king. It was God's method for disciplining wrongdoers. A just war brought order back into the world whereas an unjust war brought additional disorder into the world. But what else, besides being declared by a lawful authority, made a war just or unjust? Because Augustine made the Sermon on the Mount a guide for interior attitudes and not a teaching that could guide action, the teachings of Jesus were rendered irrelevant to Augustine's world of statecraft. Augustine, therefore, needed some practical guide to help Christians decide what made a war just or unjust. He needed some practical principles that could guide thinking about war. He found it in his classical hero, Cicero.

Augustine had great respect for Cicero. He thought him to be "among the most learned and eloquent of all mankind."[19] He quotes him no less than eighteen times in the City of God.[20] Cicero's writings contain the rudiments of the theory of just war that Augustine will take up and refine.

Just Cause

Cicero writes in *De Re Publica*, "A war is never undertaken by the ideal state except in defense of its honor or its safety."[21] No war can be considered just that is not preceded by some wrongdoing by an enemy. Wars fought for honor include wars fought to defend or aid allies. In fact, in such wars, Cicero declares with some satisfaction,

---

[18]Brown, *Augustine of Hippo*, 240.
[19]Augustine, *City of God*, XXII.6, 1030.
[20]Mattox, *Saint Augustine and the Theory of Just War*, 14. This summary of Cicero's teaching is a condensed version of John Mark Mattox's treatment of the topic.
[21]Cicero, *De Re Publica* (libertyfund.org, Francis Barham translation), Book 3, verse 23.

"Our people by defending their allies have gained dominion over the whole world."[22] Cicero also countenances wars fought for glory, but considers glory to be a much less compelling reason for war than honor, revenge, or self-defense. Augustine will disagree on this point—glory is not for him a justifying cause for war.

Public Declaration and Last Resort

For Cicero, "No war is just unless after a formal demand of satisfaction for injury, or after an express declaration and proclamation of hostilities."[23] This requirement was part of a long religious tradition in Rome. Rome had special priests, *fetiales,* who conducted religious ceremonies that prefaced the declaration of war and who determined whether a state had committed an injustice against Rome. The offending state was given a period in which to make satisfaction. This ultimatum and period of grace was regarded as a last resort.

Peace as the Ultimate Objective of War

Cicero declared "The only excuse for going to war is that we may live in peace without injury."[24]

Proportionality

Cicero says, "For there is a limit to revenge and punishment—nay I know not whether it may not be enough for him who gave the provocation to repent of his wrong-doing, so that he may not do it again, and that others may be the less disposed to do as he has done."[25]

Discrimination

Soldiers who cease hostilities should not be victims of punishment because they were acting as instrumentalities of the state not on their own behalf.

---

[22]Ibid.
[23]Cicero, *De Officis* (libertyfund.org, Andrew Peabody translation, 1887), Book 1, Chapter 11.
[24]Ibid.
[25]Ibid.

Augustine takes up this line of thinking from Cicero and Ambrose because he has already concluded that wars are inevitable—given the evil drives in humans as a result of the Fall. The best humans can do as they wait for the final reckoning is labor to build a "kind of peace." War is required to stop the wicked from doing harm and prevent even more disorder from entering the world. The most one can hope for is to make sure that the wars that Christians participate in meet minimal standards of decency—that most reasonable humans can agree to—these criteria of just war thinking. The most humans can hope for, given the inevitability of war, is to at least participate only in *just* wars.

Augustine: An Appraisal

To summarize the differences between Augustine and the practices of the early church and the stance of the early Church Fathers: For the early Fathers Rome was the corrupting force in the world, filled with pagan beliefs and worship, given to unending violence and insatiable thirst for greater reach and glory, rewarding with laurels and honors those who killed the greatest number. For Augustine Rome was the *patria,* the partner with the church in ruling the world—under the guidance of the church. Augustine wrote about church leaders: "You teach kings to rule for the benefit of their people; and it is you who warn the people to be subservient to their kings."[26] Walter Wink wrote, "The Church no longer saw the demonic as lodged in the empire, but in the empire's enemies."[27]

In the early church, baptism changed everything for newly baptized Christians. They were filled with God's grace and released from the clutches of sin and evil, freed to live the life of the kingdom of God in this world and dedicated to loving even their enemies, even Rome — with the power that dwelled in them. For Augustine, even the baptized were still part of the *massa damnata,* still in the clutches of the three lusts of avarice, domination, and sex. For Augustine, Romans 7:18–20 described the deepest truth about him and about other Christians: "For even though the desire to do good is in me, I am not able to do it. I don't do the good I want to do; instead I do the evil that I do not

---

[26] Augustine, *De Moribus Ecclesiae Catholicae et De Moribus Manichaeorum* I, 30, 63 as quoted in Pagels, *Adam, Eve, and the Serpent,* 123.

[27] Walter Wink, *Engaging the Powers* (Minneapolis: Augsburg Fortress Press, 1992), 150.

want to do. If I do what I don't want to do, this means that I am no longer the one who does it; instead it is the sin that lives in me." The early church recognized the truth of this passage but they read further—Romans 7:25 and 8:2. "Thanks be to God, who does this through our Lord Jesus Christ! . . . For the law of the Spirit, which brings us life in union with Christ Jesus, has set me free from the law of sin and death." They could confront the evils of this world with the weapons of love and nonviolence, not out of their own strength, but because of the Spirit who had filled and freed them and given them strength.

The ways that the early Church Fathers and Augustine read the Old Testament are very different. Unlike the Montanists and the Donatists, the early Church Fathers accepted Judaism as the ground from which Christianity had sprung and therefore accepted the Old Testament. They recognized, however, that Jesus read and taught passages from the Old Testament selectively. If his disciples thought that the Old Testament promised them a savior who would lead a fight against the occupying forces, Jesus patiently pointed out selected passages that would lead them to a different conclusion. Passages such as Second Isaiah pointed to a savior who would show a third way—not resignation, not violent revolt—but the way of the cross, the way of suffering love. The early Fathers did not feature the warrior God of the Old Testament—they found the wars of the Old Testament to be an embarrassment if taken literally—given the life and revelation of Jesus. Augustine, however, approvingly quotes the passages that had Yahweh ordering wars. God uses wars, Augustine claims, to punish evildoers, to correct the strays. His wisdom is beyond human wisdom. If God orders them or at least permits them, war must be a good.

The Fathers of the early church were sure that they were making progress in the progressive fight against violence and war—that the prophecies of Micah and Isaiah were coming true in their midst—that spears were being turned into pruning hooks and swords into plowshares. Augustine taught war as inevitable. Augustine responded to the criticism that Christianity had made Rome vulnerable and soft by writing the *City of God*. Christians had to take up the sad "necessities" of life in this city of man while they waited for the advent of the City of God. They had to do their part in protecting Rome as the force for order against the chaos of the barbarians—even though, by the time he wrote *The City of God*, he had an attitude toward Rome very different from that of his early years as a bishop. Rome had been overcome by Alaric. In *The City of God*, Augustine makes it very clear that no human government can bring the fullness of peace. That cannot be enjoyed until the final coming.

The Fathers of the early church read the Sermon on the Mount and especially the instructions on loving one's enemies and doing good to those who persecute you and turning the other cheek and going the extra mile; these were their marching orders, their practical guide for negotiating the days and nights, the turmoil and obstacles that came at them. Augustine interpreted those passages as invitations to keep one's internal motivations pure. They had nothing to do with behavior according to Augustine.

The early Fathers believed that faith could not be coerced. Humans had to respond to the message of Christianity from their hearts and with their free will. As Clement of Alexandria wrote: "Above all, Christians are not allowed to correct by violence sinful wrong-doings. For it is not those who abstain from evil by compulsion, but those who abstain by choice, that God crowns. For it is not possible for a man to be good steadily except by his own choice."[28]

Augustine not only accepted the state's power of the sword in matters of the faith, he provided a detailed rationale for the state compelling heretics, such as the Donatists, back into the fold of the Catholic Church. The forces of the emperor were unleashed on the Donatists—their churches were confiscated, their bishops exiled, their adherents forcibly brought into the Catholic churches. The bloody alliance between the Catholic Church and the empire, the state, had begun. What even Constantine had refused to do, Augustine did—and he legitimated it.

Augustine strongly influenced the subsequent history of Christianity. After him the church continued to work hand in hand with the state—with the church for the most part having the upper hand, the guiding hand. As the relationship took more definite form through the centuries as "Christendom," Augustine's teachings on the inevitability of war and the corollary that Christians should participate only in wars that were *just* continued to hold sway. The theory of justifiable war continued as the presumptive teaching on the relationship between a

---

[28]Clement, *Fragment in Maximus Confessor*, Sermon 55.

Christian and war right on through the centuries. Thomas Aquinas, for example, more or less repeated what Augustine had written.[29] The earlier tradition of active, confident peacemaking was for the most part submerged with only traces of it surviving—such as monks and clergy not being allowed to fight in wars. Periodically clusters of Christians, such as Franciscans and Quakers, would rediscover the "hard sayings" and try to put them into practice.

What is somewhat difficult to understand is that even as the just war theory has endured, the foundational teachings of Augustine that shaped his just war theory have been rejected.

Augustine's interpretation of the Fall and his theory of the state undergird and lead to the just war theory. For him the Fall means humans are so helpless and given to lusts of avarice, domination, and sexual predation that war is inevitable. The state's power is all that keeps humans from eating one another alive. The state is all that keeps some semblance of order in the City of Man. The state therefore needs to be protected and defended. Citizens have a duty to shoulder the "necessities," including war, to defend the keeper of order. But an unjust war will introduce even more chaos into the universe. The all-important thing therefore is for the leader (king or emperor, e.g.) to make sure that the war is just. A just war will by definition bring order to the world. The individual Christian's responsibility is to obey the leader. No need to worry as long as the leader has proclaimed the war just. The individual Christian should only worry about keeping love in his heart for the one he or she kills.

Many have disputed Augustine's teaching on the Fall—that Adam and Eve fundamentally contaminated the whole universe through their disobedience and pride, that humanity is a *massa damnata*, that the sin is passed on through semen, and that very few people have been predestined for salvation. For example, Thomas Merton writes: "Note of course that the doctrine of original sin, properly understood, is *optimistic*. It does not teach that man is by nature evil, but that evil in him is unnatural, a disorder, a sin. If evil, lying, and hatred

---

[29]The history of the just war theory and of pacifism and how they evolved over the centuries is told in many places, including *Christian Attitudes to War, Peace, and Revolution* by John Howard Yoder (Grand Rapids, MI: Brazos Press, 2009), *The Catholic Peace Tradition* by Ronald Musto (New York: Peace Books, 2002), *Christian Attitudes toward War and Peace* by Roland Bainton (Nashville, TN: Abingdon Press, 1960), and *Peace Be with You* by Eileen Egan (Maryknoll, NY: Orbis Books, 1999).

were natural to man, all men would be perfectly at home, perfectly happy in evil."[30] Robert Daly writes: "The story of the primordial sin of Adam and Eve recounted in Genesis 3, as it is now understood by most mainline Christian theologians, is not to be read as a literal description of a historical first sin, but as a psychological description of all sin, reminding us of what is repeatedly happening in our own sinful existence."[31]

Augustine's theory of the state—that the king is God's steward, that all power flows from the top—has been in dispute for centuries. What seemed to be power residing in the king has actually been shown to reside in the subjects, the citizens, the people, and given to the king, the president, the führer, the premier. Power is now recognized as rising. No leader has power unless it is given to him, unless he or she enjoys legitimacy, unless people decide to obey. As soon as they decide otherwise, the leader is finished—especially if the people succeed in cutting the cord between the "ruler" and those equipped to compel compliance, the armed forces. Once the enforcers take back their loyalty, the leader is really finished. Duane Friesen writes, "The hidden power of every state, even the most totalitarian, resides to a great extent in the consent, either overt or passive, of the governed."[32] Citizens have to decide for themselves whether or not a given war is one in which they should participate. Blind obedience to the king, the president, the führer, is unworthy of a free people.

Many are distrustful of Augustine's markedly vertical structures of dominance. Michael Nagler reminds us: "The infamous Milgram experiments [which had innocent college students upping the doses of shock to other students just because the one in authority kept telling them to do it—even to the point of death if it had been real] have shown how dangerous obedience to authority can be as an enabling condition for violence."[33] The lashes and corrective punishment of a supposedly loving paterfamilias as a model for how the world should work is no longer spontaneously accepted. The common maxim "spare

[30]Thomas Merton, *Conjectures of a Guilty Bystander* (Garden City, NY: Doubleday Image Books, 1968), 85.

[31]Robert Daly, SJ, "Phenomenology of Redemption?" *Theological Studies* 74, no. 2 (2013): 356.

[32]Duane Friesen, *Christian Peacemaking and International Conflict* (Scottdale, PA: Herald Press, 1986), 38.

[33]Michael Nagler, "Eternal Peace," in *Peace Movements Worldwide*, ed. Marc Pilusik and Michael Nagler (Santa Barbara, CA: Praeger, 2011), 12–13.

the rod and spoil the child" is increasingly called into question as the link between abuse in childhood and later adult abuse of others is established. As Marc Pilusik has written: "Historical data include accounts of widespread abusive child-rearing practices in Germany at the turn of the 20th century that probably contributed to the child traumatization of many who later became Nazis. Hitler's own background is one example affirming Stephenson's studies of 14 modern tyrants. All had suffered multiple childhood humiliations, were shame based, and had grown up in violent authoritarian families."[34]

Augustine's assumption that war, if just, brings order back into the world, is hardly borne out in the history of wars. One war seems to lead to the next. Mattox indicates that "given the political-military circumstances of the Roman Empire at the dawn of the fifth century, Augustine's personal acquaintance with war came largely in the form of internal police actions. Hence when he refers to just wars, he almost certainly has in mind wars intended to quell internal rebellions . . . or defensive wars waged to protect the borders of the Empire."[35] In any case, Augustine at times greatly overstates the positive impact of war on the human condition. For example, he wrote that "war is oftentimes the vehicle by which regretfully but necessarily, the carnal lusts . . . are thoroughly subdued so that unruly and unjust men can be brought into subjection first to reason, and ultimately to God himself.[36]

As for his fundamental belief, given his view of human nature, that war is inevitable, many disagree. For example, Pope John Paul II increasingly taught the priority of nonviolence and the need to end war. In his speech at Drogheda in Ireland in 1979 he argued that violence, under the illusion of fighting evil, only makes violence worse. He exhorted persons not to follow leaders "who train you in the way of inflicting death. . . . Give yourself to the service of life, not the work of death. Do not think that courage and strength are proved by killing and destruction. True courage lies in working for peace. . . . Violence is the enemy of justice. Only peace leads to true justice."[37]

The Seville Statement on Violence, issued under the auspices of the United Nations in 1986 had eighteen distinguished ethnologists, psy-

---

[34]Marc Pilusik, "Psychology and Peace," in *Peace Movements Worldwide,* ed. Marc Pilusik and Michael Nagler (Santa Barbara, CA: Praeger, 2011), 61.

[35]Mattox, *Saint Augustine and the Theory of Just War,* 36.

[36]Ibid., 115.

[37]John Paul II, *Homily at Drogheda,* 1979, 18–20.

chologists, and bioscientists systematically refute the assumptions that humans by nature are defined by competitive behaviors and biologically inclined to waging war. They recognized that the myth that war is intrinsic to our nature is a significant obstacle to progress toward peace. War is a human construct and as such can be deconstructed. Humans are as wired for cooperation as they are for violence. Humans have outlawed slavery. When dueling was labeled murder, it disappeared. Margaret Mead wrote in her essay "War Is Only an Invention" that in order for an invention to become obsolete, "people must recognize the defects of the old invention, and someone must make a new one. In this way, trial by jury supplanted trial by ordeal or combat."[38]

Finally, writers have questioned Augustine's belief that killing can be done in war, and one can still be a faithful Christian as long as one's intention is pure and one keeps love in one's heart. This stems from his belief that actions are not as important as intentions. Lisa Sowle Cahill puts it simply: "In presenting killing as an act of love for the killed, Augustine barely avoids an aura of disingenuousness."[39] Erasmus refused to accept the opinion taught since Augustine that the act of killing a human being could be accomplished while maintaining a loving disposition. He refused to accept the split between the inner disposition and the external act. He writes: "Augustine approves of it [war] in some instances, and St. Bernard praises some soldiers. But Christ himself and Peter and Paul everywhere teach the opposite. Why is their authority less with us than that of Augustine or Bernard?"[40]

Even in Augustine's day, as Roland Bainton points out, there was another viable way other than war to solve the problem of the barbarians at the gate.

Under Valens, the Visigoths pressed by the Huns asked permission to settle in the empire with their families, to the number of a million souls. They were for the most part Christian. Fritigern was their leader. The Emperor Valens promised admission. The horde came over the Danube, but instead of being settled were corralled by the forces of Rome and kept alive by a supply of dead dogs. The price for each dog was a child to be sold into

---

[38]Margaret Mead, "Warfare Is Only an Invention," *Asia* (August 1940).

[39]Lisa Sowle Cahill, *Love Your Enemies* (Minneapolis: Fortress Press, 1994), 233.

[40]Erasmus, *The Education of a Christian Prince*, trans. Lester K. Born (New York: Columbia University Press, 1936), 257.

slavery. The guard of Fritigern was treacherously murdered by the Romans. The Goths broke loose and ravaged Thrace. Valens met them in battle. The emperor himself perished, together with two-thirds of the Imperial army. Then it was that the Spanish general Theodosius restored order by honorably granting the settlement promised at the outset.

Had Rome practiced her ancient virtue of bona fides, the barbarian invasions might have continued to be a controlled immigration.[41]

The theory of the just war has been dominant within the Christian churches for all these centuries since Augustine. At long last, however, in the twentieth and into the twenty-first centuries the church has begun to rediscover its earlier tradition—the animating power of Jesus' nonviolent example, the dynamism of the Sermon on the Mount and its relevance for issues of war and peace, the power and potential of nonviolence and the centrality of the Christian's vocation to be a peacemaker. In the next chapter I trace that development and the Catholic Church's return to a gospel-based theology of peace.

---

[41]Bainton, *Christian Attitudes toward War and Peace*, 100.

6

Tracing the Catholic Church's Journey Back to a Gospel-based Theology of Peace

Since the 1960s the Catholic Church has taken important steps back to a gospel-based theology of peace. One of the basic differences in the church's approach has been in the move away from the traditional debate between pacifism and just war theory. The church instead has focused on the challenge of *peacemaking*. In that shift the church begins to come back to the challenging, open-ended spirit of the gospels. No longer is there an exclusive focus on whether or not a given war is just, but instead the focus is much broader—how to build a culture and a world of peace. Fundamental to that shift is a move away from a negative definition of peace, namely, the absence of war, to a positive vision of peace. Also fundamental to that shift will be the acceptance and exploration of nonviolence as a viable way of exercising power and a substitute for violent power. That shift began in 1963, when Pope John XXIII issued his encyclical *Pacem in Terris*, Peace on Earth.

1963: *Pacem in Terris, Peace on Earth*: An Encyclical from Pope John XXIII

John XXIII came from a simple farm family in Bergamo, Italy. Growing up, he and his parents were part of a huge Catholic Action initiative led by their local bishop involving some two hundred thousand people. Before becoming the patriarch of Venice, Angelo Roncalli was a member of the diplomatic corps and was widely revered in his posts in France and later in UNESCO where he learned that many people of different backgrounds could work together to benefit humanity. In

1962 he was utilized by Nikita Khrushchev and John F. Kennedy as a backchannel negotiator during the Cuban Missile Crisis. He witnessed personally how close we had come to a world conflagration. His personal history and the way he came to experience the modern world shaped his teachings.

As stated in the Introduction to this book, John used natural law thinking[1] in this encyclical. The Sermon on the Mount did not enter into his discussion of peace on the earth. Nonetheless, *Pacem in Terris* made three contributions to the unfolding gospel-based theology of peace.

First, it questioned the long hallowed distinction between just and unjust wars. Many interpreted John XXIII as saying that, given the monstrous destruction of modern wars, no modern war could be just. He wrote: "Humans are becoming more and more convinced that disputes which arise between States should not be resolved by recourse to arms, but rather by negotiation. . . . In an age such as ours which prides itself on its atomic energy it is contrary to reason to hold that war is now a suitable way to restore rights which have been violated."[2]

John is using natural law thinking when he says "contrary to right reason" modern wars cannot be just because in their mass, indiscriminate killing, they violate fundamental criteria of the just war theory, namely proportionality and discrimination. Ronald Musto writes, "First, Pope John is not condemning nuclear war alone, but all war waged in the nuclear age. Second . . . in rejecting the suitability of war as a means of restoring violated rights he explicitly rejects the theory of the just war."[3]

The savagery and unrestrained nature of modern war leads ineluctably to a development of doctrine and the need for another approach to the problems of war and peace—the just war theory is no longer

---

[1]A brief explanation of the term "natural law thinking" may be helpful. Natural law thinking prescinds from scripture and revelation and using the power of human reasoning reflects on how humans are put together, what is built into them from creation, for what purposes they are made, and what it takes to fulfill those purposes, and then natural law thinking draws out a set of rational conclusions. In this case by reflecting on how humans are put together, the ultimate purposes for which they are made, and what is required for reaching those ends, John XXIII came to see that humans have a set of inalienable rights—among them "the right to life and the means suitable for the proper development of life—primarily food, clothing, shelter, rest, medical care, and finally the necessary social services." This is the first (in paragraph 11) of the many rights listed in the document. He goes on to say that "the natural law" gives to humans these human rights—social, religious, cultural, and economic—all of which are required if humans are to live their lives to the full.

[2]John XXIII, *Pacem in Terris,* 126–27.

[3]Ronald Musto, *The Catholic Peace Tradition* (New York: Peace Books, 2002), 190.

an ineffective guide. There must be another way to approach the question of war and violence. That opens the door to an exploration of nonviolence, which will emerge in the Second Vatican Council and which will be emphasized more and more in official church teaching in subsequent years. Francis X. Meehan writes, "The very principles of the just war theory, which require moderation and discrimination, enable us to point to the evil of indiscriminate killing and to name it as evil . . . It was the just war theory teaching itself which became the catalyst for Vatican II to call for an 'entirely new attitude.'"[4]

Second, Pope John called for an end to the arms race and the ban of nuclear weapons. The arms race not only is a danger to the world; it also robs the poor, wasting resources while deepening fear between peoples. He wrote: "Justice, then, right reason and consideration for human dignity and life urgently demand that the arms race should cease, that the stockpiles which exist in various countries should be reduced equally and simultaneously by the parties concerned, that nuclear weapons should be banned, and finally that all come to an agreement on a fitting program of disarmament, employing mutual and effective controls."[5]

Third, John XXIII defined peace broadly and positively. Peace must be built. It goes well beyond the mere cessation of hostilities. Many peace treaties end up broken, and violence breaks out again. Deep divisions between people need to be healed through patient peacebuilding. The pope offered an expansive vision of peacemaking: "Peace is had when people enjoy the full panoply of their natural human rights." Any state that protected and encouraged the full flowering of these rights would be at peace. If the whole world protected and encouraged these rights, the world would be at peace.

John's vision of peace is like Gandhi's Constructive Program. Gandhi focused on three main topics in his Constructive Program: eliminate untouchability, bring a decent standard of living and dignity to the million small villages of India through a program of social uplift, and eliminate enmity between and bring together in friendship Muslims and Hindus—huge long-term programs of social justice, conflict resolution, and human development. He knew that India would not

---

[4]Francis X. Meehan, in *The Catholic Bishops and Nuclear War*, ed, Judith Dwyer (Washington, DC: Georgetown University Press, 1984), 92.
[5]John XXIII, *Pacem in Terris*, 112.

really be free, *swaraj,* unless all these positive peace-building efforts were brought to fulfillment. Real freedom went well beyond simple political independence from Great Britain. In some ways Pope John XXIII's vision is even more challenging—when one reads the long list of rights that he feels are commensurate with peaceful living. As John sees it, the Christian's call to peacemaking begins with a full, expansive vision of what really makes for peace.

This emphasis on peacemaking and a positive vision of peace brings the church closer to the call of the gospels. It is important to work to end war and reduce violence, but lasting peace calls for even more—bringing people together and addressing the underlying causes of violence. If there is great disparity within a society or between societies in terms of basic human rights, peace will not endure.

A gospel-based theology of peace benefits from language that is not too restrictive. Some terms do not adequately express a positive vision of peace. For example, the Latin word for peace is *pax,* a pact—understanding peace to be just an agreement not to fight. The Greek term for peace is *eirene,* from *ar,* which means to piece together an agreement, cessation of hostilities. The German word for peace is also restrictive—*gewaltlosigkeit,* means the absence of violence. In contrast, *shalom,* the Hebrew word for peace, refers to the fullness of right relationships and overflowing bounty. The Indian word, *shanti,* has a semantic range that covers all human longings. The Philippine word for peace means to offer dignity. They are closer to the meaning of peace in the gospels. Jesus said: "Blessed are the peacemakers, for they shall be called the children of God." Some expressions are worse than restrictive and are misleading. For example, the Department of the Navy refers to peace as "perpetual prehostility." Ronald Reagan talked of "peace through strength." The MX missile was named the "Peacemaker." Pope John, in contrast, offers a definition of peace that opens a pathway to a lifetime of creative peacemaking practices. If peace is the enjoyment of the full gamut of human rights for all, there is much positive, challenging work to do.

In the fifty plus years since *Pacem in Terris* was published, much has been done and accomplished. It was the first time in the history of the church that the church embraced the idea of human rights. Before *Pacem in Terris* it had always emphasized "duties" not rights. *Pacem in Terris* proposed a structure of peace built on the recognition, respect, protection, and promotion of human rights. In his commemorative piece on the fiftieth anniversary of *Pacem in Terris,* Drew Christiansen writes:

In the years that followed, national conferences of bishops, dioceses and religious orders opened human rights offices to address offenses in Latin America, Africa and Asia. These groups worked through the Pontifical Council for Justice and Peace with politically influential national bishops' conferences in the West and with secular human rights agencies to defend people against repressive regimes. . . .The secular world was likewise undergoing an awakening to human rights during this time. Amnesty International began making appeals for prisoners of conscience in 1961. The adoption of the Helsinki Accords in 1968 . . . gave rise to new civil rights groups like the Helsinki Group and Human Rights Watch.[6]

The call to defend human rights has been heard by many quarters of the church. The church in Guatemala, for example, set a magnificent example when it not only brokered an end to Guatemala's thirty-five-year civil war but also labored by might and main to defend the human rights of the Mayan people during the period of ethnic cleansing of the Mayans in Guatemala. The Archdiocesan Human Rights Office of the Guatemalan Church issued a massive four-volume report documenting the systematic harassment, torture, disappearances, and massacres of the Mayan people. The bishop who had supervised the project was murdered a few days after the report was issued.

Gerald Schlabach, in a lecture for the Presentation Sisters' Peace Studies Forum, quoted Mario Hugueros, a Guatemalan and dean of the Mennonite Seminary for Central America, who during his address to the joint Mennonite and Catholic conference for Promoting Church Unity in 2000, held up the Catholic Church in Guatemala as a model "peace church,"—much to the surprise of the Catholic participants.[7] Hugueros was recognizing that the Catholic Church in Guatemala, in the spirit of Pope John's *Pacem in Terris*, had become the country's foremost defender of human rights.

Pope John's *Pacem in Terris* was issued between the first and second sessions of the Second Vatican Council. It was addressed to all humanity, but it especially heartened those who were already peace-minded.

[6]Drew Christiansen, "A Vision of Peace," *America*, April 8–15, 2013.
[7]Gerald Schlabach, "Meeting in Exile: Historic Peace Churches and The Emerging Peace Church Catholic," a lecture for Presentation Sisters' Peace Studies Forum, Fargo, North Dakota, January 23, 2004.

A group of fifty women from various backgrounds decided to journey to Rome as "mothers of peace" to thank Pope John for his message of peace. Among them was Dorothy Day, the co-founder of the Catholic Worker Movement and a firm believer in the power and potential of gospel nonviolence. They hoped for a private audience with the pope, but instead they were asked to attend a public audience in St. Peter's. After blessing all present, the pope began to speak about the "Pilgrims of Peace." Eileen Egan described the scene: "A young woman translated his words as he spoke, and kept beaming at the group as did other members of the audience. They were wearing buttons, almost as large as saucers, bearing the legend 'Madre per la Pace.' The young woman, indicating first the pope, and then the group, wanted to let them know that he was speaking to them especially."[8] Dorothy Day reflected on the moment: "It seemed too good to be true, and if all those around us had not kept assuring us that he was speaking to us, I would have considered it but a coincidence. Our messages had reached him, we felt, impossible though it had seemed they would."[9] On the day Dorothy Day arrived back in the States, June 3, 1963, she received news that Pope John had died. His spirit and his writings continued to influence the council. As Pope John wrote in *Pacem in Terris*: "Every believer must be a spark of life, a center of love, a vivifying leaven amid his fellow humans."[10]

1965: *Gaudium et Spes, Joy and Hope,*
The Pastoral Constitution on the Church in the Modern World:
Issued by all the World's Catholic Bishops
at the Second Vatican Council

Each time the church has taken a step closer to returning to a gospel-based theology of peace, it has been the result of many people behind the scenes working to clarify, communicate, and demonstrate gospel nonviolence in their own lives. That is especially true of the document, *Gaudium et Spes, Joy and Hope,* Vatican II's document on the Church in the Modern World and, in particular, the section on war and peace adopted in the final session of the council by the council fathers, which

---

[8]Eileen Egan, *Peace Be with You* (Maryknoll, NY: Orbis Books, 1999), 286.
[9]Dorothy Day, a notebook of Day's cited in William Miller, *All Is Grace* (Garden City, NY: Doubleday, 1987), 172.
[10]John XXIII, *Pacem in Terris,* 164.

called for "an evaluation of war with an entirely new attitude."[11]

That behind-the-scenes story might well begin with Jean Goss and his wife Hildegard Goss-Mayr. Jean Goss was a prisoner of war in the Second World War, and through his experiences vowed to work in whatever way he could to end war. He became a railroad union leader after the war. He happened to hear about a cardinal in Rome, by the name of Ottaviani, who after touring the war-torn south of Italy, declared publicly "bellum omnino interdicendum," "war is to be altogether forbidden." Jean set out to meet with him, arriving at the headquarters of the Holy Office in Rome only to be stopped by a Swiss Guard. Jean yelled as loud as he could: "bellum omnino interdicendum" which brought the cardinal out of his office and resulted in a sit-down meeting. Jean subsequently introduced the cardinal to his wife, Hildegard, a PhD in philosophy, and the daughter of one of the founders of the International Fellowship of Reconciliation. They hit it off, and the cardinal introduced them to the bishops and theologians preparing the document on the Church in the Modern World.

Jean Goss went on to help organize a "peace lobby." The English-speaking peace lobby consisted of Barbara and Bernard Wall, of English Pax—Barbara had an official press pass to the Vatican II Masses in St. Peter's—Richard Carbray, a university professor and a Latinist who was able to translate the group's suggestions into Latin and get them submitted into the discussions on the council floor; Eileen Egan, the founder of the American branch of Pax; Gordon Zahn, whose book *German Catholics and Hitler's Wars* had received much attention from the bishops; and James Douglass, whose book *The Nonviolent Cross* had introduced many of the bishops to the tradition of nonviolent action and Mahatma Gandhi's contemporary relevance. The group proceeded to visit personally with dozens of bishops, bringing with them a special edition of the *Catholic Worker,* written by Eileen Egan, outlining suggested priorities for the schema.

Jean and Hildegard also helped Lanza and Chanterelle del Vasto, leaders of the Arc, a Gandhi-like ashram in France and a long-time supporter of gospel nonviolence, bring to Rome a group of women, including Dorothy Day, who fasted and prayed for the council fathers.

On the last day of open debate on the schema, one of the most powerful and, by reputation, conservative officials in the Vatican, Cardinal

---

[11]Pastoral Constitution on the Church in the Modern World, no. 80.

Ottaviani, stood up to speak. Thomas Cornell described the action: "Ottaviani . . . rose to defend Schema XIII and to urge its acceptance against the efforts of some American bishops, led by Cardinal Spellman to weaken the text. Ottaviani was given the longest and loudest ovation of the council and *Gaudium et Spes* was accepted resoundingly."[12]

What did this work of many hands and hearts produce? *Gaudium et Spes* devoted the last chapter of its second part to "The Fostering of Peace and the Promotion of a Community of Nations," and pushed the church ever closer to its earlier stance of gospel-based nonviolence.

First, it underlines the positive, expansive vision of peace enunciated by Pope John, and makes peacemaking a central priority for all Christians: "Peace is not merely the absence of war. Nor can it be reduced to the maintenance of a balance of power. Nor is it brought about by dictatorship. Instead it is rightly and appropriately called 'an enterprise of justice. . . . Hence peace is likewise the fruit of love, which goes beyond what justice can provide. . . . For this reason, all Christians are urgently summoned 'to practice the truth in love' (Eph. 4:15) and to join all true peacemakers in pleading for peace and bringing it about. "[13]

Second, it explicitly commends, for the first time ever in an official document of a church council the stance of nonviolence: "Motivated by this same spirit, we cannot fail to praise those who renounce the use of violence in the vindication of their rights and who resort to methods of defense which are otherwise available to weaker parties too, provided that this can be done without injury to the rights and duties of others or to the community itself."[14]

Third, for the first time the church makes a clear statement supporting conscientious objection: "Moreover, it seems right that laws make humane provision for the case of those who by reason of conscience refuse to bear arms, provided, however, that they accept some other form of service to the human community."[15]

Before the council, if Catholics approached a draft board in the United States with a petition to be declared a conscientious objector, they would be automatically refused and be told—your church teaches

---

[12]Thomas Cornell, "How Catholics Began to Speak Their Peace," *Salt of the Earth* (Claretian Publications, 1999).

[13]Church in the Modern World, no. 78.

[14]Ibid., no. 78.

[15]Ibid., no. 79.

the just war theory, and it is not possible for you to claim conscientious objector status. That possibility is only open, in the American selective service system, to all-war objectors. Ever since Augustine the common teaching was that when a ruler declared a war, the citizen had to give obedience and was obliged to fight. In the 1960s conscientious objection became a burning issue in the United States with the escalation of the Vietnam War. It was very important, especially for young American Catholics, that the Catholic Church clarify its stance on conscientious objection. Kenneth Himes writes, "In the space of nine short years church teaching had undergone a dramatic change from Pius XII's opposition to conscientious objection to Vatican II's endorsement of the idea."[16]

Musto adds, "There had only been 4 Catholics among the 3,989 conscientious objectors to World War I, only 135 among the 11,887 COs classified as IV-E during World War II; by 1969, 2,494 Catholics had received CO status among the 34,255 so classified, the single largest percentage of all American religious bodies."[17]

Finally, the council condemned any act of war that ignored the difference between combatants and noncombatants—any act of war that aimed at the destruction of cities or population centers. The documents of previous ecumenical councils in the history of the church had been filled with "anathemas" or condemnations. The following statement, in Section 80 of *Gaudium et Spes,* stood out starkly as the only condemnation of the Second Vatican Council: "With these truths in mind, this most holy synod makes its own the condemnations of total war already pronounced by recent popes, and issues the following declaration: Any act of war aimed indiscriminately at the destruction of entire cities or of extensive areas of population is a crime against God and humanity. It merits unequivocal and unhesitating condemnation."[18]

In this declaration the council, in effect, condemned retroactively the carpet and obliteration bombing that both Germany and the Allies did in World War II, the bombing of Hiroshima and Nagasaki by the United States, and all future destruction of population centers through the air or through other means.

---

[16]Kenneth R. Himes, "Pacifism and the Just War Tradition," in *One Hundred Years of Catholic Social Thought,* ed. John A. Coleman, SJ (Maryknoll, NY: Orbis Books, 1991), 333.

[17]Musto, *Catholic Peace Tradition,* 254.

[18]*Gaudium et Spes,* no. 80.

1983: *The Challenge of Peace*
A Pastoral Letter of the American Catholic Bishops

An additional step toward recovering the church's early posture of nonviolence was taken by the American Catholic Bishops in 1983 when they issued their pastoral letter, *The Challenge of Peace*. Not as much is known about who behind the scenes contributed to this achievement, but it is clear that a priest of the Archdiocese of Boston, Bryan Hehir, the secretary for peace and justice issues for the National Conference of Catholic Bishops, played a major role in the formulation of the pastoral letter—as did Cardinal Joseph Bernardin, the head of the ad hoc committee of five bishops delegated the responsibility of preparing the statement by the National Conference of Catholic Bishops.

First, *The Challenge of Peace* condemned any use of nuclear weapons—not first strike use, not defensive use, not "limited" use. After consulting with many experts in the field, they concluded that there could be no guarantee that a so-called limited nuclear war could be contained and not escalate. The use of nuclear weapons would be the "crime against God and humanity" that the council described. The bishops wrote: "Our 'no' to nuclear war must, in the end, be definitive and decisive."[19]

Second, the American Catholic Bishops condemned nuclear deterrence but did not insist on immediate, unilateral disarmament—allowing the deterrence system to stay in place in the short term as long as leaders of countries with nuclear weapons took quick and deliberate actions to rid the world of nuclear weapons. Musto writes: "On the practice of deterrence, they note that the peace brought by the balance of power is not really Christian peace and is more like the peace of terror imposed by the Pax Romana. While they admit that deterrence is not fully moral and has not led to arms reductions, the bishops accept Pope John Paul II's formula for deterrence as not an end in itself, but as a temporary transition to true disarmament."[20] The Catholics in the United States were confronted, in *The Challenge of Peace*, with a stance diametrically opposed to the stance of the United States government concerning the value of nuclear deterrence.

---

[19]*Challenge of Peace*, no. 138.
[20]Musto, *Catholic Peace Tradition*, 263.

Third, the American bishops praised those who practice nonviolence and commended nonviolence as the way to resolve conflicts and fend off aggression that best reflects the call of Jesus. "We believe work to develop nonviolent means of fending off aggression and resolving conflict best reflects the call of Jesus both to love and to justice. Indeed, each increase in the potential destructiveness of weapons and therefore of war serves to underline the rightness of the way that Jesus mandated to his followers."[21]

The bishops of the United States then devote an entire section of the letter to the "Value of Nonviolence." They briefly trace its history in the life of the church and indicate that the vision of Christian nonviolence is not passive or indifferent to the defense of the rights of others; they go on to cite the contributions of Mahatma Gandhi, Martin Luther King Jr., and Dorothy Day and their impact on the life of the church in the United States. The "entirely new attitude" toward war and peace recommended in *Gaudium et Spes* begins to take shape in this letter from the American Catholic bishops. They understand that the nonviolent stance is not a turning away from the world's evils and is a real alternative to violent power. They write:

> We see many deeply sincere individuals who, far from being indifferent or apathetic to world evils, believe strongly in conscience that they are best defending true peace by refusing to bear arms. In some cases they are motivated by their understanding of the Gospel and the life and death of Jesus as forbidding all violence. In others, their motivation is simply to give personal example of Christian forbearance as a positive, constructive approach to loving reconciliation with enemies. In still other cases, *they propose or engage in "active nonviolence" as programmed resistance to thwart aggression, or to render ineffective any oppression attempted by force of arms.*[22]

In other words the bishops do not equate nonviolence with pacifism—understood as simply the refusal to bear arms or fight in a war—they understand that nonviolence is another way to fight. They understand that it has been successfully used to defend, to disrupt, to

---

[21]*Challenge of Peace*, no. 78.
[22]Ibid., no. 73 (emphasis mine).

overcome, that it is another kind of power. They recognize that when people speak of an "obligation to defend" they usually mean to defend with force of arms. The bishops in the statement above acknowledge an alternative way to "defend"—using the power of nonviolent action. "Defending the innocent" or defending one's country, or defending one's way of life does not have to mean through force of arms. There is indeed an alternative.

This is a substantial step back to a gospel-based theology of peace. Not only do the bishops put forward and praise the nonviolent way, they defend it and explain it to a country that is steeped in the traditions of war and the nobility of the fighting man. They also say clearly that it is the way that best reflects the call and the teachings of Jesus.

Nonetheless, the bishops also claim the importance still of the just war theory. Although they say that the possibility of "taking even one human life is a prospect that we should consider in fear and trembling,"[23] they nonetheless confirm the Augustinian tradition that allows for the use of lethal force to prevent aggression against innocent victims—the "presumption that we do no harm, even to our enemy, yielded to the command of love understood as the need to restrain an enemy who would injure the innocent."[24] The bishops then lay out the conditions to be met in order to overcome the presumption for peace and against war—the criteria of the just war theory. The bishops then use the just war theory and its criteria—especially the criteria of proportionality and discrimination, to reason to their conclusions forbidding any use of nuclear weapons and to their strictly provisional acceptance of deterrence.

The bishops go on to say that nonviolence and just war theory are distinct but interdependent methods of evaluating warfare and are complementary to each other. They wrote: "They diverge on some specific conclusions, but they share a common presumption against the use of force as a means of settling disputes. Both find their roots in the Christian theological tradition; each contributes to the full moral vision we need in pursuit of human peace. We believe the two perspectives support and complement one another, each preserving the other from distortion."[25]

---

[23]*Challenge of Peace*, sec. C.3, no. 80.
[24]Ibid., sec. C.3, no. 81.
[25]Ibid., sec. C.2, no. 74.

This statement has caused some confusion and controversy. Some interpreters simply deny that nonviolence and the just war theory are complementary. For example, J. Milburn Thompson writes: "In actuality pacifism and just war positions are objectively opposed to one another. The bishops rightly emphasize the strong presumption against war that is at the basis of the just war position, but pacifism holds that war and violence are absolutely illegitimate. Nonviolent activists and just war adherents can walk together down the road to last resort, but once there they part company."[26]

Others can see what the bishops are trying to express. For example, David Hollenbach writes:

> The link which binds the two perspectives together and prevents them from being simply contradictory is the presumption they share against the use of force. This strong presumption against the use of force is the central thread of the Christian tradition on the morality of warfare both for individuals and for governments. . . . The suggestion that non-violence is the norm and the legitimacy of the resort to force must be seen as an exception to be justified in every case is an important new emphasis of a perspective at the heart of Catholic tradition.[27]

Hollenbach in effect understands that the just war theory and nonviolence have in fact switched positions. If in the past the just war theory was equated with the church's stance on war and peace; now nonviolence is the norm to which the just war theory is subordinated and to which it has to answer.

A third way of understanding how the bishops can promote nonviolence as more faithful to the teachings of Jesus and at the same time hold and utilize the just war theory and then call the relationship between nonviolence and the just war theory complementary is to appreciate the two different audiences the bishops are addressing and the two different "hats" the bishops are wearing—the two different voices they are using. The bishops, on the one hand, are addressing, in their role as moral leaders all the citizens of the United States, all people of

---

[26]J. Milburn Thompson, *Introducing Catholic Social Thought* (Maryknoll, NY: Orbis Books, 2010), 129.

[27]David Hollenbach, "*The Challenge of Peace* in the Context of Recent Church Teachings," in *Catholics and Nuclear War*, ed. Philip J. Murnion (New York: Crossroad, 1983), 8.

good will. On the other hand, they are also addressing a subset of the population—believing Christians. Addressing the citizenry as a whole, they use natural law thinking, assuming that if they present a reasoned argument based on solid first principles, they may have a positive effect on the debate over nuclear weapons. As moral teachers, the bishops attempt to clearly demarcate for the citizenry the line between right and wrong, where the line is between what the United States can and cannot do with its nuclear weapons. To the subset of the population, believing Christians, the bishops endorse Jesus' call to nonviolent peacemaking. The bishops recognize that Christians, believing in the way of Jesus' suffering love, may want to go much further—to build a world and culture of peace, go beyond mere self-protection to assertive works of reconciliation and restorative justice. Just war thinking establishes the floor of morality; the gospel of nonviolence calls people to go well beyond what is right—to do what is more. Nonviolence accepts the minimum floor of morality established by the just war theory, namely—do not drop a nuclear bomb—and goes on to the follow-up work of peacemaking— to push for disarmament, to establish international arbiters of compliance, to build strong grassroots movements at the societal level to demand nuclear disarmament from governments, to encourage mutual understanding across the political divides of East and West and social justice between the countries of the North and South, and so on. They are complementary in that the one provides the floor for the other to build on.

In section 3 of the letter, nos. 223–30, the bishops spell out some of the practical applications that could and should come to pass as a result of their giving nonviolence such pride of place—everything from training in nonviolent civilian defense, the development of a US Academy of Peace, the development of university-level peace programs of interdisciplinary research, education, and training, especially at Catholic universities, and the teaching of nonviolent conflict resolution in primary schools across the country. One senses just how dynamic and creative would be a consistent embrace by the church of the power and potential of nonviolence and what might happen if the church turned its full attention to peacemaking as the central vocation of all Christians.

If the *Challenge of Peace* in 1983 accepted and featured nonviolence as a legitimate choice for individuals, the document issued ten years later on the anniversary of *Challenge of Peace,* would take the church one additional step closer to its earliest tradition of nonviolence.

**1993: *The Harvest of Justice*: A Follow-up Letter
on the Tenth Anniversary of *The Challenge of Peace*
by the National Conference of Catholic Bishops of the United States**

On the tenth anniversary of *The Challenge of Peace*, the National Conference of Catholic Bishops established a second subcommittee to update what had been written in *The Challenge of Peace*. Once again people were in place who made a real difference. Drew Christiansen, SJ, a noted scholar of social justice, who through much of the 1990s was the director of the United States Catholic Conference's Office of International Justice and Peace, served as staff to the committee. Once again, Cardinal Bernardin chaired the group, and the committee brought in a number of experts to advise them. This time they asked not just Catholic moral theologians for their input. According to Father Christiansen they also asked John Howard Yoder, an eminent Mennonite theologian teaching at the University of Notre Dame who had published a groundbreaking book, *The Politics of Jesus*, and other important works elucidating a deep understanding of the scriptures and the nonviolent peacemaking modeled by his Mennonite tradition, and Gene Sharp of the Einstein Institute who had written many works documenting the theory and practice of successful nonviolent action, including *Waging Nonviolent Struggles* and *The Politics of Nonviolent Action*. Gene Sharp's writings were later used as blueprints for action by the successful Otpor revolution in Serbia against Milosevic and the Arab Spring revolutions in Tunisia and Egypt.

By 1993, the world had recently witnessed a good part of the earth changed through the power of nonviolent struggle. The former Soviet Union had been fragmented through individual nonviolent revolutions in East Germany, Poland, and Czechoslovakia. The Philippines had nonviolently overcome a dictator, and South Africa an apartheid regime. No one could miss at this point in history the epoch-making power of nonviolent action.

The first contribution of *Harvest of Justice* is to accentuate the call of Christians as peacemakers. The bishops begin their letter with reflections on the spirituality of peacemaking. Again the emphasis is not on pacifism but on peacemaking, not on simply saying no to war and violence but embracing the vocation to build a world and culture of positive peace. "Part of the legacy of the *Challenge of Peace* is the call to strengthen peacemaking as an essential dimension of our faith, remind us that Jesus called us to be peacemakers."[28]

Second, the bishops expanded the scope of nonviolence from a merely personal option to an option for states and public bodies. It is perhaps no surprise that, given the signs of the times, and the presence of special advisers such as John Howard Yoder and Gene Sharp, that the bishops expanded their understanding of the potential for nonviolent action: "Although nonviolence has often been regarded as simply a personal option or vocation, recent history suggests that in some circumstances it can be an effective public undertaking as well. Dramatic political transitions in places as diverse as the Philippines and Eastern Europe demonstrate the power of nonviolent action, even against dictatorial and totalitarian regimes."[29]

Father Christiansen reflected on the development of the *Harvest of Justice* statement at a meeting on peacebuilding at the University of Notre Dame in 2009. He said that, when they were done, Cardinal Bernardin looked at him and said—concerning this expanded appreciation for the nonviolent option as an option for public bodies and not just individuals—"We have definitely moved the discussion and the teaching a step forward."

Up to 2013: The Teachings of Pope John Paul II, Pope Benedict XVI, and Pope Francis

Both Pope John Paul II and Pope Benedict XVI have continued to echo these main themes that bring the church back to its earliest tradition of peacemaking and the virtue of nonviolent action.

On the positive definition of peace Pope John Paul II, in a homily at Covington England in 1982, said: "Peace is not just the absence of war. It involves mutual respect and confidence between people and nations. It involves collaboration and binding agreements. Like a cathedral, peace must be constructed patiently and with unshakeable faith."[30]

On the link between peace and the enjoyment of human rights Pope John Paul II said in his World Day of Peace message in 1982 and in

---

[28]*Harvest of Justice*, Introduction.
[29]Ibid., sec. B, no. 1.
[30]John Paul II, "Homily at Bagington Airport, Coventry, 2, *Origins* 12 (1982): 55.

his address to the General Assembly of the United Nations in 1979: "Unconditional and effective respect for each one's unprescriptable and inalienable rights is the necessary condition in order that peace may reign in a society. . . . In a society in which these rights are not protected, the very idea of universality is dead as soon as a small group of individuals set up for their own exclusive advantage, a principle of discrimination whereby the rights and even the lives of others are made dependent on the whim of the stronger."[31]

Pope John Paul was intimately involved with the Polish people in their Solidarity struggles—through his words, actions, and visits. He could not help but be overwhelmed by what nonviolent action accomplished for his own people. He recognized the power of nonviolence as a fruitful and still to be explored alternative to violence.

On the power and potential of nonviolence, Pope John Paul II wrote: "It seemed that the European order resulting from the Second World War . . . could only be overturned by another war. Instead, it has been overcome by the nonviolent commitment of people who, while always refusing to yield to the force of power, succeeded time after time in finding effective ways of bearing witness to the truth."[32]

In the Introduction some of the striking recent sayings by Pope Benedict XVI on nonviolence in the life of Jesus have already been quoted. They are worth repeating here. In 2007 Pope Benedict XVI said:

> Above all we want to make the voice of Jesus heard. He was always a man of peace. It could be expected that, when God came to earth, he would be a man of great power, destroying the opposing forces. That he would be a man of powerful violence as an instrument of peace. Not at all. He came in weakness. He came with only the strength of love, totally without violence, even to point of going to the cross. This is what shows the true face of God, that violence never comes from God, never helps bring anything good, but is a destructive means and not the path to escape difficulties. . . . This is Jesus' true message: seek peace with the means of peace and leave violence aside.[33]

---

[31]John Paul II, "World Day of Peace Message, 1982," 9, cited.
[32]John Paul II, in *Centesimus Annus, On the Hundredth Anniversary of Rerum Novarum*, no. 23.
[33]Pope Benedict XVI, *Midday Angelus*, 2007.

On nonviolence as the keystone of the Christian revolution and discipleship, Pope Benedict in 2011 said:

Love your enemies. . . . This page of the Gospel is rightly considered the *"magna carta"* of Christian nonviolence; it does not consist in surrendering to evil—as claims a false interpretation of "turn the other cheek" (Luke 6:29)—but in responding to evil with good (Romans 12:17-21), and thus breaking the chain of injustice. It is thus understood that nonviolence for Christians, is not mere tactical behavior but a person's way of being, the attitude of one who is convinced of God's love and power, who is not afraid to confront evil with the weapons of love and truth alone. Loving the enemy is the nucleus of the "Christian revolution."[34]

In an address to the faithful gathered in St. Peter's square in 2013, Pope Francis said: "The true force of the Christian is the force of truth and of love, which means rejecting all violence. Faith and violence are incompatible! Faith and violence are incompatible! But faith and strength go together. The Christian is not violent but he is strong. And with what strength? That of meekness, the force of meekness, the force of love."[35]

In summary, ever since John XXIII's encyclical *Pacem in Terris* in 1963, the Catholic Church has step by step come back to its precious heritage of Jesus' nonviolence and his call to peacemaking. At the Second Vatican Council, in 1965, in *Gaudium et Spes*, the church legitimated conscientious objection and for the first time in a document of an ecumenical council praised those who choose the way of nonviolence. The American Catholic bishops went even further in their instruction of 1983, *The Challenge of Peace*. They recognized nonviolence as an effective way to use power—effective for protecting people from oppression, for overturning dictatorial regimes, and overcoming injustice, racial and otherwise. They put it forward as the approach most faithful to the teaching of Jesus and spelled out some of the implications for peacemaking that would come with an adoption of a nonviolent way of life. In 1993, the tenth anniversary

---

[34]Pope Benedict XVI, *Good Friday Sermon*, 2011.
[35]Pope Francis, *Homily before the Angelus*, at St. Peter's Square, August 18, 2013.

of *The Challenge of Peace*, the American Catholic bishops issued *The Harvest of Justice*. In it they celebrated the successful nonviolent campaigns that had changed the face of the earth over the previous five years—the revolutions in Eastern Europe, the Philippines, and South Africa—and they suggested that nonviolence was an appropriate stance for public bodies—not just individuals—to take to confront evil and combat injustice. Finally the recent popes, John Paul II, Benedict XVI, and Francis in their pastoral preaching hold up nonviolence as the ideal way of life for Christians precisely because it was the way of Jesus—even to the cross. They point us back to the way the early church practiced it and how the early Church Fathers taught it. They summon all Christians to be peacemakers. If the Catholic Church cannot technically be called a "peace church" yet—in the same way as the traditional peace churches, Mennonites, Quakers, and the Disciples of Christ, can be called "peace churches"—at least it has clearly become a "peacemaking" church. The church is once again calling its members to be peacemakers and to explore and practice the virtue of nonviolence.

In the following and final chapter I explain the components of a gospel-based theology of peace, suggest peacemaking practices that flow from a gospel-based theology of peace, and offer examples of a gospel-based theology of peace in action.

7

A Gospel-based Theology of Peace

Until relatively recently, Catholic moral theology was leery of using the gospels to elucidate a theology of peace. It was felt that the gospels did not and could not give detailed moral guidance for complicated contemporary problems. Suspicious of biblical fundamentalism, it turned to other sources to found its thinking on peace and war. In his book *Tranquilitas Ordinis,* for example, George Weigel quoted the great Jesuit theologian, John Courtney Murray, about his introduction to the issues of morality and foreign policy:

> My introduction to the state of the problem took place . . . in a conversation with a distinguished journalist who is now dead. In public affairs he was immensely knowledgeable; he was also greatly puzzled over the new issue that was being raised. What he asked, has the Sermon on the Mount got to do with foreign policy? I was a little taken aback by this statement of the issue. What, I asked, makes you think that morality is identical with the Sermon on the Mount?[1]

The assumption was that the exigencies of the age would be better served through cool reasoning than evangelical fervor. As a result, the traditional Catholic moral theology approach was to use reason to reflect on the natural law, abstract some universal principles, and then apply those principles to contemporary situations.

In recent times, however, a more refined and robust approach to

---

[1]John Courtney Murray, *We Hold These Truths: Catholic Reflections on the American Proposition* (New York: Doubleday Image Books, 1964), 262, as quoted in George Weigel, *Tranquilitas Ordinis* (New York: Oxford University Press, 1987), 25.

the gospels and how they can inform our thinking and action—even on contemporary issues of war, terrorism, and peace—has taken hold among scholars. This new hermeneutic is, however, far from biblical fundamentalism. This approach stems from two sources: historical Jesus studies and a fuller understanding of the meaning of classical texts.

Historical Jesus Studies

Biblical scholarship's increasingly in-depth understanding of the cultural, economic, political, and religious milieus of Jesus' time has led Christian theology to focus not first on Jesus the Christ, but first on Jesus of Nazareth, the flesh-and-blood human being, and Jesus' life—the way he lived and confronted the evils of his time, the way he struggled to renew his Jewish faith, the way he resisted the temptation to the violence of his time, and the way that he pulled people together into a nonexclusive community. The way Jesus lived is paradigmatic for Christians. This Christology is intent on presenting an accurate historical representation of Jesus in his own context. It is a Christology, as Karl Rahner described it, "from below."[2] It begins with Jesus of Nazareth and finds in his humanity, on through his resurrection, the revelation of his divinity. This is in contrast to traditional Christology, which unfolded from above, beginning with an understanding of an exalted Christ as presented in the Johannine tradition, and then accounted for his humanity. The monumental two-volume work of Edward Schillebeeckx, is representative of this Christology from below. He begins with a careful understanding of the New Testament texts in their historical context in *Jesus*,[3] and then in *Christ*[4] develops a narrative Christology that brings the biblical witness into dialogue with contemporary situations and problems. The work of Jon Sobrino is another important example of a Christology from below. In his *Christology at the Crossroads*[5] he interprets the events of Jesus' life as demonstrations of liberating people from their suffering and then brings those actions into dialogue with the plight of social injustice in Latin America.

---

[2]Karl Rahner, "The Two Basic Types of Christology," in *Theological Investigations*, vol. 13 (New York: Seabury Press, 1975), 213–23.

[3]Edward Schillebeeckx, *Jesus: An Experiment in Christology* (New York: Seabury Press, 1979).

[4]Edward Schilebeeckx, *Christ: The Experience of Jesus as Lord* (New York: Seabury Press, 1980).

[5]Jon Sobrino, *Christology at the Crossroads* (Maryknoll, NY: Orbis Books, 1978).

Such a Christology from below with its emphasis on Jesus' humanity and his real-life struggles to resist evil and bring a positive peace to his world is a very different starting point for constructing a theology of peace than an approach that begins with a study of natural law in the spirit of Cicero. In fact to the degree that theology is understood as reflection on the revelation given to us through the scriptures and especially the gospel portraits of Jesus, it is hard to see that traditional just war theory is theology at all—given a methodology that does not begin with the gospels. As Mary Evelyn Jegen puts it, "In general, it is accurate to say that a theology of positive peace, as distinct from a moral theology dealing with guidance about participation in war, resonates with an ascending Christology, a Christology from below, that puts the accent on the humanity of Jesus and his historical experience without prejudice to the mystery of his divinity."[6]

An Enriched Understanding of How Past Texts Can Provide Meaning for Present Concerns

For contemporary biblical scholarship the meaning of biblical texts is not confined to the meaning the author intended when the text was written. Whenever new questions are posed to the tradition, in some measure new answers will be given. New meaning will be found. As Sandra Schneiders expresses it:

> The scholar interprets the text as always speaking in the present because of the transcendent and ever-active power which can be found in all classical texts and *a fortiori* in the scriptures which are our primary witness to divine revelation. . . . There seems to be a move away from moral reasoning based on a somewhat static theology that uses God's creation as the framework . . . an unchanging natural law from which we can deduce what is acceptable behavior. The transition is toward a more dynamic theology of salvation in which Jesus . . . is seen as the primary expression of a new humanity.[7]

---

[6]Mary Evelyn Jegen, "Peace and Pluralism," in *One Hundred Years of Catholic Social Thought*, ed. John A. Coleman, SJ (Maryknoll, NY: Orbis Books, 1991), 290.

[7]Sandra M. Schneiders, "New Testament Reflections on Peace and Nuclear Arms," in *Catholics and Nuclear War*, ed. Philip J. Murnion (New York: Crossroad, 1983), 94–95.

This new emphasis on the importance of placing the scriptural text in dialogue with the "signs of the times" and letting the meaning of the scriptures emerge afresh is why the participants at the Second Vatican Council said that the encounter between the word of God and the realities of twentieth-century existence compelled them to "undertake an evaluation of war with an entirely new attitude."[8]

The "sign of the times" that was at the forefront of their minds at the time of the council was the looming threat of nuclear weapons on the world, the potential for omnicide, the destruction of the entire human race, and the MAD ("mutually assured destruction") stance of the contending super powers. The twentieth century had been the bloodiest in human history, and it seemed at the time that it just might get even worse.

There is, however, another important sign of the times that, put in dialogue with the sacred scriptures, also prompts an entirely "new attitude" toward the issues of war and peace. This sign of the times is a profoundly positive one. It is the fact of Gandhi and what his discovery of *satyagraha*[9] has come to mean for the world.

The witnesses to the importance of this sign of the times are many and varied. Leo Tolstoy wrote a letter to Gandhi way back in 1910, the last letter of his life, telling Gandhi that what he was doing in South Africa with his *satyagraha* campaign was the most important thing for the future of humanity going on in the world at the time.[10] Hannah Arendt, the eminent political theorist, has written that the theory and practice of nonviolence is the most important political theory discovery of the twentieth century.[11] Andre Trocme, the pastor of the church in Chambon, France, that saved thousands of Jews under the noses of the Nazis during the Second World War wrote:

---

[8] *Gaudium et Spes,* no. 80.

[9] Satyagraha is Gandhi's term. It literally means "holding strongly to the truth." It has also been translated as "soul force." It refers to his method of fighting evil and injustice with loving, nonviolent, willing-to-suffer power—using mass, collaborative action. For a full explanation of this all-important concept and technique of action, a synthesis of Eastern and Western thought, see the chapter on satyagraha in my book *Gandhi and Jesus: The Saving Power of Nonviolence* (Maryknoll, NY: Orbis Books, 2008).

[10] Leo Tolstoy, letter of September 7, 1910: "Your work in Transvaal, which seems to be far away from the center of our world, is yet the most fundamental and the most important to us." As quoted in Rajmohan Gandhi, *Gandhi: The Man, His People, and the Empire* (Berkeley: University of California Press, 2008), 143.

[11] Hannah Arendt, as quoted by Michael True in "Defining Nonviolence: Sharp's Dictionary," *Peace Chronicles* (Spring–Summer 2012): 10.

The coming of Mahatma Gandhi, whose life and teaching surprisingly resemble those of Jesus, revived the whole issue of nonviolence just when majority theology thought it had already answered the question negatively. . . . Gandhi showed that the Sermon on the Mount can be politically effective.[12]

Martin Luther King Jr. has written:

Gandhi was probably the first person in history to lift the love ethic of Jesus above mere interaction between individuals to a powerful and effective force on a large scale. Love for Gandhi was a potent instrument for social and collective transformation. It was in this Gandhian emphasis on love and nonviolence that I discovered the method of social reform. . . . Gandhi resisted evil with as much vigor and power as the violent resister, but he resisted with love instead of hate.[13]

The reason why Gandhi is such an important sign of the times is that he and those who have followed in his spirit have revealed tellingly and clearly that there is another kind of power loose in the world—the power of collaborative nonviolent action—a power truer and more effective than violence. The assumption at work in the world through the centuries was that the only way to protect the innocent, defend one's country, overcome oppression, or defeat a tyrant, was—when it came right down to it—the power of the sword, the power of the bigger gun. As much as we have hated to admit it, our deeper unspoken belief has been that one has to stand up to bullies and the only way to do that effectively is to put them down. As the common wisdom has it, if you want peace, prepare for war. Gandhi and those who have followed in his train over the last sixty years have demonstrated time and again that there is another way more effective than violence, more lasting than violence, a way that breaks the iron cycle of violence in which humanity has been caught.

That realization has been played out dramatically before us over

---

[12]Andre Trocme, *Jesus and the Nonviolent Revolution* (Maryknoll, NY: Orbis Books, 2004), 153, 156.

[13]Martin Luther King Jr., *Stride toward Freedom* (New York: Harper and Brothers, 1958), 97–98.

the last sixty years, but it is still hard for many of us to believe—given the deep culture of violence that we have grown up in.

We have seen Solidarity in Poland grow into a free trade union of ten million members through concerted nonviolent action, enduring martial law, and staying the course, withstanding the threat of Soviet tanks and staying together—until the government that had lost all citizen support came crumbling down. We saw their courage. We saw their creativity. We saw their careful organization. We saw their tenacity in the face of great odds. We saw their joy in facing down violence and defeating it through their nonviolent spirits and nonviolent strategies. We saw that there is indeed a power more powerful than the gun.

We saw the rapid progress that the liberation movement in South Africa generated once it had given up violent rebellion and turned to a disciplined, willing-to-suffer nonviolent movement. How the evil of apartheid became all too obvious to the world and even to many of the White citizens of South Africa. We saw, when so many feared a bloodbath, the creative, nonviolent way the people of South Africa achieved reconciliation through their Truth and Justice Commission. As long as people admitted to their violent deeds, as long as those who were on the receiving end of the violence had a chance to tell their stories and get their bitterness and lingering sense of injustice out in the bright light of day, people could begin to put behind their anger and build together a new South Africa.

We have witnessed the people power of the Philippines that united to resist the tyranny and corruption of the dictator Ferdinand Marcos and his cronies in power. As he sought to steal an election from Cory Aquino, thousands of poll watchers who had been carefully trained in the principles and techniques of nonviolent action foiled his efforts. When a faction of the army rebelled against Marcos he sent the rest of his army to crush them. The populace was called by Cardinal Sin of Manila to come and stand unarmed between the two factions of the army. Nuns gave the soldiers loyal to Marcos rosaries. Young women gave them flowers. A million people turned out to resist Marcos's faction nonviolently. Marcos gave the orders to his army to fire on the people. He gave orders to his air force to bomb them. His orders were refused. He was revealed as a man who had no power. The people had taken it from him nonviolently. He was out of the country in two weeks. The real power, as Gandhi taught, belonged to the people. Once they decided not to cooperate in evil any longer and once they stood together in their nonviolent power, violence was rendered limp and ineffectual.

It is not necessary to repeat all the great stories of nonviolent action over the last sixty years—the heroic civil rights movement and the saga of the farmworkers in our own country, the Orange Revolution, the Velvet Revolution, the Otpor movement in Serbia that threw out the "butcher of the Balkans," the Arab Spring. What is important is that we recognize this new and mighty alternative to violence that has been unleashed for us. Gandhi rightly serves as a flesh-and-blood symbol of this power. He was confident that many would come after him to use and refine and perfect this power—he said it was as electricity was at the time of Edison. No one quite understood electricity and its power back then, and all the ways it could be used were not apparent, but it would become ever more effective and useful. So also with the power of nonviolent action.

Gandhi then becomes an important "sign of the times." The scriptures read with Gandhi and the great stories of effective nonviolent action in mind will give us new perspectives into the meaning of the scriptures. Reading the scriptures this way will allow us to understand violence and war with an "entirely new attitude." Gandhi gives us a new lens with which to read the scriptures and understand the life of Jesus. New situations bring new questions to the scriptures, and in turn the scriptures provide us new answers.

Jesus' Life as Normative for a Theology of Peace

How do we know how to think about and act as Christians when it comes to issues of war and peace and violence? We first follow the arc of Jesus' life and determine if and how he confronted similar situations and issues. If he did face similar issues and if he did show us a way to face them, then that is our first clue as to how we must act.

Tracing the arc of Jesus' life reveals that he was an ardent, dedicated peacemaker. Peace in this context is not a negative peace. In chapter 6 I described the difference between a negative and positive peace. A negative peace is simply the absence of war and violence. As in— peace is had when the fighting stops; peace as the interlude between wars; peace as "*gewaltlosigkeit*," the absence of war. A positive peace, in contrast, is best described and translated, when used in the New Testament, by the word "*shalom*." *Shalom* is a very rich and resonant word as used in the scriptures. It means at one and the same time—relief from oppression and suffering, overflowing life, both in terms of fulfillment of potential and plenitude of health and well-being, and smiling relationships between people within community.

As discussed in chapter 3 the early Fathers of the Church rejoiced that the message of *shalom* that they read in Isaiah and Micah had come true through Jesus in the way he lived and loved, which is the way they were living and why they were having such a profound influence on the empire. One after another the Fathers found in those quotations a way to express what they were experiencing. They all quoted Isaiah and Micah: swords are turned into plowshares and spears into pruning hooks, and each person sits under his or her own vines and fig tree—an image that symbolizes harmony as well as plenitude. Securing a positive peace means focusing on the underlying causes of war and violence and fixing those causes. Securing a positive peace means supplanting a culture of war with a culture of peace. Building a positive peace means reconciling peoples who have been sundered and disfigured from extended violence and finding ways to heal those wounds and bring the people together. Securing a positive peace means finding the ways to bring authentic human development so people can live in harmony and plenitude. As significant and important as it is to end a war, that is typically just the beginning of what needs to happen. A full, positive peace is the work of, and the challenge that awaits, peacemakers.

Reflecting on the challenge of bringing positive peace into a society, it seems there are at least four directions the peacemaker needs to pursue, four challenges that peacemakers need to meet. They are the following: First, in their fight to build a positive peace, peacemakers have to do all they can to relieve the suffering that results from oppression. There is no positive peace when people are under the bootheel of oppression and cowering in fear of violence. Second, peacemakers are called to address and change the structures of evil and oppression that keep people in line. Structural evil extends beyond the evil that people do; it extends to institutions and cultural norms and habits that harden injustices in place. Those institutions, cultural norms, and habits need to be changed for there to be positive peace. Third, peacemakers must turn enemies into friends. There is no lasting, positive peace if enmity still reigns between peoples. Especially when there has been long-lasting violence between people—memories are long, stories are told and retold, vengeance is just beneath the surface—the task of building trust and achieving reconciliation is herculean. In a time of terrorism and blind outbursts of counterviolence, and then counter-counterviolence, the cycle becomes more and more difficult to break. The fourth important task of the peacemaker is to work at the cultural level to change cultural norms concerning peace and war and violence. Full, positive peace endures in a culture of peace. That requires an alternative community to demonstrate peaceful practices. As long as people continue to devote great resources to be ready for violence and war, they will get war. As long as they are constantly looking out for and expecting the next attack, the next slight, the next affront from outside their inner circle, they will find those affronts and remain stuck in a culture of violence. Positive peace will elude them.

In chapters 1 and 2, I reviewed Jesus' life and teaching. I summarize those findings here to see again how Jesus took on the challenges of peacemaking. He gave his followers a vivid sense of how to confront the issues of peace, war, and violence. A theology of peace can and should rest on the life and teachings of Jesus.

Tracing the arc of his life, we find that it was framed and filled with the message of peace (*shalom*). At his birth the angels sang to the shepherds a song and message of peace—"peace [*shalom*] on earth, good will to men." At the end, after his resurrection, he came to the apostles who had deserted him and announced the message of peace. "Peace [*shalom*] is what I leave with you; it is my own peace that I give you; I do not give it as the world does. Do not be worried and upset; do not be afraid" (John 14:27). In the middle of his public life the explicit purpose for which he commissions his disciples, when he sent them out to the villages of Galilee, is peace. "Into whatever house you enter, first say 'Peace [*shalom*] to this house' " (Luke 10:5).

First, Jesus battled as hard as he could to overcome the evils and oppression that bound and prostrated the people of his time. The main hardships suffered by his people were first, economic injustice—the result of the system set up by the powers that be, starting with the taxes levied by Rome, coupled with the exaction of multiple taxes and tithes for the priests and the Temple and the taxes paid to support the local kings in their mad desire to curry favor with Rome. As a result of this economic injustice, many were thrown off their lands and forced into penal servitude. Those at the top of the social structure, especially the high priest and the priestly class, enriched themselves at the expense of the rest of the population—even using their Temple police, or, as Josephus described them, "thugs," to steal grain from the peasants. Second, through a perverted reading of their religious tradition a huge portion of the populace was treated as outcasts by their own religious leaders. Third, people suffered from disease both physical and mental.

Jesus, in opposition to the economic injustice, revived the Deuteronomic jubilee teaching of compassion for those who were the weakest and poorest—especially the orphans, the widows, and the sojourners. The jubilee tradition provided for food for the poor and restoration of land and freedom for those in servitude. He took the side of the poor and warned and invited the rich to change their ways. In the teeth of fierce opposition he battled the scribes and Pharisees on their interpretation of the Torah, the Sabbath, and the Temple. He pointed out the inclusive nature of their religion. He endured the scorn of the society leaders and practiced what he preached by eating with, socializing with, and inviting people society leaders labeled as unclean and outcast to be part of his inner circle of disciples. He showed compassion for the confused, depressed, and ill with an aggressive ministry of healings and exorcisms.

There may not have been full-scale war in Jesus' time, but there was hardly positive peace in the land. Instead, there was seething resentment and injustice. And hanging over the heads of the populace was the constant threat of the sword and worse, crucifixion, for those who fought the system. The first job of the peacemaker is to resist injustice. Jesus did what he could. Walter Wink concluded that "Jesus resisted evil with every fiber of his being."[14]

On this front Gandhi's life and actions offer some illumination. The focus of his satyagraha campaign in India was from the beginning more than a campaign to bring political freedom to India, independence from Britain. Gandhi understood *swaraj,* an ancient Indian word that meant much more than mere political independence, to be their goal. *Swaraj* meant full freedom, freedom from covetousness, freedom to act in harmony with others, freedom to serve and uplift the poor, freedom from want and hunger. He constantly reminded his followers of the fuller meaning of *swaraj.* He warned that if they did not aim

---

[14]Walter Wink, *Engaging the Powers: Discernment and Resistance in a World of Domination* (Minneapolis: Fortress Press, 1992), 113.

at real, full freedom when they were free from Britain, they ran the risk of falling into the same patterns as the British in their rule of the country and would end up trading one tyranny for another. With that in mind the preponderance of Gandhi's time and political organizing was his constructive program—the uplift of the million impoverished villages of India, instilling a spirit of fearless self-improvement. As Gandhi said, "My real politics is constructive work."[15] His aim was a full, positive peace for India.

Second, Jesus not only resisted the injustices of his time, he also went after the structures that embodied unjust cultural norms and attitudes. Jesus attacked the way the Torah had become a tool for ostracizing people, fomented a spirit of hatred for outsiders and, through the hundreds of rules governing food, had become another way to squeeze money from the poor. Jesus went to Jerusalem to oppose the way the Temple institution had become a place that sat at the pinnacle of a system that robbed the poor. "You have made my Father's house a den of thieves" (Luke 19:46). Even the sacred Sabbath had been made into an oppressive institution—people were afraid to do even the most obvious good for others for fear of violating the Sabbath. The fundamental problem that Jesus had with the institutions of his time was that the religion he cherished and had come to fulfill, instead of fostering a spirit of compassion, justice, and inclusiveness, had become a buttress and pillar of a terribly unjust social and economic system that systematically transferred wealth from the peasant class to the priestly and royal class. There can be no positive peace if the institutions of society have injustice baked into them.

Gandhi too risked his life to change the institutions in India that were, in effect, structures of evil. The institution of the "untouchables," the Harijan, as he called them, "the beloved of God," has existed in Hinduism and in India from time immemorial. They are the lowest class, set apart, deemed suitable only for such activities as carrying out night soil and cleaning latrines. Gandhi said: "I believe implicitly that all men are born equal. Untouchability has to be rooted out completely."[16] He labored unceasingly to bring the untouchables into a place of respect-

---

[15]Gandhi, as quoted in Michael Nagler, *Is There No Other Way?* (Berkeley, CA: Berkeley Hills Books, 2001), 146.

[16]Quoted in J. T. F. Jordens, *Gandhi's Religion: An Interpretation* (New York: Palgrave, 1998), 114.

ability. He even conducted a fast unto death to make sure they were treated fairly in the emerging laws of the new India. He came a whisper away from death before laws were written to his satisfaction.

Third, Jesus not only taught that we should love our enemies, he worked very hard to turn enemies into friends by removing the sources of misunderstanding between himself and the scribes and Pharisees who saw him as their enemy. He used many approaches to bring them along. As shown in chapter 1, at times he entered into vigorous debate with the Pharisees. Other times he answered the questions intended to trap him with clever, straightforward answers, which prompted admiration from his questioners. In one instance, when some scribes of the Pharisee party saw him eating with tax collectors and, in their mind, sinners, they said to his disciples: "Why does he eat with tax collectors and sinners?" (Mark 2:16). Jesus overheard them, but he did not respond with anger or denunciation or with halakhic disputation. In this situation, he took another approach—he invited them to look at the situation more deeply, and he patiently clarified what he did and "why he did it in order to help his critics understand the meaning of his actions," as Thomas Schubeck writes.[17] Jesus responded: "It is not the healthy who need the doctor, but the sick. I came to call not the upright, but sinners" (Mark 2:17). At other times he tried to shame his critics and have them reconsider their approach, as when he reminded them of their acceptance of *korban*, the dedication of funds to the Temple that allowed people to be free of their obligation to care for their elderly parents. As Benedict XVI wrote: "He made impassioned efforts to elicit from the Holy City a positive response to the message he must proclaim."[18]

The Samaritans were inveterate enemies of the Jews, dating back to the time of Alexander the Great, who had given them permission to build their own temple on Mount Gerizim. Political and religious issues kept them in enmity with one another. Not only did Jesus reach out to the Samaritan woman at the well, he held up a Samaritan as the loving hero in his tale of the Good Samaritan. Jesus urges active, converting love of enemies. As Miroslav Volf wrote: "At the heart of the cross is Christ's stance of not letting the enemy remain an enemy

---

[17]Thomas L. Schubeck, *Love That Does Justice* (Maryknoll, NY: Orbis Books, 2007), 57.
[18]Benedict XVI, *Jesus of Nazareth* (San Francisco: Ignatius Press, 2011), 24.

. . . the victim who refuses to be defined by the perpetrator."[19] Even on the cross he said, "Father, forgive them, for they know not what they do" (Luke 23:34).

Gandhi saw this element of Jesus' praxis very clearly. He said in 1920: "Buddha and Christ were for intensely direct action. But even as Buddha and Christ chastised, they showed unmistakable gentleness and love behind every act of theirs."[20]

Gandhi in South Africa and later in India labored to make his opponents his friends—through demonstrating his respect for them and consistently showing kindness to them. General Smuts in South Africa and the Viceroy of India, Lord Irwin, became very close friends with Gandhi. As General Smuts's secretary wrote: "I do not like your people, and do not care to assist them at all. But what am I to do? You help us in our days of need. How can we lay hands upon you? I often wish you took to violence like the English strikers, and then we would know at once how to dispose of you. But you will not injure even the enemy. You desire victory by self-suffering alone . . . and that is what reduces us to sheer helplessness."[21]

Another peacemaker in the Gandhi and Jesus tradition, Martin Luther King Jr., insisted that love was the only force capable of transforming an enemy into a friend. King wrote: "We never get rid of any enemy by meeting hate with hate; we get rid of an enemy by getting rid of enmity. By its very nature, hate destroys and tears down; by its very nature, love creates and builds up. Love transforms with redemptive power."[22]

Fourth, Jesus worked to supplant the culture of violence that was taking deep root in the hearts of his people and substitute for it a culture of peace. As we have seen, Israel at the time of Jesus was seething with anger. Jesus could see what was developing—a headlong rush into violent rebellion against the occupying power, Rome. He predicted that his countrymen would bring upon themselves a time of great desolation. The Temple and their whole country would be destroyed if they kept nursing violence in their souls. He tried to instill in them

---

[19]Miroslav Volf, *Exclusion and Embrace* (Nashville, TN: Abingdon Press, 1996), 126.

[20]Mohandas Gandhi, quoted in *Gandhi's Experiments with Truth*, ed. Richard Johnson (Lanham, MD: Lexington Books, 2006), 120.

[21]Mohandas Gandhi, *The Collected Works of Mahatma Gandhi* (New Delhi: Publications Division, Ministry of Information and Broadcasting, 1958-95), 34:267 [hereinafter CWMG].

[22]Martin Luther King Jr., *Strength to Love* (New York: Harper and Row, 1963), 46.

an alternative to violent rebellion, a way of suffering love, a way of courageous, nonviolent resistance to violence and domination.

James Douglass writes, "The fundamental purpose of his life—to save the city and its people from destruction—the city that Jesus wept over."[23] Many of Jesus' countrymen refused to listen to his message. The culture of violence continued to intensify until, in the year 66 CE, they rose up in violent rebellion against Rome. All factions entered into the fray, including the Pharisees and the Essenes. Rome crushed them and step by step obliterated their Temple and their country, including the last-stand hideout at Masada. The weeping and desolation Jesus foretold came to pass. One group did understand and began to live out his message. The band of people who refused to enter into the fighting would later be called Christians. According to Josephus, they removed themselves entirely from the fray and moved to the city of Pella across the Jordan. That group, as shown in chapter 3 on the early church, practiced and nurtured a culture of peace, and their numbers continued to grow because of the attraction of their nonviolent, loving lifestyle. It grew into a religion professed by the majority of the people of the empire. The way of Jesus proved to be more powerful than the culture of violence. In the words of K. S. Latourette, a leading historian of the period:

> Never in so short a time has any other religious faith, or, for that matter, any other set of ideas, religious, political or economic, without the aid of physical force or of social or cultural prestige, achieved so commanding a position in such an important culture . . . even as their rulers spared no cruelty in the ten major persecutions which were launched against Christians. Under Nero, Christians were torn by dogs or nailed to crosses and set on fire at night to serve as living torches.[24]

Gandhi is well known for inspiring an entire nation to resist calls for violent revolution and instead participate in a nonviolent resistance

---

[23]James Douglass, *The Nonviolent Coming of God* (Eugene, OR: Wipf and Stock, 2006), 118.

[24]K. S. Latourette, *A History of the Expansion of Christianity*, vol. 1: *The First Five Centuries* (New York: Harper and Brothers, 1937), 369, as quoted by Lawrence Espy, "How Transforming Power Has Been Used in the Past by Early Christians," in *Nonviolence in Theory and Practice*, ed. Robert Holmes and Barry Gan (Long Grove, IL: Waveland Press, 2005), 33–35.

movement for freedom and for building, to support the movement, a culture of positive peace. After the Salt March in 1930, hundreds of thousands people of all ages and classes participated in the civil resistance movement, making salt, boycotting British cloth and liquor, risking violent retribution and jail. Tens of thousands filled the jails, and going to jail became a badge of honor instead of a stigma. All was done nonviolently.

Not as well known was Gandhi's Muslim compatriot, Abdul Ghaffar Khan, who organized and led history's first nonviolent army in the part of India called then the Northwest Territories, the mountainous area on the border between what is now Pakistan and Afghanistan. The hundred-thousand-member army consisted of young Pashtuns, a tribe with a long history of assertive violence when crossed. This army of young Muslims was totally committed to nonviolence, inspired by the Koran and influenced by Gandhi's thought. They served their people by building schools, promoted a culture of positive peace while, at the same time, entering wholeheartedly into the nonviolent campaign against British rule. Khan wrote: "There is nothing surprising in a Muslim or a Pathan [Pashtun] like me subscribing to the creed of nonviolence. It is not a new creed. It was followed fourteen hundred years ago by the Prophet all the time he was in Mecca. . . . But we had so far forgotten it that when Gandhiji placed it before us, we thought he was sponsoring a novel creed."[25]

Within the living memory of many people today, great swaths of people have had their cultures of violence changed to cultures of positive, risk-taking peace. It does not happen just in a Bible story. It happens in history—in our time.

This brief review of Jesus' life underlines how central peacemaking was to his mission. It shows us that Jesus modeled a way to think about and act on the issues of war, peace, and violence. That way is called the way of the cross. He said many times to his followers: "If any one wants to come with me, he must forget himself, take up his cross every day, and follow" (Luke 9:23). A Christian theology of peace begins with that call to peacemaking. Peacemaking is the thrust of a Christian theology of peace. As Schneiders writes:

[25]Abdul Ghaffar Khan, as quoted in Eknath Easwaran, *Nonviolent Soldier of Islam: Badsha Khan, a Man to Match His Mountains* (Petaluma, CA: Nilgiri Press, 1999), 183.

In other words, the Gospel's contribution to our reflection on war and peace is neither accidental nor purely exhortatory. It is substantive and structural. . . . One of the most encouraging signs of the maturity and commitment of Christians in our time is that increasing numbers of Christians are making those choices and making it clear that the source of their convictions and their actions is the Gospel they profess.[26]

The Thrust of a Gospel-based Theology of Peace Is Peacemaking

The old debate between pacifism and the just war theory is superseded by the call to peacemaking. It is not enough to say I will not participate in war and violence. Christians are called to go far beyond saying no—we are called to be peacemakers—to resist oppression nonviolently, to confront and change the structures of evil, those attitudes and cultural values and institutions that make violence the priority solution to problems, that champion God-awful investments in arms, that name, label, and then fear enemies; to remove the injustices that cause war and violence; to find ways to reconcile people and change enemies into friends; to build a positive culture of peace—as Jesus did. As Glen Stassen writes, "To raise issues of pacifism or just war as we approach the brink of war is almost always too late. . . . Just peacemaking theory focuses attention on prevention and conflict resolution early in a conflict. . . . It keeps pacifists from being narrowed down to simply saying 'no.' "[27]

Peacemaking also takes us beyond the limits of the just war tradition. The just war theory still has some value. It provides to reasonable people a way to evaluate the morality of a given war using some criteria of natural law reasoning. It does not, however, bring into the discussion how Jesus confronted issues of war and peace and violence, nor how, as followers of Jesus, *we* should act. It is in effect, not a specifically Christian way to confront the contemporary issues of war, peace, violence, and terrorism. It is instead a philosophical tradition—stemming from classical, pagan philosophy. "Just peacemaking

---

[26]Schneiders, "New Testament Reflections on Peace and Nuclear Arms," 104.

[27]Glen Stassen, *Just Peacemaking*, 1st ed. (Louisville: Westminster/John Knox Press. 1992), 233–34.

is emerging as the new paradigm that parallels but pushes past the just war tradition," as Maryann Cusimano Love writes.[28]

Why is it important that a Christian theology of peace break out of the just war tradition? First, peacemaking makes prevention of war, not participation, the central issue. Second, peacemaking entails positive, transformative action—not armchair theorizing. Third, peacemaking calls us to unfetter our imaginations. We are to envision all the ways to build positive peace, ways currently undreamed of. Who would have thought that the techniques of creative conflict resolution would have been so successful? Who would have thought that the United Nations would launch a brand-new movement enlisting dozens of countries and their citizens into coming up with new ways to build cultures of peace? Who would have thought that nonviolent accompaniment by neutral parties between fighting factions as practiced by the Peace Brigades or the Nonviolent Peaceforce would be so effective? Who knows what peacemakers will come up with next, once their imaginations are freed and they don't limit themselves to checking off a list of just war criteria and think their job is done? Eileen Egan, one of the founders of Pax Christi in the United States, put it very well when she said, referring to the strongly held belief that the just war theory was *de riguer,* the last word of the Catholic Church on the issues of war and peace: "Nothing closes the mind more than calling it a settled question. . . . How much creative energy might have been released. . . . How many more examples of speaking truth to power might we have seen?"[29]

A Gospel-based Theology of Peace Rejoices in the Newfound Power of Nonviolence

We are fortunate in our time to benefit from a rich, recent tradition of thinking about the nature of power. Gandhi's theory of power is a watershed. As Theodor Ebert, an important theorist of nonviolent power, wrote: "Gandhi represents a Copernican revolution in politics."[30]

Contrary to the popular assumptions that "power grows out of the

---

[28]Maryann Cusimano Love, "What Kind of Peace Do We Seek?" in *Peacebuilding: Catholic Theology, Ethics, and Praxis,* ed. Robert J. Schreiter, R. Scott Appleby, and Gerard F. Powers (Maryknoll, NY: Orbis Books, 2010), 74.

[29]Eileen Egan, *Peace Be with You* (Maryknoll, NY: Orbis Books, 1999), 104.

[30]Theodor Ebert, "Preparations for Civilian Defense," in *Civilian Defence: An Introduction,* ed. Gene Sharp, T. K. Mahadevan, and Adam Roberts (New Delhi: Gandhi Peace Foundation, 1967), 198.

barrel of a gun" and that "the only way to defeat a strong military power is through a stronger military power," Gandhi asked a simple question. He asked how can a little over 100,000 British dominate a country of 350 million, the population of India at the time. His answer: we let them. From that answer he went on to develop his theory of power—that power rises. Leaders have their power because the people give it to them. If a populace stops giving it to them, if they stop going along, if they unite in a refusal to cooperate with the powers that be, the powers that be will be powerless. If the powers that be respond to noncooperation with force, they lose legitimacy. If the populace stays united and responds to violence with disciplined nonviolent action and resistance, they will eventually win—especially if they conduct a nonviolent campaign aimed at the regime's vulnerabilities and turn their sources of support against them. All the findings of theories of warfare that have been developed through the centuries such as—identify the weakest spot in the opponent's defenses, concentrate your forces *en masse* at those places, keep the enemy off balance through the element of surprise—can be switched over and used by the nonviolent strategist just as effectively. Again and again we have seen nonviolent power, when pitted against violent "power," be a force more powerful.

The power of nonviolence has been amply demonstrated in the decades since Gandhi. In fact, looking back, we can now see that the power of nonviolence has been at work in our own US history. Historians are recovering, for example, how the United States achieved its independence; they conclude that we were freed *before* the War of Independence through the concerted nonviolent noncooperation and resistance of colonists all across the colonies. For example, in response to the Stamp Act of 1765 passed by Britain, which required the purchase of an official stamp from Britain to be placed on every legal document signifying a transaction, lawyers and judges all across the colonies simply refused to comply. Port authorities up and down the coasts refused to comply. As a result, Britain took the law off the books. Britain had collected less than the costs of printing the stamps. In 1767 Britain passed the Townshend Acts, placing a tax on all purchases made by the colonies of British goods such as cloth, glass, and furniture. Merchants refused to pay the tax and led a boycott of such goods—to their own detriment, but in united resistance. The colonies stopped exporting the materials and goods Britain wanted and needed from us, such as lumber and tobacco. At their commencement students of what became known as Brown University took pride in their home-spun cloth outfits, spurning the fancy imports from Britain. A young girl, invited to tea by the royal governor of New Jersey, took a cup and then flung the tea out the window. All across the country young and old united in resistance to and noncooperation with Britain. The colonies developed their own mechanisms of self-government before the Articles of Confederation. Britain tried to put the colonies back in line when they declared war. It was too late. We were already free. We had achieved our freedom from Britain nonviolently. We celebrate the soldiers of the Revolutionary War. We should celebrate even more vigorously the many nonviolent resisters and noncooperators who actually forged our freedom.[31]

Nonviolence can accomplish just about anything, it would seem. It can overthrow dictators, gain civil rights, garner economic rights, wrest independence from an imperial power, secure peace between warring factions.

Why is this heritage of theory and praxis of nonviolent power important for a theology of peace? One, it helps us appreciate afresh just how "realistic" Jesus' message of the Sermon on the Mount really is. Gandhi recognized the deep truth of Jesus' message of the Sermon on the Mount from the moment he read it as a young man. He said, "It went straight to his heart"; it confirmed for him what he was experiencing in his own nonviolent campaigns.

Two, nonviolence shows us a way to promote peace and oppose injustice and oppression at one and the same time. In answer to Augustine and Ambrose who taught that the ones who refused to defend the innocent were worse than those who hurt the innocent, Martin Luther King Jr. responded to that contention by asking Augustine and Ambrose if that meant "by any means necessary?" According to William D. Watley, King "argued that a symmetrical response to a violent act has led to legitimating everything from maiming a rapist to an apology for the Vietnam War. Violence takes the form of altruism by claiming to prevent suffering. Its method is to inflict so much more suffering that one must surrender unconditionally. King rejected this kind of altruism and insisted that suffering can only be stopped when

---

[31]Walter Conser, "The United States: Reconsidering the Struggle for Independence, 1765–1775," in *Recovering Nonviolent History,* ed. Maciej J. Bartkowski (Boulder, CO: Lynne Rienner, 2013), 299–318.

it is endured rather than increased."[32] Nonviolence offers a way to protect the innocent without violence.

Three, nonviolence gives us a way to fight without turning into what we oppose—what Albert Camus yearned for in his book *The Plague*—how can we fight the plague without contracting it ourselves? How can we fight violence and not turn violent ourselves?—through fighting with nonviolence.

Four, it can hearten us to move forward with our peacemaking knowing we have weapons of our own that can be every bit as powerful as weapons of violence. If violence can employ rifles and tanks and drones and bombers, nonviolence can employ weapons such as cooperatives, demonstrations, strikes, boycotts, noncooperation campaigns, go-slow campaigns, and suffering.

Five, nonviolence helps us to not be afraid of conflict, to recognize it as part of the human condition. War is not inevitable, but conflict is. In addition, it gives us a method to not only face up to conflict but an assured way to resolve conflict. The nonviolent way in the spirit of Gandhi brings both parties together in a search for a larger truth that more fully satisfies the underlying needs of both parties. The approach includes deep listening, unfailing regard for a partner in conflict, and a willingness to suffer for the truth if it comes to that. A leading Catholic moral theologian, Kenneth Himes, has commented that traditional Catholic approaches to war and peace have lacked a vigorous conflict resolution mechanism and have too often relied, especially in papal teaching, on rather vague appeals to rationality or appeals to the better angels of our natures. "Missing in the tradition is a theory of conflict resolution. . . . A weakness of Catholic social teaching stemming from its communitarian vision is that conflict is viewed as more apparent than real; the organic metaphor of society, so prevalent in Catholic social teaching, induces a belief that harmony and cooperation are easier to achieve than is the case."[33] Nonviolent conflict resolution fills in that lacuna in Catholic social justice teaching.

Sixth, nonviolence offers what William James asked for in his fa-

---

[32]William D. Watley, "Martin Luther King Jr.," in *Nonviolence—Central to Christian Spirituality*, ed. Joseph T. Culliton, CSB (New York: Edwin Mellen Press, 1982), 150.
[33]Kenneth Himes, "Peacebuilding and Catholic Social Teaching," in *Peacebuilding: Catholic Theology, Ethics, and Praxis*, ed. Robert J. Schreiter, R. Scott Appleby, and Gerard F. Powers (Maryknoll, NY: Orbis Books, 2010), 282.

mous essay "The Moral Equivalent of War"[34]—a moral alternative to war. Nonviolent power can be the final arbiter of conflicts every bit as effectively as has war been the final arbiter.

At the same time that nonviolence has been attracting followers and advocates, violence is increasingly revealed as a sham. In fact military power at its apex, at its purest and most deadly form, is revealed to be not powerful but self-annihilating. As James Douglass writes: "The new threat of global suicide has redefined military power at its height as ultimately powerless. What we thought was power turns into sure self-destruction. This should force us to look for an alternative approach to power."[35] Hannah Arendt writes: "Hence warfare—from time immemorial the final arbiter in international disputes, has lost much of its effectiveness and nearly all of its glamor."[36]

A Gospel-based Theology of Peace Puts the Cross Back into the Political Arena

Much of Christian theology, especially since Anselm in the eleventh century, with his satisfaction theory of salvation, has placed the cross in a place outside of history. Anselm's theory has been called, as Elizabeth Johnson writes, the "most successful theological construct of all time," in its longevity and pervasiveness.[37] Anselm's theory puts God's mercy and justice in conflict, and then makes justice win out with a picture of God as a righteous judge who could not simply forgive sin without receiving some satisfaction. Because humankind had committed an infinite offense against God in its original sin, only a God-man could offer a sacrifice of sufficient worth that God's justice could be satisfied. So Jesus, the God-man, came into the world, offered his life on the cross, and sufficient satisfaction was gained to offset humankind's sin. Then the merit gained from that act was transferred to humanity. God makes a declaration from outside time that the merit gained by Christ on the cross is sufficient for humanity's salvation.

---

[34]William James, "The Moral Equivalent of War," in *William James: The Essential Writings,* ed. Bruce W. Wilshire (New York: Harper Torchbooks, 1971).

[35]James Douglass, *The Nonviolent Cross* (London: Macmillan, 1968), 6.

[36]Hannah Arendt, *On Violence* (New York: Harcourt, Brace and World, 1969), as quoted in Mark Kurlansky, *Nonviolence: The History of a Dangerous Idea* (New York: Modern Library, 2008), 155.

[37]Elizabeth A. Johnson, "Jesus and Salvation," *Proceedings of the Catholic Theological Society of America* 49 (1994): 5.

In recent years such a theory has come in for much criticism. Joseph Ratzinger, who, before he became Pope Benedict XVI, was among the first to offer a contemporary critique, declared that the theory was unbiblical in that it makes God the object of the saving action, thereby reversing the meaning of the cross: "In other world religions expiation usually means the restoration of the damaged relationship with God by means of expiatory actions on the part of men. . . . In the New Testament the situation is almost completely reversed. It is not man who goes to God with a compensatory gift, but God who comes to man, in order to give to him."[38]

More to the point for a gospel-based theology of peace, the expiatory theory of satisfaction locates salvation in the cross alone, taking the life of Jesus entirely out of the picture. The brutal death of Jesus becomes a cosmic drama played out within the Godhead, between the Father and the Son, outside of time, rather than an event that releases liberating power for the struggles people face in this life. A Christology from below, in contrast, with its emphasis on the life of Jesus and his peacemaking actions, preserves the vital link between the life and death of Jesus. He died because of the way he lived. He died because he confronted the powers of evil and showed us a new way to fight. The cross is a sacred symbol not because it symbolizes a transaction in God outside of time. It is a sacred symbol because it stands for a historical life given fully, and to the end, for the liberation of humankind through nonviolent power.[39] As Marcus Borg and John Dominic Crossan write, "One may speak of Jesus sacrificing his life for his passion, for his advocacy of the kingdom of God. . . . Did Good Friday have to happen? As divine necessity? No. As human inevitability? Virtually. Good Friday is the result of the collision between the passion of Jesus and the domination systems of his time."[40]

A gospel-based theology of peace not only restores the cross to the political order, it also highlights how suffering, of which the cross is the culminating moment, exerts its power in history.

From the beginning of his active life Jesus seemed to understand

---

[38]Joseph Ratzinger, *Introduction to Christianity* (New York: Herder and Herder, 1970), 214.

[39]For a fuller critique of the Anselmian theory of salvation, see Terrence Rynne, "The Multiple Versions of Salvation Theologies," in *Gandhi and Jesus: The Saving Power of Nonviolence* (Maryknoll, NY: Orbis Books, 2008), 133–52.

[40]Marcus J. Borg and John Dominic Crossan, *The Last Week* (San Francisco: HarperSanFrancisco, 2007), 162.

the power of suffering. He knew how the prophets had been treated before him. Early in his public life Matthew quotes Jesus saying, "Happy are you when people insult you and persecute you and tell all kinds of evil lies against you because you are my followers. . . . This is how the prophets who lived before you were persecuted" (Matt. 5:11). When James and John's mother, the wife of Zebedee, came to him to request that her sons be placed one at his right and one at his left when he came into his kingdom, Jesus responded to the sons: "You don't know what you are asking for. Can you drink from my cup?" As peacemakers who would come after him and follow in his footsteps, they were destined to receive the same kind of resistance that he had engendered from the powers that be.

That is the key to understanding the kind of suffering Jesus predicted for himself and for his disciples. Not just any suffering—physical ailments or psychological pain or family troubles—but the suffering that comes specifically from the trouble the peacemaker stirs up, the violent reaction from the powers that be when they are threatened. As Jon Sobrino writes, "Spirituality based on the cross does not mean merely the acceptance of sadness, pain, and sorrow; it does not mean simply passivity and resignation. . . . Rather, it is a spirituality focused on the following of Jesus. Not all suffering is specifically Christian, only that which flows from the following of Jesus."[41]

The suffering Jesus endured stemmed directly from what he was trying to accomplish—the ushering in of God's kingdom. But by refusing to return violence for violence and patiently enduring the suffering, he signaled something else about the significance of suffering patiently endured in the midst of conflict—its power to reach the one inflicting the suffering. Suffering voluntarily endured is a method of reaching the humanity of the oppressor. Instead of responding to violence with violence—the usual, expected response—bearing the suffering attempts to break through to the heart and emotions of the one inflicting the suffering. In that way suffering, as well as the cross, its culmination, were brought into the historical, political struggle. Jesus' suffering is creative, not just unmerited.

Jesus did reach many of his enemies. John wrote in his gospel: "Even then, many Jewish authorities believed in Jesus; but because of the Pharisees they did not talk about it openly, so as not to be expelled from

---

[41]Sobrino, *Christology at the Crossroads*, 215.

the synagogue" (John 12:42). Many, however, continued to see him as their enemy. But he said that his followers would do even greater things than he. "I am telling you the truth: whoever believes in me will do what I do—yes, he will do even greater things, because I am going to the Father" (John 14:12). In the light of the resurrection the disciples understood more clearly what Jesus meant and the significance of the way he lived and died. They felt compelled to go and do likewise. And they, through their suffering and nonviolent, loving lifestyle, were successful in converting enemies into friends. Suffering does not always work its power, but often it does. And it always does better than the alternative—violence. Gandhi and King came along and brought out more clearly than ever the political magic that suffering can, at times, fashion and the inner dynamics of how it works.

As Gandhi constructed his marvelous synthesis of Eastern and Western thought, *satyagraha*, to describe and explain the method of peacemaking he had discovered, he included as a constituent part of the method—*tapasya*, self-suffering. As I have written elsewhere, "The tapasya component of satyagraha means that when push comes to shove in a dispute, rather than retaliate with force, the satyagrahi takes it, endures the suffering—not out of passivity, but knowing first, that retaliation never goes anywhere, and second, that the opponent's heart can be reached by the witness of voluntary suffering endured for the truth."[42]

As Gandhi noted: "Far from seeking revenge, a votary of non-violence would pray to God that he might bring about a change of heart of his opponent, and if that does not happen he would be prepared to bear any injury that his opponent might inflict upon him, not in a spirit of cowardice or helplessness, but bravely with a smile on his face. I believe implicitly in the ancient saying that 'nonviolence real and complete will melt the stoniest of hearts.' "[43]

For Gandhi self-suffering has power to reach hearts. How? Richard Gregg, in his book *The Power of Nonviolence*[44] describes how it works in psychological terms. He described the three faces that nonviolence presents to the one who is doing violence to another. The first is the suffering face of the person who is being violated. That can be upsetting

---

[42]Rynne, *Gandhi and Jesus*, 65–66.
[43]Gandhi, *CWMG*, 68:64.
[44]Richard Gregg, *The Power of Nonviolence* (New York: Schocken Books, 1966).

in itself—the spontaneous human emotion of sympathy for one who is suffering. The second face is the one in the mirror. It is difficult for a person who is dealing violence to another to square that with their own carefully constructed self-image. "How can I come to terms with the fact that I am being brutal to another human being? How can 'I' be causing this suffering?" The third face is the loving face of the one who is being harmed. "How can this person whom I am treating so badly still look at me without hate and even, apparently, with love. I want to be worthy of that love."

Gandhi maintained that any and every human being could be reached with nonviolence and the power of suffering, no matter how far, apparently, they were beyond the pale. He was not underestimating the amount of evil in the world, however. He admitted that if persons had hardened themselves, if their violence had become so great and had lasted so long, it would take an equivalently great amount of nonviolent, self-suffering love to break through to them. The longer evil and violence are allowed to build and engrain themselves in a culture, the more monumental is the challenge of overcoming them with nonviolence. Bernard Häring said that if all the Christians in Germany had put on the yellow star when it was required of the Jews, that would have been the beginning of the end of Hitler. The problem was that they did not, and the evil was allowed to grow. Gandhi wrote: "It is therefore a matter of a rule of three to find out the exact amount of non-violence required to melt the hearts of the Fascists and Nazis."[45] The rule of three means three times as much nonviolence is required to counter a significant amount of violence in order to be successful.

We know that the firefighters in Selma refused to turn their hoses on children when ordered by Bull Connor. We know that instead they knelt and wept. We know that George Wallace later apologized publicly for his role in Jim Crow. We know that the soldiers in the Philippines refused to fire on their fellow countrymen when they were ordered to do so by Marcos—because they were greeted with nonviolent love and willingness to suffer. Suffering clearly has power. It does not always work. But it often does.

I quoted Doctor King's powerful testimony earlier: "We will match your capacity to inflict suffering with our capacity to endure suffering.

---

[45]Gandhi, *CWMG*, 69:122.

. . . But we will soon wear you down by our capacity to suffer, and winning our freedom we will so appeal to your conscience that we will win you in the process."[46]

Some authors dismiss nonviolence as powerless against adversaries who use brutal methods; they think it is only successful with those who have a moral code that prevents them from killing unarmed civilians. Michael Walzer, a prominent just war theorist, for example, writes that the practice of nonviolent resistance is unrealistic against tyrants such as Hitler or Stalin. It is either a "disguised form of surrender or a minimalist way of upholding communal values after a military defeat."[47] Walzer's understanding of how nonviolence works, however, is truncated.

The power of suffering to reach the heart of the oppressors is only one strand of nonviolent strategy. It is typically coupled with vigorous direct action. As David Cortright explains:

Nonviolent action does indeed try to reach the heart of the oppressor, but its effectiveness does not depend on an appeal to conscience. Rather, nonviolent resistance seeks to alter the political dynamics in a struggle by appealing to and winning sympathy from third parties and thereby undermining the power base of the oppressor. . . . Direct dialogue is often necessary to negotiate the resolution of a conflict, as Gandhi and King demonstrated, but this stage of the struggle usually comes after other forms of direct action and mass noncooperation have created conditions conducive to bargaining.[48]

Suffering voluntarily endured can be not only demoralizing to those who use violence without having it returned to them; it can also upset the consciences of those on the outside of the conflict—as happened around the world as people saw the violence of the British revealed in India, as happened with the world community in the case of apartheid in South Africa, as the world witnessed Marcos's violence against his

---

[46]King, *Stride toward Freedom*, 217.

[47]Michael Walzer, *Just and Unjust Wars: A Moral Argument with Historical Illustrations*, 2nd ed. (New York: Oxford University Press, 1987), 157.

[48]David Cortright, *Peace: A History of Movements and Ideas* (Cambridge: Cambridge University Press, 2008), 229.

own people in the Philippines, and as happened in our own struggle for civil rights.

A Theology of Peace Grounded in the Gospels Does Not Propose a Set of Rules: It Sounds a Call to Discipleship

The ethic proposed by a gospel-based theology of peace is a response to a call, the call to discipleship. The way forward for a disciple is not preset or laid out in great detail; it is discovered through action. As Christian peacemakers follow in the Way that Jesus blazed, they frequently find themselves in hard, challenging situations that call for, not only courage, but also the ability to forge new approaches and new answers. Loving one's enemy is not the safe, the convenient, the comfortable lifestyle. As John Howard Yoder wrote: "Nonviolent resistance is not legalism but discipleship, not 'thou shalt not' but 'as he is so are we to the world.'"[49]

It is important to understand why and how Christian peacemakers are able to act in this way, why they are able to do more (*perisson*) than the usual or expected. As Jesus said in effect in the Sermon on the Mount: "If you only love your neighbors, what makes you any different from the gentiles—what *more* do you do you, what do you do beyond what is the typical and the minimum and the 'natural'?" As Lisa Sowle Cahill writes, "Life in Christ is the root and commitment to nonviolence is a branch."[50] Christian peacemakers can aim high and deliver on their aspirations because they are inspired by the life of Jesus, gospel teaching, and the witness of other nonviolent peacemakers. Peacemaking is an experience of grace. The message of Jesus and the example of his life stir a sense in believers that they can do great things for peace. They do not have to be humdrum. As Pope Benedict wrote: Love can be commanded because God has first given love; we respond to a gift versus give an assent to duty, rule or command."[51] Or as C. F. Andrews wrote: "Agape begins where the individual experiences the

---

[49]John Howard Yoder, *The Politics of Jesus*, 2nd ed. (Grand Rapids, MI: William B. Eerdmans, 1994), 37.

[50]Lisa Sowle Cahill, *Love Your Enemies* (Minneapolis: Fortress Press, 1994), 168.

[51]Bendict XVI, as quoted in *Peace Movements Worldwide*, ed. Mark Pilusik and Michael Nagler, vol. 1: *History and Vitality of Peace Movements* (Santa Barbara, CA: Praeger, 2011), 139.

love of God in personal redemption and regeneration. . . . Love is not the upward movement of the human soul seeking the divine love, it is the reverse. A Christian can outlast, outlive and outlove the forces of unrighteousness, in spite of suffering.[52]

Jesus' ethic of love of enemies is rooted in God's boundless love even for sinners. The "realist" ethical thinkers, such as Reinhold Niebuhr, so emphasize the sinfulness of humankind that they overlook some basic promises in the gospels. Richard Hays underlined how Matthew assures his readers in numerous ways of the powerful, ongoing presence of Jesus with his people.[53] "Wherever two or three gather in my name, I am there in the midst of them." "I will be with you always, even unto the end of time." Hays points out that Niebuhr's focus on chapter 7 of Romans on the corruption of human nature ignores chapter 8 of Romans that describes the transformed life in the spirit.[54]

Participating in the work of Christian peacemaking is to experience the mysterious relationship between nature and grace. Grace does not undercut what is natural; grace transforms every "natural" pattern of behavior. When people participate in nonviolent resistance, they typically experience something of their higher selves. As Hays writes: "God broke through the borders of our standard definition of what is human and gave a new formative definition in Jesus."[55]

The ethic proposed by a gospel-based theology of peace is not a static ethic. It is a dynamic ethic. The disciples of Jesus, immersed as they are in the ever-changing passage of time, encounter new situations—of oppression, alienation, injustice, discord—and, guided by the example and teaching of Jesus, are able to enter into those situations with confidence and resourcefulness. They come up with ever-new peacemaking solutions.

If one were to take the saying "turn the other cheek," to be a rule, one would make a serious mistake. The saying presents a vivid example of how to live in the way Jesus did, an example of how to respond creatively and resourcefully and bravely to a situation of violence and disrespect. That is the power of such examples—they light up life as

---

[52]C. F. Andrews, *The Sermon on the Mount* (London: G. Allen and Unwin, 1942), 94–95.
[53]Richard Hays, *The Moral Vision of the New Testament* (San Francisco: Harper San-Francisco, 1996), 105.
[54]Ibid., 221.
[55]Ibid., 243.

lived and invite imaginative responses for new situations. They invite Jesus' followers to walk in his way, to unleash the power of their imaginations to bring to their times and places the way that Jesus modeled. Reading the scriptures and following the arc of Jesus' life reaches the heart and the emotions, the deeper level of our moral sense and challenges us to personal transformation. "The Sermon on the Mount is binding on Christians; it is the utopian-critical goad in every human ethic practiced by Christians—it is binding but can never be codified in laws," as Schillebeeckx writes.[56] In this context we can see peacemaking not as a summons to obey a set of rules but as a virtue to be practiced and, and through practice, to be strengthened. As Eli Sasaran McCarthy puts it, "Virtues are habits responsive to the good rather than acting from duty or fear of punishment."[57]

Disciples of Jesus, as John Howard Yoder writes, "do not repeat a mantra, they join a movement."[58] A theology of peace grounded in the gospels, therefore, gives central importance to the church as the community that should support growth in the virtue of peacemaking—by helping people, through mutual support, to unlearn the habits of violence and to learn the habits of nonviolent peacemaking. The church is to be, as Hays writes, "an ecclesia . . . a disciplined community of followers who put his teachings into practice. The Church is a demonstration plot in which God's will can be exhibited. For that reason, the righteousness of Jesus' disciples must exceed that of the scribes and Pharisees; otherwise the Church will not be a paradigm of the kingdom Jesus proclaimed."[59]

When the church reduced its teaching on issues of war and peace to the just war theory, it lost, or allowed to be muted, the strong, prophetic teaching of the gospels. Rarely was the bold call to peacemaking greatness in the Sermon on the Mount heard in the church. No longer was the example of Jesus' nonviolent life held up for study and emulation. Strangled was the call to restless, creative peacemaking. As Wink writes, "The removal of nonviolence from the gospel blasted

---

[56]Schillebeeckx, *Christ,* 597.

[57]Eli Sasaran McCarthy, *Becoming Nonviolent Peacemakers* (Eugene, OR: Pickwick, 2012), 32.

[58]John Howard Yoder, *The War of the Lamb* (Grand Rapids, MI: Brazos Press, 2009), 169.

[59]Hays, *Moral Teaching of the New Testament,* 96.

the keystone from the arch, and Christianity collapsed into a religion of personal salvation."[60]

That is why the developments of the twentieth and twenty-first centures are so exciting. These centuries have been the bloodiest in human history. They are also the time when nonviolent power has been rediscovered as a political ethic and an alternative to war and violence to settle conflicts. The life of the nonviolent Jesus is once again being placed at the center of the church's reflections on war and peace and violence. The keystone of the arch is being set in place once again. Christianity once again has much to say and offer the world in the arena of politics. This invigorated discipleship is manifested and strengthened through practices of peacemaking.

A Gospel-based Theology of Peacemaking Generates Imaginative Peacemaking Practices

Nonviolent resistance theory has continued to be enriched as it has been practiced over the last sixty-five plus years since the death of Gandhi in 1948. Gene Sharp's work has been particularly important for the recording and the codifying of the many nonviolent struggles over these years. He and others have also continuously analyzed nonviolent initiatives and campaigns to determine what has worked and what has not worked. Gene Sharp personifies a type of nonviolent action that does not depend on a system of beliefs to support and undergird it. Gandhi and most committed Christian peacemakers depend on their faith to provide a deep well of motivation and staying power in what typically are long and drawn-out struggles for justice. Gene Sharp professes a nonsectarian faith in the power of nonviolence. He finds that the strategies and tactics of nonviolence stand on their own, work in a way that is much superior to violence, and can be practiced by believers and nonbelievers alike.

In any case, as the theory has been enriched over these decades, so has been the practice of nonviolent peacemaking. In fact, whole new subcategories of peacemaking practice have begun to emerge. Three are worth commenting on in the light of a gospel-based theology of peace: (1) unarmed civilian peacemakers accompanying people under the constant threat of violence; (2) peace or healing circles; and (3) peace-

---

[60]Wink, *Engaging the Powers*, 217.

building, a subset of peacemaking to resolve and transform situations of long-term violence between peoples. Each of these breakthrough approaches to peacemaking has been developed only recently. They demonstrate just how creative a focus on active peacemaking can be. Emboldened and inspired by the teachings and example of Jesus, the peacemaking imagination will, in the future, no doubt be a cornucopia of innovative peacemaking practices.

Unarmed Civilian Peacekeepers

Unarmed civilian peacekeepers accompany peoples under the constant threat of violence. Growing out of Gandhi's idea of a *Shanti Sena,* or a peace army, a number of organizations have developed an approach to moderating conflict in situations of great violence that involves sending neutral outsiders to accompany groups of people at risk of violence. William James's famous essay "The Moral Equivalent of War" accurately analyzed what was so appealing to humanity about war. He identified the traditions of heroism that have been handed down for generations. He pointed out that war brings out the higher ideals of service and sacrifice.[61] "War is the strong life. . . . The advocates of war point to the great virtues of the martial spirit—fidelity, cohesiveness, tenacity, heroism, discipline, physical fitness."[62] James wondered if there was a way to channel these same virtues in the pursuit of peace. We have already seen the examples of Gandhi's dedicated satyagrahi and Abdul Ghaffar Khan's brave army of nonviolent Pashtun youth that made up the Khudai Khitmagar, the nonviolent army from what is now Pakistan. Organizations of unarmed peacekeepers continue to demonstrate that the virtues of hardihood so celebrated in war can be lived out in the service of peace. Among the unarmed peacekeeping organizations are the Peace Brigades, Witnesses for Peace, Christian Peacemaker Teams, and the Nonviolent Peaceforce.

The practice of unarmed civilian peacekeepers has been surprisingly successful wherever it has been tried. The underlying dynamic seems to be the following: both sides of a conflict care what the international community thinks of them. They know that a negative reputation might

---

[61]James, "Moral Equivalent of War," 340–59.
[62]Cortright, *Peace,* 308.

bring their opponents aid from the outside; it might bring sanctions upon them; it might sever the supply lines of external support already established. As a result, both sides of a conflict take care to not harm outside, neutral parties or international observers. Into that opportunity a number of organizations are inserting unarmed civilian peacekeepers to be with and thus protect peoples threatened by violence.

Peace Brigades International has provided trained volunteers in conflict zones to monitor ceasefires, offer mediation services, and help with reconciliation. Teams were first deployed in Guatemala in 1983, and later teams served in El Salvador, Sri Lanka, Colombia, and Haiti.

Witnesses for Peace was started in 1985 by US peacemakers who had been startled by what they had learned on a fact-finding mission to Nicaragua that the US-supported Contra militias were murdering innocent civilians in villages across the country. As a result, they "arranged for four hundred U.S. activists to live in communities across Nicaragua to discourage U.S. organized Contra attacks," as Robert Burrowes reports.[63] They effectively prevented additional Contra attacks on those communities.

Christian Peacemaker Teams were developed under the auspices of the traditional peace churches after Ronald Sider, an author, activist, and leader of Evangelists for Social Action, laid down a challenge at the 1984 Mennonite World Conference. Cortright explains: "Sider challenged his listeners to show the same level of courage in working for peace as soldiers display in their willingness to die in battle. . . . The founders of CPT sought consciously to emulate the spirit of disciplined self-sacrifice that is characteristic of armies facing battle. . . . CPT volunteers attempt to 'get in the way' when acts of abuse and injustice are occurring."[64] They have been deployed in Gaza and the West Bank, Chechnya, Haiti, Bosnia, Colombia, Iraq, and in Arizona along the border with Mexico.

The Nonviolent Peaceforce was started by David Hartsough and Mel Duncan in 1999 to provide teams of trained nonviolent activists to intervene in armed conflicts to protect human rights, deter violence, and facilitate peacemaking. The first teams were deployed to Sri Lanka and the Philippines. They have since responded to requests for their

---

[63]Robert J. Burrowes, *The Strategy of Nonviolent Defense* (Albany: State University of New York Press, 1996), 260.

[64]Cortright, *Peace,* 312.

services from South Sudan. The Nonviolent Peaceforce recruits staff members from all over the world, preferring people who have already had significant cross-cultural experiences. They undergo rigorous training in cross-cultural understanding and conflict mediation before being deployed. Not only do they maintain neutrality, they also develop strong community partnerships, while paying careful attention to local customs and traditions and being ready to instantly accompany participants whenever requested.

One particularly striking example of their work in Sri Lanka featured some of their staff accompanying a group of mothers whose children had been abducted by a local militia who intended to make them into child soldiers. The mothers and the Nonviolent Peaceforce staff members entered the camp of the militia and began to dialogue with the militia leaders. As a result of the intervention, the children were allowed to go home again with their mothers.

The Nonviolent Peaceforce is currently considering sending a contingent into Syria. A recent article appeared in the newsletter *Waging Nonviolence,* titled "Can Unarmed Peacekeeping Work in Syria? It Has in South Sudan."[65]

Peace or Healing Circles

Peace or healing circles are an innovative and very effective peace-making practice. Healing or peace circles come from the American Indian tradition and are similar to the approach of the Maori people of New Zealand to handling and resolving conflict. The rules for participating in a circle are straightforward. The circle is a shape that makes all participants equal. All voices need to be heard. When a person in the circle speaks, he or she is handed a symbol of peace. It can be anything that has meaning for the group, an Indian peace pipe or a talisman of courage. Holding the symbol obligates the speaker to speak the truth as he or she perceives it and to speak from the heart. Each person in the circle, one at a time, speaks his or her truth. All participants pledge to listen respectfully and attentively. No interruptions or challenges are allowed, although questions for clarification are permitted. Participants are encouraged to withhold judgment until

---

[65]Stephane van Hook, "Can Unarmed Peacekeeping Work in Syria? It Has in South Sudan," *Waging Nonviolence,* October 31, 2013.

they have heard everyone out. The experience of being listened to with respect and without judgment gradually generates trust between members of the group, and trust begins to generate a sense of community.

These peace circles are now being used as instruments of peace in a number of different settings and for a number of purposes. Among the purposes are reconciliation, prevention, and teaching the skills of conflict resolution.

The use of peace or healing circles for reconciliation of people is an outgrowth of the restorative justice movement. The restorative justice movement attempts to augment and, in some instances, replace the dominant mode of justice in our society—retributive justice. For the most part the justice system in the United States is designed as a retributive justice system. In such a system justice is symbolized by the woman with a blindfold holding a scale. Crime is understood as a violation of laws and an unbalancing of the scales of justice. This system in all its component parts is of unending interest to the American public. The most popular and longest lasting television shows (*Law and Order* surpassed *Gunsmoke* as the television show with the longest reign) feature one or another of the components of the retributive system. The system is designed to first investigate the crime and unearth the evidence (*CSI*), find and arrest the criminal (*Hill Street Blues, Cagney and Lacey, Person of Interest,* and police shows too numerous to count) and then put the perpetrators on trial, convict them (*Law and Order, Law and Order SVU*), and put them in jail (*Orange Is the New Black*). The system is designed to balance the scales of justice. A punishment is given that fits the crime, thus rebalancing the scales of justice.

The biblical symbol of justice, which guides the restorative justice movement, is not the blindfolded woman with scales but a surging river that waters dry land and restores the land to health. The aim of biblical/restorative justice is reconciliation of people. Out of this tradition has come a restorative justice movement. In this system a criminal violates not just a law but harms people. Justice is not served until the perpetrators recognize the harm they have done; the one harmed has been acknowledged; the offenders have turned away from their crime; and both parties have been reconciled. The retributive justice system, for the most part, pays little attention to the victim—assuming that punishment of the criminal will be enough for the victim. The punishment of the criminal does not go nearly far enough to restore to wholeness a person who has been on the receiving end of a serious crime—a woman who has been raped, a victim of soul-shattering assault, a family that has lost a loved one to violence. The restorative justice movement begins, therefore, with the victims and their need for healing.

One example of this movement—which has growing advocates all across the country—is the Marquette University Law School's Restorative Justice Initiative, founded by an eminent jurist, Janine Geske. Ms. Geske was a Wisconsin Supreme Court justice who left the bench to start the initiative. One of the principal activities of the center is to conduct "healing circles" composed of victims, surrogate victims, offenders, community members who may have been affected by the crime, and members of community resources who may play a part in healing the wounds of crime.

With the consent of the victim the healing circle is convened—at times in the place where the offenders have been incarcerated. They proceed in three stages: all those involved have a chance to say how the crime has affected them and their feelings about the crime. Often enough, it is the first time that perpetrators have really understood the effect their actions have had on others. The criminals review what led them to commit the crime. Participants then brainstorm on what could be done to fix the wounds that have been felt. Often, through the healing circle, criminals fully face what they have done and express a desire to make amends. Often the victims find it in their hearts to move on from the crime and even to forgive and be reconciled.

The second peacemaking use for which peace circles have been used is for prevention of crime and violence. For example, a prosecutor from the Milwaukee States Attorney's office, Paul Dedinsky, has led numerous peace circles involving at-risk young people after they have done something to come to the notice of law enforcement. In this situation the peace circles involve not just the at-risk young person but also members of their families; concerned community members; and, if appropriate, school representatives. The intent of the peace circles is to interrupt the potential progression toward criminal behavior and to offer concern and support to the young person. The peacemaking circles in this situation are useful not only for reconciling people but also for preventing crime and violence.

Finally, healing or peace circles provide an excellent medium for teaching young people the skills of nonviolent conflict resolution. For example, Peace Works, the curriculum of twenty-three interactive modules, developed by the Marquette University Center for Peacemaking to teach middle and high school students the skills of nonviolent conflict resolution, uses peace circles as the medium for learning the skills. From deep listening to tapping nonviolent strategies to how to respond to a bully, students in a circle practice those skills with and on one another.

Peacebuilding

Peacebuilding is the peacemaking practice aimed at building a sustainable peace after protracted violence between peoples. These skills are hard won and are gradually being formulated through the creative work of people in the field who are committed to peacemaking. Typically, these conflicts have deep historical roots, sometimes lasting not just decades but for generations, and typically, they involve horrendous violence between ethnic groups. This kind of violence—in countries such as Somalia, Colombia, Cambodia, Nicaragua, Northern Ireland, the Philippines, Sri Lanka, Burundi, and Sudan—typically has many forms and complications, from drug-related assassinations to kidnapping and rape to government corruption to militias gone wild to abduction of children. John Paul Lederach writes, "This sustained experience of violence affecting a wide swath, often of the rural and poorest communities, has left for many a legacy of trauma, lost childhood, displaced populations, the bitterness of lost life and often a daily search for survival."[66] The peacemaking task in such situations goes well beyond simple mediation. In these situations typically there are great differences in leverage and power between the parties. To simply mediate and stop the violence—as important as that would be—could result in a continuation of the power imbalance and a continued state of oppression. Situations such as these require, at the same time, significant changes in the structures of power. Peacebuilding is the set of skills and practice that addresses these volatile and imbalanced situations. Peacebuilding is a term to describe this subset of peacemaking and is a term of recent usage. As Scott Appleby wrote: "It first came into widespread use . . . only after 1992, when Boutros Boutros-Ghali,

---

[66] John Paul Lederach, "The Long Journey Back to Humanity," in *Peacebuilding: Catholic Theology, Ethics, and Praxis,* ed. Robert J. Schreiter, R. Scott Appleby, and Gerard F. Powers (Maryknoll, NY: Orbis Books, 2010), 27.

then Secretary-General, announced his Agenda for Peace. . . . Under Kofi Annan's leadership of the United Nations, peacebuilding was construed as post-conflict structural transformation, with a primary focus on institutional reform."[67]

The United Nations realized that 50 percent of the time-negotiated peace agreements fall apart within five years. No part of the United Nations addressed the challenge of helping countries with the transition from war and violence to sustainable peace, so in 2005 Kofi Annan created the UN Peacebuilding Commission. Since then it has had difficulties securing adequate funding, and it is still developing its skills and credibility in the field of postconflict peacebuilding.

The Department of Defense of the United States began recognizing the challenges of postconflict peacebuilding when it officially claimed in 2005 in Iraq, that it had postconflict reconstruction obligations, labeled "nation building," as a core mission—even in the face of misgivings within the military that such an emphasis would diminish war-fighting capabilities. Unfortunately, the efforts of the Department of Defense in the area of postconflict transformation end up focusing mainly on issues of security and rebuilding shattered infrastructure, and do not address adequately the underlying challenges of unjust structures and systems in the country or the groups within the country who are still deeply at odds with one another.

Productive work in this difficult field is, however, being carried out by civilian nongovernmental organizations around the globe. The field of peacebuilding is being developed piece by piece by people on the ground. John Paul Lederach, a long-time Mennonite mediator and currently on the faculty of the Joan Kroc Institute for International Peace Studies at the University of Notre Dame, is a leading practitioner of peacebuilding. In his various books Lederach documents how he has gradually discovered the keys to successful peacebuilding—a work that is still unfolding.

For example, he recounts learning from priests serving in Colombia the importance of face-to-face dialogue with armed actors and the importance of treating them with respect even when appalled by the violence they are inflicting on others. He quotes Father Dario, a Clar-

---

[67]R. Scott Appleby, "Peacebuilding and Catholicism," in *Peacebuilding: Catholic Theology, Ethics, and Praxis*, ed. Robert J. Schreiter, R. Scott Appleby, and Gerard F. Powers (Maryknoll, NY: Orbis Books, 2010), 27.

etian priest in Colombia: "How do I look in the eyes of people and try to dialogue with people who have destroyed the lives of so many and so cruelly broken every sense of human rights? . . . I work very hard to find ways to show them respect."[68] That dialogue opened the way to find common ground between various armed actors from the right and left and began to end the violence.

In his book, *The Journey toward Reconciliation*, Lederach describes what he discovered during his work in Cambodia in 1994 with officials from all the factions that participated in the genocide, perpetrators and victims. He asked the participants how they could now work with their enemies. He heard from them a common answer: We do it so my children and grandchildren will never have to suffer as we did. Lederach writes:

> With a focus on future generations, they were able to work with former enemies. . . . The framework of past-present-future suggested that we must first cast out the demon of the past to make peace with our enemies in the present. Yet in Cambodia, the future, the shared common hope for future generations pro-vided a space within which they could relate and work together in the present. . . . This has been a common approach in the field of conflict transformation. . . . It is this intense weight of responsibility for preventing future victimization that motivates a person to engage in the vulnerable journey of confronting the injustice and the enemy. . . . This procedure has helped them cope with *the present*. Later, perhaps, they can address the *personally painful past*.[69]

Working in Somalia during the nineties to mediate between various warlords involved in the violence, Lederach acquired another insight into peacebuilding. "Each of them took pains to rehash the history of the Somalian conflict. Each then concluded with fiery statements of accusation and justification. . . . That experience and others led me to a deeper conviction. In Somalia, one could not effectively approach the building of peace by relying exclusively on the high-level negotiations

---

[68]Lederach, "Long Journey Back to Humanity," 34–35.
[69]John Paul Lederach, *The Journey toward Reconciliation* (Scottdale, PA: Herald Press, 1999), 76–77.

between faction leaders. . . . We made the case for building peace from the bottom up. . . . We helped to achieve the participation of women, religious leaders, and the Somalian nongovernmental organizations."[70]

Unarmed civilian peacekeeping, peace circles, and peacebuilding are among the peacemaking practices that have emerged as peacemakers focus on building a positive, sustainable peace. No less important is the emergence of the field of peace studies itself. Hundreds of leading universities around the world now offer degrees in the field. The field of peace studies rigorously examines the causes of violence and war, explores ways that violence and war can be prevented, mitigated, and ended, and introduces students to the power of nonviolence. In addition, traditional fields of study are reexamining themselves in the light of peace studies. Many historians, for example, realize that history all too often has been taught as a sequence of wars. Peace historians focus instead on humanity's long efforts to build a rich culture of peace, harmony, and security. Peace journalism is beginning to generate a new generation of investigators and scholars highlighting the many stories of peacemaking and conflict transformation. These stories are often at least as compelling as the stories of violence and mayhem that typically lead the nightly news. Peace communications is a discipline pioneered by Marshall Rosenberg and has gained worldwide acceptance and support. Economists are increasingly tuned in to the ways that economic policies contribute to continuing conflict and violence or support peace and peacemaking.

A gospel-based theology of peace invites disciples of peace to use their imaginations. That is precisely what Jesus did when he laid out a series of examples of conflict in the Sermon on the Mount and invited his disciples to think of their own situations of conflict and reflect on how they would handle them—now that they had witnessed how Jesus behaved. Jesus asked them to go beyond whatever rules and dictums they may have heard—to use their imaginations and bring *more* into the world, something new that the world had not yet seen. As Albert Einstein said: "Logic will get you from A to B. Imagination will take you everywhere."[71]

70Ibid., 83–84.

[71]As quoted in John Paul Lederach, *The Moral Imagination: The Art and Soul of Building Peace* (Oxford: Oxford University Press, 2005), 171.

Nonviolent Peacemaking: Churchwide and Parish Deep

As the church reclaims the gospel call to active peacemaking as central to Christian discipleship and as the church continues to embrace and explore the power of nonviolence, one can envision the church making great contributions to the world's search for lasting peace. The church not only has global reach, it is also has thousands of bastions of local influence and action through its many parishes and institutions. It can contribute from the top down and from the bottom up.

As we saw in chapter 6, recent popes have been doing their part. They have clearly embraced Jesus' call to peacemaking and nonviolence. Pope John Paul II made solidarity with the poor in the pursuit of just development the heart of his social teaching—positive peace as the fruit of justice enlivened by charity. Benedict XVI eloquently placed the Sermon on the Mount, love of enemy, and the challenge of building a positive, lasting peace at the center of his teaching. Pope Francis continues that teaching.

The Vatican has formal diplomatic relationships with 177 countries and has emphasized preventive diplomacy. Kenneth Himes writes:

> Various conferences of bishops as well as individual bishops have offered to assist in mediating disputes and peacemaking. The work of the episcopacy in Guatemala is one example of a sustained effort at peacemaking during the country's civil war and subsequent civil unrest. Bishops Oscar Romero of El Salvador, Laurent Monsengwo of the Democratic Republic of Congo, Samuel Ruiz of Mexico, and Carlo Belo of East Timor are individual church leaders who have been widely hailed for their efforts at bringing peace and reconciliation to violent societies.[72]

Catholic Relief Services (CRS), the global outreach arm of the American Catholic Church, has gone through a top to bottom reorientation of its identity and mission to become a self-identified peacebuilding organization. That story is, perhaps, an exciting harbinger of what is to come for the Catholic Church as a whole. CRS had already evolved

---

[72]Kenneth R. Himes, *Christianity and the Political Order* (Maryknoll, NY: Orbis Books, 2013), 336.

from being an aid or relief organization—working in over a hundred countries since the end of World War II, aiding people after calamities had struck and helping them get back on their feet—to a development organization, not just bringing aid but helping communities develop their own capacities, from water and irrigation projects to strengthening education and health capabilities. Then came the genocide in Rwanda. CRS had worked in Rwanda for decades. Most of their staff on the ground were native Rwandans—both Tutsis and Hutus. As the word came in that dozens of their own staff members and their families had been slaughtered in the genocide, CRS was shaken to the core. They realized that they had sensed, over time, the ongoing conflict between the Tutsis and Hutus but, over the years, had not really addressed it—and perhaps they may have even contributed to the conflict by working with one group more than the other. As a result CRS did a deep soul searching. They set out to delve as deeply as they could—the whole organization worldwide—into the social teachings of the church and make them the touchstone of all that they did. As a result of this reflection and education, they came to see that building relationships between people, especially in situations of conflict, had to be at the center of their mission. They are now clearly a peacebuilding organization.

The challenge from here will be to energize and equip members of the church at the grass roots to see themselves as peacemakers, to read the gospels with fresh eyes and discover Jesus' clear call to nonviolent peacemaking, to tell one another the great stories of successful nonviolent action, and to make every parish a cockpit of active, nonviolent peacemaking.

One group that has tuned in to the need to train people at the grass roots in nonviolent action is Pace e Bene. Pace e Bene was founded in the spirit of Saint Francis of Assisi, the great peacemaker. The title of the organization is Italian for peace and all good blessings. Pace e Bene was founded and is led by Friar Louis Vitale, a Franciscan priest, and Ken Butigan, a noted teacher and scholar of peace studies, and now joined by Father John Dear. It has trained thousands of local community and church groups in the skills and philosophy of nonviolent action. They are currently working with the Archdiocese of Chicago, for example, to train cadres of committed, nonviolent peacemakers to serve and offer ongoing training for every deanery (division) of the archdiocese.

We look forward to the day when every future priest receives intensive instruction in a gospel-based theology of peace so that all priests can enthusiastically preach the gospel of peace to people seeking an alternative to our culture's commitment to violence; when all converts to the church receive as part of their Rite of Christian Initiation of Adults (RCIA)—evangelization in gospel-based peacemaking; when all the children in Catholic schools learn gospel-based peacemaking and receive training in conflict resolution; when every Catholic university offers degrees in peace studies; when intellectual leaders in the church move beyond the just war theory to a gospel-based theology of active peacemaking, when each and every parishioner understands his or her mission in the world to be a peacemaker in the spirit of the nonviolent Jesus. The mission of making nonviolent peacemaking churchwide and parish deep continues. We take heart that the good news of Jesus, his call to peacemaking, and his example of suffering love is being heard today in the church from the top and from below. We take heart from the initiatives under way and the many disciples who are following the nonviolent way of Jesus.

Appendix

There are promising signs and experiments afoot.

There is a need for sharing what is happening at the grass roots.

One experiment that is worth sharing is happening in the Archdiocese of Chicago.

In 2011 some forty people, concerned in various ways about peacemaking, were called to a planning session by two chancery employees, the director of human resources, and the director of lay ministry. The group was already calling itself Catholics for Nonviolence. The group was asked to identify some priorities for peacemaking action. The five priorities:

1. Decreasing gun, street gang violence. Some pastors in the group talked movingly about the unending number of funerals at which they were presiding and the grief and trauma for families.

2. Domestic violence. Father Chuck Dahm, a long-term peace and justice advocate and Dominican priest, currently working in the Latino community, described the seriousness of the problem and his frustrations trying to alert the church to the problem.

3. Catholic schools. Training for teachers and students in conflict resolution and peacemaking

4. Parishes. Parish priests need help in speaking about peace and nonviolence. Most feel uncomfortable addressing the topic of peace. Parents, especially in the inner cities, need support in parenting skills.

5. Training of archdiocesan personnel. The bishops, chancery office staff, parish staffs, and so on would benefit from training in peace and nonviolence.

After identifying the priorities champions of each of the areas stood up and committed themselves to develop and follow through on a plan of action.

As a result, progress is already evident:

1. Gang violence. The Black Catholic Deacons have sponsored sun-

rise liturgies at a number of locations along Lake Michigan to bring publicity to the problem and organize people who want to help. Five parishes in the inner city have organized "Take Back Our Streets" initiatives—flooding areas of potential violence on Friday and Saturday nights with peaceful parishioners.

A young man, Vince, from St. Sabina's, recently gave this update:

> St. Sabina has sponsored a Peace Basketball Tournament. Every Friday evening, traditionally the time of the highest crime rate in the area, teams representing the eight gangs from the area play one another at 5:30 and then 7:30. In order to participate they have to come to a 4:30 session on conflict resolution. Chicago Bulls players Joachim Noah and Derrick Rose have attended. Joachim Noah donated 40 tickets to a Bulls game with the stipulation that five representatives from each of the gangs attend and socialize together. In addition, St. Sabina parishioners and staff do outreach to the corners where gang members gather on Friday nights. They show their interest in them, invite them, if they are ready to come, to Sabina's full-time GED program and full-time job placement program. They do not just try to attract people out of the gangs, they are there to provide support and concrete alternatives in terms of education and jobs.
>
> They may have pants that hang way down but they are just like you and me, they want a hug. . . . *The only thing that defeats violence is love.*

Author's comment on Vince's final statement: So obvious, so true, so much in the spirit of the nonviolent Jesus.

2. Domestic violence. Father Chuck Dahm's voice is being heard. He was recently named the Archdiocesan Director of the Domestic Violence Program. He has spoken in thirty pulpits across the archdiocese and has conducted a workshop for the seminarians at the major seminary. At each parish where he speaks, a group of parishioners committed to helping with the problem sustains the work.

3. Catholic schools. The Peaceworks program in conflict resolution and peacemaking has been provided to five schools in the Pilsen area over the last two years. Twice a week all the students, from fourth grade through eighth grade, received intensive training in conflict

resolution and peacemaking. Significant decreases in violent behavior have resulted, and ongoing skills in handling conflict go with the students into the future.

4. Parishes. A Parenting for Peace program has been developed with the theme "Too Blessed to Be Stressed" and is now being offered at five inner city parishes.

5. Training. The bishops of the archdiocese, chancery office personnel, and local deanery staff have gone through Pace e Bene's training program in peace and nonviolence. Ken Butigan, the executive director of Pace e Bene, and the Director of Peace and Justice for the Archdiocese are rolling out a plan to provide each deanery with a well-trained cadre to support ongoing training for parishes in peacemaking and nonviolence.

Bibliography

Andrews, C. F. *The Sermon on the Mount*. London: G. Allen and Unwin, 1942.
Appleby, R. Scott. "Peacebuilding and Catholicism." In *Peacebuilding: Catholic Theology, Ethics, and Praxis,* edited by Robert J. Schreiter, R. Scott Appleby, and Gerard F. Powers. Maryknoll, NY: Orbis Books, 2010.
Arendt, Hannah. *On Violence*. New York: Harcourt, Brace and World, 1969.
Arment, J. Frederick. *The Elements of Peace*. Jefferson, NC: McFarland, 2012.

Bainton, Roland. *Christian Attitudes toward War and Peace*. Eugene, OR: Wipf and Stock, 1960.
Bartkowski, Maciel, ed. *Recovering Nonviolent History*. Boulder, CO: Lynne Rienner, 2013.
Beilby, James K., and Paul Rhodes Eddy, eds. *The Historical Jesus: Five Views*. Downers Grove, IL: IVP Academic, 2009.
Benedict XVI. *Good Friday Sermon*. 2011.
———. *Jesus of Nazareth*. San Francisco: Ignatius Press, 2011.
———. *Midday Angelus*. 2007.
Borg, Marcus. *Conflict, Holiness and Politics in the Teaching of Jesus*. Harrisburg, PA: Trinity Press International, 1998.
———. *Meeting Jesus Again for the First Time*. San Francisco: HarperSanFrancisco, 1994.
Borg, Marcus J., and John Dominic Crossan. *The Last Week*. San Francisco: HarperSanFrancisco, 2007.
Brown, Peter. *Augustine of Hippo*. Berkeley: University of California Press, 1967.
Brueggeman, Walter. *The Prophetic Imagination*. Minneapolis: Fortress Press, 2001.
Burckhardt, Jacob. *The Age of Constantine the Great*. Berkeley: University of California Press, 1949.
Burrowes, Robert J. *The Strategy of Nonviolent Defense*. Albany: State University of New York Press, 1996.

Cadoux, C. John. *The Early Christian Attitude to War*. London: Headley Bros., 1919.
Cahill, Lisa Sowle. *Love Your Enemies*. Minneapolis: Fortress Press, 1994.
Carroll, James. *Constantine's Sword*. New York: Houghton Mifflin, 2001.

Carter, Warren. *What Are They Saying about Matthew's Sermon on the Mount?* New York: Paulist Press, 1994.

Chase, Kenneth R., and Alan Jacobs, eds. *Must Christianity Be Violent?* Grand Rapids, MI: Brazos Press, 2003.

Chernus, Ira. *American Nonviolence: The History of an Idea.* Maryknoll, NY: Orbis Books, 2004.

Christiansen, Drew. "A Vision of Peace." *America*, April 8–15, 2013.

Coleman, John A., SJ, ed. *One Hundred Years of Catholic Social Thought.* Maryknoll, NY: Orbis Books, 1991.

Conser, Walter. "The United States: Reconsidering the Struggle for Independence, 1765–1775." In *Recovering Nonviolent History,* edited by Maciej J. Bartkowski. Boulder, CO: Lynne Rienner, 2013.

Cortright, David. *Peace: A History of Movements and Ideas.* Cambridge: Cambridge University Press, 2008.

Cortright, David, and George Lopez, eds. *Uniting against Terror.* Cambridge, MA: MIT Press, 2007.

Crocker, Chester A., Fen Osler Hampson, and Pamela Aall, eds. *Leashing the Dogs of War.* Washington, DC: United States Institute of Peace Press, 2007.

Crossan, John Dominic. *God and Empire.* San Francisco: Harper, 2007.

———. *The Greatest Prayer.* New York: HarperCollins, 2011.

Culliton, Joseph T., CSB., ed. *Nonviolence—Central to Christian Spirituality.* New York: Edwin Mellen Press, 1982.

Curran, Charles. *Catholic Social Teaching.* Washington, DC: Georgetown University Press, 2002.

Daly, Robert, SJ. "Phenomenology of Redemption?" *Theological Studies* 74, no. 2 (2013): 347–71.

Deane, Herbert A. *The Political and Social Ideas of St. Augustine.* New York: Columbia University Press, 1963.

Dear, John. *The God of Peace.* Eugene, OR: Wipf and Stock, 1992.

———. *Living Peace.* New York: Image Books, 2001.

Deats, Richard. *Marked for Life: The Story of Hildegard Goss-Mayr.* Hyde Park, NY: New City Press, 2009.

Douglass, James. *The Nonviolent Coming of God.* Eugene, OR: Wipf and Stock, 2006.

———. *The Nonviolent Cross.* London: Macmillan, 1968.

Drake, H. A. *Constantine and the Bishops.* Baltimore: Johns Hopkins University Press, 2000.

Duffey, Michael K. *Peacemaking Christians.* Kansas City, MO: Sheed and Ward, 1995.

———. *Sowing Justice, Reaping Peace.* Franklin, WI: Sheed and Ward, 2001.

Dunn, James D. G. *Jesus Remembered.* Vol. 1. Grand Rapids, MI: William B. Eerdmans, 2003.

Ebert, Theodor. "The Crisis." In *Civilian Defence: An Introduction*, edited by T. K. Mahadevan, Adam Roberts, and Gene Sharp. New Delhi: Gandhi Peace Foundation, 1967.

———. "Preparations for Civilian Defense." In *Civilian Defence: An Introduction*, edited by T. K. Mahadevan, Adam Roberts, and Gene Sharp. New Delhi: Gandhi Peace Foundation, 1967.

Egan, Eileen. *Peace Be with You*. Maryknoll, NY: Orbis Books, 1999.

Eknath Easwaran. *Nonviolent Soldier of Islam: Badsha Khan, a Man to Match His Mountains*. Petaluma, CA: Nilgiri Press, 1999.

Erasmus. *The Education of a Christian Prince*. Translated by Lester K. Born. New York: Columbia University Press, 1936.

Espy, Lawrence. "How Transforming Power Has Been Used in the Past by Early Christians." In *Nonviolence in Theory and Practice*, edited by Robert Holmes and Barry Gan. Long Grove, IL: Waveland Press, 2005.

Eusebius. *The History of the Church from Christ to Constantine*. Translated by G. A. Williamson. New York: Dorset Press, 1965.

———. *The Life of Constantine*. In *Select Library of Nicene and Post-Nicene Fathers of the Christian Church*, edited by P. Schaff and H. Wace. New York, 1890.

Fox, Michael Allen. *Understanding Peace*. New York: Routledge, 2014.

Francis, Pope. *Homily before the Angelus*. St. Peter's Square. August 18, 2013.

Friesen, Duane. *Christian Peacemaking and International Conflict*. Scottdale, PA: Herald Press, 1986.

Friesen, Duane K., and Gerald W. Schlabach, eds. *At Peace and Unafraid*. Scottdale, PA: Herald Press, 2005.

Furnish, Victor Paul. *The Love Commandment in the New Testament*. Nashville, TN: Abingdon Press, 1972.

Gandhi, Rajmohan. *Gandhi: The Man, His People and the Empire*. Berkeley: University of California Press, 2008.

Gaudium et Spes. The Church in the Modern World. 1965.

Gittings, John. *The Glorious Art of Peace*. New York: Oxford University Press, 2012.

Gorringe, Timothy. *God's Just Vengeance*. Cambridge: Cambridge University Press, 1996.

Gregg, Richard. *The Power of Nonviolence*. New York: Schocken Books, 1966.

Grossman, Dave. *On Killing*. New York: Back Bay Books, 2009.

Hamm, Dennis, SJ. *Building Our House on Rock*. Frederick, MD: The Word Among Us Press, 2011.

Hardin, Michael. *The Jesus Driven Life*. Lancaster, PA: JDL Press, 2010.

Häring, Bernard. *The Healing Power of Peace and Nonviolence.* New York: Paulist Press, 1986.

Harnack, Adolf. *The Mission and Expansion of Christianity in the First Three Centuries.* New York: Harper Torchbooks edition, 1961. Originally published by Williams & Norgate, London, 1908.

Hays, Richard. *The Moral Vision of the New Testament.* San Francisco: Harper SanFrancisco, 1996.

Heagle, John. *Justice Rising: The Emerging Biblical Vision.* Maryknoll, NY: Orbis Books, 2011.

Hedges, Chris. *War Is a Force That Gives Us Meaning.* New York: Anchor Books, 2002.

Helgeland, John, Robert Daly, and J. Patout Burns. *Christians and the Military: The Early Experience.* Philadelphia: Fortress Press, 1985.

Himes, Kenneth R. *Christianity and the Political Order.* Maryknoll, NY: Orbis Books, 2013.

———. "Pacifism and the Just War Tradition." In *One Hundred Years of Catholic Social Thought,* edited by John A. Coleman, SJ. Maryknoll, NY: Orbis Books, 1991.

Hollenbach, David, SJ. "*The Challenge of Peace* in the Context of Recent Church Teachings." In *Catholics and Nuclear War,* edited by Philip J. Murnion. New York: Crossroad, 1983.

———. *Nuclear Ethics: A Christian Moral Argument.* Ramsey, NJ: Paulist Press, 1983.

Holmes, Robert, and Barry Gan, eds. *Nonviolence in Theory and Practice.* Long Grove, IL: Waveland Press, 2005.

Hornus, John-Michel. *It Is Not Lawful for Me to Fight.* Eugene, OR: Wipf and Stock, 1980.

Horsley, Richard. *Bandits, Prophets and Messiahs.* Harrisburg, PA: Trinity Press International, 1985.

———. *Jesus and the Powers.* Minneapolis: Fortress Press, 2011.

———. *Jesus and the Spiral of Violence.* Minneapolis: Fortress Press, 1993.

Jegen, Mary Evelyn. "Peace and Pluralism." In *One Hundred Years of Catholic Social Thought,* edited by John A. Coleman, SJ. Maryknoll, NY: Orbis Books, 1991.

Jeremias, Joachim. *The Sermon on the Mount.* Philadelphia: Fortress Press, 1963.

John XXIII. *Pacem in Terris.* 1963.

John Paul II. *Centesimus Annus,* On the Hundredth Anniversary of *Rerum Novarum.* 1991.

———. *Homily at Bagington Airport,* Coventry, 2. *Origins* 12 (1982): 55.

———. *Homily at Drogheda.* 1979.

———. *World Day of Peace Message.* 1982.

Johnson, Elizabeth A. "Jesus and Salvation." *Proceedings of the Catholic Theological Society of America* 49 (1994): 1–18.

Johnson, James Turner. *The Quest for Peace*. Princeton, NJ: Princeton University Press, 1987.

Johnson, Richard, ed. *Gandhi's Experiments with Truth*. Lanham, MD: Lexington Books, 2006.

Jordens, J. T. F. *Gandhi's Religion: An Interpretation*. New York: Palgrave, 1998.

Kelly, Matthew. *Rediscovering Catholicism: Rediscovering Catholicism: A Spiritual Guide to Living with Passion and Purpose*. Cincinnati, OH: Beacon Publishing, 2010.

King, Martin Luther, Jr. *Strength to Love*. New York: Harper and Row, 1963.

———. *Stride toward Freedom: The Montgomery Story*. New York: Harper and Row, 1958.

Kissinger, Warren. *The Sermon on the Mount: A History of Interpretation and Bibliography*. ATLA Bibliography Series, no. 3. Metuchen, NJ: Scarecrow Press and the American Library Association, 1975.

Kruger, Thomas. "'They Shall Beat Their Swords into Plowshares': A Vision of Peace through Justice and Its Background in the Hebrew Bible." In *War and Peace in the Ancient World*, edited by Kurt A. Raaflaub. Malden, MA: Blackwell, 2007.

Kurlansky, Mark. *Nonviolence: The History of a Dangerous Idea*. New York: Modern Library, 2008.

Latourette, K. S. *A History of the Expansion of Christianity*, vol. 1: *The First Five Centuries*. New York: Harper and Brothers, 1937.

Lederach, John Paul. *The Journey toward Reconciliation*. Scottdale, PA: Herald Press, 1999.

———. "The Long Journey Back to Humanity." In *Peacebuilding: Catholic Theology, Ethics, and Praxis*, edited by Robert J. Schreiter, R. Scott Appleby, and Gerard F. Powers. Maryknoll, NY: Orbis Books, 2010.

———. *The Moral Imagination: The Art and Soul of Building Peace*. Oxford: Oxford University Press, 2005.,

Lelyveld, Joseph. *Great Soul: Mahatma Gandhi and His Struggle with India*. New York: Alfred A. Knopf, 2011.

Lohfink, Gerhard. *Jesus of Nazareth*. Collegeville, MN: Liturgical Press, 2012.

Love, Maryann Cusimano. "What Kind of Peace Do We Seek?" In *Peacebuilding: Catholic Theology, Ethics, and Praxis*, edited by Robert J. Schreiter, R. Scott Appleby, and Gerard F. Powers. Maryknoll, NY: Orbis Books, 2010.

Mahadevan, T. K., Adam Roberts, and Gene Sharp, eds. *Civilian Defense: An Introduction*. New Delhi: Gandhi Peace Foundation, 1967.

Markus, Robert. *Christianity and the Secular*. Notre Dame, IN: University of Notre Dame Press, 2006.

———. *Saeculum: History and Society in the Theology of Augustine*. London: Cambridge University Press, 1970.

Marshall, Christopher. *Beyond Retribution.* Grand Rapids, MI: William B. Eerdmans, 2001.

Mattox, John Mark. *Saint Augustine and the Theory of Just War.* New York: Continuum, 2006.

McCarthy, Eli Sasaran. *Becoming Nonviolent Peacemakers.* Eugene, OR: Pickwick, 2012.

McMorrow, Marilyn. "Creating Conditions of Peace: A Theological Framework." In *Peacemaking: Moral and Policy Challenges for a New World,* edited by Gerard F. Powers, Drew Christiansen, and Robert T. Hennemeyer. Washington, DC: United States Catholic Conference, 1994.

McSorley, Richard. *It's a Sin to Build a Nuclear Weapon.* Baltimore: Fortkamp, 1991.

Mead, Margaret. "Warfare Is Only an Invention." *Asia* (August 1940).

Meehan, Francis X. In *The Catholic Bishops and Nuclear War,* edited by Judith Dwyer. Washington, DC: Georgetown University Press, 1984.

Meier, John P. *A Marginal Jew: Rethinking the Historical Jesus.* Vols. 1–3. New York: Doubleday, 2001.

Merton, Thomas. *Conjectures of a Guilty Bystander.* Garden City, NY: Doubleday Image Books, 1958.

———. *Faith and Violence.* Notre Dame, Ind.: University of Notre Dame Press, 1968.

———. *Passion for Peace.* New York: Crossroad, 2006.

Miller, William. *All Is Grace.* Garden City, NY: Doubleday, 1987.

Monden, Louis. *Sin, Liberty and Law.* New York: Sheed and Ward, 1965.

Mueller, Tom. "King Herod Revealed." *National Geographic,* December 2008.

Murnion, Philip J., ed. *Catholics and Nuclear War.* New York: Crossroad, 1983.

Murray, John Courtney. *We Hold These Truths: Catholic Reflections on the American Proposition.* New York: Doubleday Image Books, 1964.

Musto, Ronald. *The Catholic Peace Tradition.* New York: Peace Books, 2002.

Myers, Ched. *Binding the Strong Man.* Maryknoll, NY: Orbis Books, 2003.

———. *Who Will Roll Away the Stone?* Maryknoll, NY: Orbis Books, 1994.

Myers, Ched, Marie Dennis, Joseph Nangle, OFM, Cynthia Moe-Lobeda, and Stuart Taylor. *Say to This Mountain.* Maryknoll, NY: Orbis Books, 1996.

Nagler, Michael. "Eternal Peace." In *Peace Movements Worldwide,* edited by Marc Pilusik and Michael Nagler. Santa Barbara, CA: Praeger, 2011.

———. *Is There No Other Way?* Berkeley, CA: Berkeley Hills Books, 2001.

National Conference of the Catholic Bishops. *The Challenge of Peace: God's Promise and Our Response.* Washington, DC: USCC Office for Publishing and Promotion Services, 1983.

———. *Harvest of Justice,* 1993.

Nolan, Albert. *Jesus before Christianity.* Maryknoll, NY: Orbis Books, 2008.

Pagels, Elaine. *Adam, Eve and the Serpent.* New York: Vintage Books, 1988.

Perkins, Pheme. *Love Commands in the New Testament.* New York: Paulist Press, 1982.

Pilusik, Marc. "Psychology and Peace." In *Peace Movements Worldwide*, edited by Marc Pilusik and Michael Nagler. Santa Barbara, CA: Praeger, 2011.

Pilusik, Marc, and Michael Nagler, eds. *Peace Movements Worldwide*. Vols. 1–3. Santa Barbara, CA: Praeger, 2011.

Pinker, Steven. *The Better Angels of Our Nature*. New York: Penguin Group, 2011.

Powers, Gerard, Drew Christiansen, and Fred Hennemyer. *Peacemaking*. Washington, DC: United States Catholic Conference, 1994.

Raaflaub, Kurt A., ed. *War and Peace in the Ancient World*. Malden, MA: Blackwell, 2010.

Rahner, Karl. "The Two Basic Types of Christology." In *Theological Investigations*, vol. 13. New York: Seabury Press, 1975.

Ratzinger, Joseph. *Introduction to Christianity*. New York: Herder and Herder, 1970.

Richard, Alain. *Roots of Violence in the U.S. Culture*. Nevada City, CA: Blue Dolphin Publishing, 1999.

Ringe, Sharon H. *Jesus, Liberation, and the Biblical Jubilee*. Philadelphia: Fortress Press, 1985.

Rudolph, Lloyd I. "Gandhi in the Mind of America." In *Gandhi's Experiments with Truth,* edited by Richard Johnson. Lanham, MD: Lexington Books, 2006.

Rynne, Terrence. *Gandhi and Jesus: The Saving Power of Nonviolence*. Maryknoll, NY: Orbis Books, 2008.

Schillebeeckx, Edward. *Christ: The Experience of Jesus as Lord*. New York: Crossroad, 1980.

———. *The Church: The Human Story of God*. New York: Crossroad, 1994.

———. *Jesus: An Experiment in Christology*. New York: Seabury Press, 1979.

Schlabach, Gerald W. *Just Policing, Not War*. Collegeville, MN: Liturgical Press, 2007.

Schneiders, Sandra M. "New Testament Reflections on Peace and Nuclear Arms." In *Catholics and Nuclear War*, edited by Philip J. Murnion. New York: Crossroad, 1983.

Schottroff, Louise, Reginald Fuller, Christoph Burchard, and M. Jack Suggs. *Essays on the Love Commandment*. Philadelphia: Fortress Press, 1978.

Schreiter, Robert, R. Scott Appleby, and Gerard F. Powers, eds. *Peacebuilding: Catholic Theology, Ethics, and Praxis*. Maryknoll, NY: Orbis Books, 2010.

Schubeck, Thomas. *Love That Does Justice*. Maryknoll, NY: Orbis Books, 2007.

Schwager, Raymond. *Jesus in the Drama of Salvation*. New York: Crossroad, 1999.

———. *Must There Be Scapegoats? Violence and Redemption in the Bible*. New York: Crossroad, 2000.

Senior, Donald. *Jesus: A Gospel Portrait*. New York: Paulist Press, 1992.

Sharp, Gene. *The Politics of Nonviolent Action*. Boston: Porter Sargent, 1973.

————. *Waging Nonviolent Struggle*. Boston: Porter Sargent, 2005.

Shifferd, Kent. *From War to Peace: A Guide for the Next Hundred Years*. Jefferson, NC: McFarland, 2011.

Shriver, Donald W. *An Ethic for Enemies*. New York: Oxford University Press, 1995.

Sobrino, Jon. *Christology at the Crossroads*. Maryknoll, NY: Orbis Books, 1978.

Stassen, Glen. *Just Peacemaking: Transforming Initiatives for Justice and Peace*. Louisville: Westminster/John Knox Press, 1992.

Stott, John R. W. *The Message of the Sermon on the Mount*. Leicester, UK: Intervarsity Press, 1978.

Swartley, Willard. *Covenant of Peace*. Grand Rapids, MI: William B. Eerdmans, 2006.

Swift, Louis. *The Early Fathers on War and Military Service*. Wilmington, DE: Michael Glazier,, 1983.

Tannehill, Robert. "The 'Focal Instance' as a Form of New Testament Speech: A Study of Matthew 5:39b–42." *Journal of Religion* 50, no. 4 (1970): 372–85.

Thompson, J. Milburn. *Introducing Catholic Social Thought*. Maryknoll, NY: Orbis Books, 2010.

Trocme, Andre. *Jesus and the Nonviolent Revolution*. Maryknoll, NY: Orbis Books, 2004.

True, Michael. "Defining Nonviolence: Sharp's Dictionary." *Peace Chronicles* (Spring–Summer 2012).

Tutu, Desmond. *No Future without Forgiveness*. New York: Doubleday, 1999.

Van Hook, Stephane. "Can Unarmed Peacekeeping Work in Syria? It Has in South Sudan." *Waging Nonviolence,* October 31, 2013.

Volf, Miroslav. *Exclusion and Embrace*. Nashville, TN: Abingdon Press, 1996.

Walzer, Michael. *Just and Unjust Wars: A Moral Argument with Historical Illustrations*. 2nd ed. New York: Oxford University Press, 1987.

Washington, James Melvin, ed. *A Testament of Hope: The Essential Writings of Martin Luther King Jr.* San Francisco: Harper and Row, 1986.

Watley, William D. "Martin Luther King Jr." In *Nonviolence—Central to Christian Spirituality*, edited by Joseph T. Culliton, CSB. New York: Edwin Mellen Press, 1982.

Weigel, George. *Tranquilitas Ordinis*. New York: Oxford University Press, 1987.

Wills, Gary. *Bomb Power*. New York: Penguin Press, 2010.

————. *Saint Augustine*. New York: Penguin Putnam, 1999.

Wilshire, Bruce W., ed. *William James: The Essential Writings*. New York: Harper Torchbooks, 1971.

Wink, Walter. *Engaging the Powers: Discernment and Resistance in a World of Domination.* Minneapolis: Fortress Press, 1992.

———. *The Powers That Be.* New York: Doubleday, 1998.

Wink, Walter, ed. *Peace Is the Way.* Maryknoll, NY: Orbis Books, 2000.

Witherington, Ben, III. *The Jesus Quest: The Third Search for the Jew of Nazareth.* Downers Grove, IL: Intervarsity Press, 1997.

Wright, N. T. *The Challenge of Jesus.* Downers Grove, IL: IVP Academic, 1999.

———. *Evil and the Justice of God.* Downers Grove, IL: IVP Books, 2006.

———. *Jesus and the Victory of God.* Minneapolis: Fortress Press, 1996.

———. *Simply Jesus.* New York: HarperCollins, 2011.

Yoder, John Howard. *Christian Attitudes toward War, Peace and Revolution.* Grand Rapids, MI: Brazos Press, 2009.

———. *The Politics of Jesus.* 2nd ed. Grand Rapids, MI: William B. Eerdmans, 1994.

———. *The War of the Lamb*, edited by Glen Stassen, Mark Thiessen Nation, and Matt Hamsher. Grand Rapids, MI: Brazos Press, 2009.

———. *What Would You Do?* Scottdale, PA: Herald Press, 1983.

———. *When War Is Unjust.* Eugene, OR: Wipf and Stock, 2001.

Index

About the Author

TERRENCE J. RYNNE is co-president of the Sally and Terry Rynne Foundation, which is dedicated to peacemaking and the empowerment of women. He is founder of Marquette University's Center for Peacemaking and currently teaches peace studies at Marquette. Previously he was president of the Rynne Marketing Group, a nationally recognized health care marketing firm. Prior to founding the firm he was a hospital administrator at Lutheran General and Westlake Hospitals. He has served as a parish priest in the Archdiocese of Chicago and was a faculty member of the Archdiocesan Seminary at Mundelein. Dr. Rynne received his MBA from Northwestern University and his PhD in theology from Marquette. He is author of *Gandhi and Jesus: The Saving Power of Nonviolence* (Orbis Books).